# QUICKSANDS

## A Memoir

Sybille Bedford

CHIVERS

**British Library Cataloguing in Publication Data available**

This Large Print edition published by BBC Audiobooks Ltd, Bath, 2006.
Published by arrangement with Penguin Books Limited

U.K. Hardcover ISBN 1 4056 3612 2
     ISBN 13: 978 1 405 63612 4
U.K. Softcover ISBN 1 4056 3613 0
     ISBN 13: 978 1 405 63613 1

Printed and bound in Great Britain by
Antony Rowe Ltd., Chippenham, Wiltshire

to Aliette

Nothing happens without consequences; nothing ever did happen without antecedents.

Anon.

Perspective—*la prospettiva*—aims at delineating solid objects on plane surfaces so as to give the same impressions of relative positions as the actual objects do. This technique may achieve images as 'real' as Uccello's pattern of lances, horses, men in battle, or as real as a *trompe-l'oeil.*

Anon.

Writing of the past, I have come to think it is memory that clarifies . . . The rest—diaries, letters, notes, are sediment . . .

Anon.

We think we know who we are and what we ought to do about it, and yet our thought is conditioned by the nature of our immediate experience . . . Life is Time's fool inasmuch as it is changing from instant to instant, changing the outside and the inner world so that we never remain the same two instants together.

from Aldous Huxley's last essay,
'Shakespeare and Religion'

. . . *Oh pauvre, oh heureux voyageur sur la terre* . . .

Anon.

# CONTENTS

*Part One*

Segments of a Circle

# CHAPTER ONE

*Geneva: one neutral day—Who was I?*
*Where am I?—Delays: events, unsuitable*
*aspirations, love of living—A kick into*
*a future*

I shall begin as I hope to continue: from the middle.

*Saturday, August 1st. Morning. Stepped off the train, still trailing a little sand, by the door banged shut last night on the platform at Cannes, followed the unhurried porter's trolley through the double customs . . .* **Douane Française . . . Douane Suisse** *. . . to the cloakroom down the station hall and walked, free for a space of hours, into the spacious sparkling luxurious town pouring with light, ablaze with water, snow-lit above the summer blue. Quai des Saules, Pont du Rhône, Pont de l'Isle, Quai des Bergues: the Lake of Geneva, wide-shored and open and there—the Jet d'Eau, slenderest, fountain shaft, white comet of water, self-flung into the sky . . .*

*Fifty steps inland and all is changed. An older smaller rooted world. The roofs are lower and the façades more simple, the dazzle of lake and mountains shut out.*

3

*There are plane trees in the square and a little shade, print-shops, flower-stalls, cafés. Women walk by with bread . . .*

*Up cork-screw lanes into the Old Town . . . a scramble over a hill top, drawing level to another change—stillness, lines of patrician streets, municipal buildings with private façades, hints of gardens behind walls . . . And so on and up, standing, drifting, walking: concentrated and aimless in the manner of a traveller who has no engagements, no duties nor homage to pay to great sights, who expects to be pleased enough with what he may find but knows he will not sleep in the town . . .*

from *A Diary in Switzerland*

Well, *yes* . . . But that August was in 1953 and the diary was not put on paper on that day nor in that summer month, it was written, exaltation unabated, the January after in an attic in the sixth *arrondissement* of Paris and now, another fifty years on, the sense of unsolicited discovery, the euphoria of those hours at Geneva are still with me. *Then*, as I stepped off that train, I felt mildly curious, on my own, uninvolved . . . Within minutes of mountain, sky and water, elation struck. It lasted through the day.

Through the brief broiling train journey in the trough of the afternoon with one last flash, stabbing bright, of Léman and Mont Blanc, past the vineyards, past grey-stone châteaux and fat-leaved slopes of the Pays de Vaud into sweet pasture country, past orchards, fir trees, cuckoo-clock houses, village spires: picture-book Switzerland. It lasted, that detached elation, through the stroll into another town along the arcaded streets of the city of Bern which looked like a handmade child-sized dream. There, the half-century old diary need not remind me, 'nothing was ugly or big or shabby or chic or new'. It lasted through the evening in another fast clean train streaking towards the Lake of Lucerne in a long twilight, lasted through the gross satisfying supper in a cheap anonymous inn, the night at a modest house of strangers, scarcely perceived (address provided by a station bureau); it lasted, in a quieter, ruminating way throughout that summer cadenza: the weeks to come . . . On *that* day, I took a tall white paddle steamer down the lake to a small resort to meet a friend.

\*     \*     \*

And what was I doing there?

Who was I, what was I at that stage? What had I come to, and from where? As time goes (age), I was in my early forties: free to live where, if not how, I chose. Unlike an unspeakably large number of my fellow beings, I had come alive and physically intact through four decades of our frightful century, and I was conscious—intermittently—of the privileges and the precariousness of my existence. I was conscious also of the pillars that more recently sustained it. The stoutest of these was the fact that I had a book published a few months ago. I was now, I told myself, I told myself quite often, *a writer.* At last. That book was not a first attempt. Writing: to be someone who wrote books of course—was what I had wished to be from childhood, seeing it as an exalted calling, a vocation, bestowed (by whom?) on me, however unworthy . . . My limitations were large: an almost entire lack of formal education; a lack of facility in getting words on paper—*la page vide que sa blancheur défend* . . . (I read French early, and it did bite deep); great natural sloth . . . Make me a writer, but not yet. So, no tales scribbled lying on the nursery floor, no essays imposed by school (hardly ever went to school); only a guilty headful of unwritten letters.

By the age of twenty—*was* it as late?—I had tortured myself through two pseudo-learned pieces, one on Baudelaire's view of *'l'infamie de l'imprimerie'*, the potential damage by cheap public print; the other on the Criminal Prosecution of Flaubert's *Madame Bovary.* One flinches at such pretentious juvenilia. And yet . . . Must I entirely repudiate that immature concern, however clumsy, with Baudelaire's foreboding about semi-literacy?

Should I shrug off my fascination with the clash between a bigoted judge and Emma Bovary a hundred years before Constance Chatterley received her judicial dressing down?

Next, in self-inflicted agony, I wrote three novels: hours, months, years of slog, rare euphoric gallops, next day's panic. *Was it good enough?* Was it *anything?* Three novels: finished, typed, re-typed (by myself ), sent the round of publishers in London and New York, read (sometimes) by the well-disposed raising slight hopes; rejected. Rightly. *They were not good enough.* For me it was devastating. Each time. Meanwhile I was supposed to find a way to earn a living (I had no money at all, nor expectations of money, having off-handedly sabotaged the source. Virtuously, I thought; irresponsibly, I thought since. That is another story. I'm afraid I shall have to come back to it at some point.)

Now I am glad that these novels never saw the light of print. In the act of writing my fourth book I became able to see them as they were. What had been wrong (beside beginner's stumble)? I had read too much and knew too little; beneath a credible bright surface I must have been what my mother often called me: a parrot. My wretched words were derivative. More whole-heartedly than other young postulants, I had stuck to an initial inspiration which in my case was an unbounded faith

7

conceived in early adolescence in Aldous Huxley's writing. His way of writing. That I was fired by his ideas goes without saying. Like so many of my contemporaries, I had been ravished by his sheer intelligence. It astonished, it exhilarated: we were led. Unfortunately for me, I also endeavoured to emulate his style. Adverbs opening a sentence, the rhythm of the sharp conclusion to a paragraph . . . All of it. I felt that one could not do better and readers would be content enough to receive the offerings of a weaker version. I say unfortunately because Aldous's ways with words on any level were quite unsuited to such talent as I may have had. I followed the master, but I followed him very poorly: watered-down Aldous Huxley, was Huxley with flat water indeed.

I had reached the age of twenty-nine when typescript number three was turned down by Chatto and by NY Harpers and this, except for a little journalism, brought me to a stop for—I must face it—many years. These and other long fragments of the life I wasted in not working lie heavy on me, and now, in the 2000s when lost time is irretrievable, I am often overcome by regret and disbelief. Oh what has remained undone by sloth, discouragement, and of course distractions . . . Distractions of living the siren song of the daily round—chance, often choice had led me to spend the squandered years in beautiful or interesting

8

places: to learn, to see, to travel, to walk in nocturnal streets, swim in warm seas, make friends and keep them, eat on trellised terraces, drink wine under summer leaves, to hear the song of tree-frog and cicada, to fall in love . . . (Often. Too often.)

\*     \*     \*

Concurrent with a number of those years, there had of course been the War.

\*     \*     \*

(Here perhaps is the place to insert a parenthesis to say that I had been a small child in the 1914 war, allowed to feel the horror and unreason of it by a mother articulately opposed to military or other violence; to say that I was born in another country of which I would have liked to know nothing— succeeding up to a point . . . That, in fact, I was born in Germany, *and* of partly Jewish descent. By a chain of circumstances—my father's early death, my mother's bolting even earlier—I too left early. Years before anyone was much concerned about Brownshirts, and the people we knew still thought in terms of the Weimar Republic, Locarno and the League of Nations. So I left by chance and stayed away for good. And that in due course, apocalypse not yet foreseen, put me on the

9

way to becoming an escapee, a survivor.)

To have survived, one has to have been alive. For many of us in the shrinking West the Twenties and the Thirties were hard times, restricting times, beginning with much hope, moving on to loss of work, inflations here, financial crashes there, covert, soon open, fears . . . (The rise of Fascism coincided with my early adolescence on our—by then—Italian doorstep; and in 1933 a worse oppression sprang upon a world that did not wish to see.) Meanwhile for a few—always only a few: the lot of men, the lot of life itself, human and animal, is to live below their par, misfortune always lurking, to kill, be killed—for a few— though, the years between the wars were good and in some enclaves talent and pleasures flourished. (Let us think of France.) The playgrounds were open again and for a brief period the players, if sheltered from private tragedy, did not have to think of closing time. Ante-bellum. By September 1939 all existences snapped in two.

\*        \*        \*

Post-bellum: the soaring relief, the lifting of that consciousness of pain and death sustained at all hours on that monstrous scale, did not outlast a few days in the summer of 1945. It was then that the facts of the unimaginable nature and immensity of the suffering wilfully

10

enacted was brought home. Then within weeks the next convulsion had to be taken in. The Bomb and what might evolve from it—would it ever have a stop, the abomination practised by men on men? Has it ever stopped? As I am writing these words in London, England, on another summer day—we have reached 1999 —French windows open to aircraft noise, not insects, 7 p.m., Radio Four has just chattered its three-minute summary of the news— Another mass-grave discovered—NATO's deal with the Russians appears to hold—Serbs in turn fleeing Kosovo—Ulster: the marching season—Digging continued for Sinn Fein victims—Brighton Bomber released after fourteen years—Congress rejects White House gun laws—The One-Hundred-Share-Index— Cricket . . .

In a measure, privately, individually, it did stop for some of us who had survived, often against odds—many of my friends were Jews and/or political refugees—and sooner or later there was a time when the impulse to turn away from what had happened, and might happen again and *was* happening, took over, and with it came a diminution of the sense of unearned acquittal and the ability to step aside from world affairs, from the events that distort what we hope to be our destinies.

\*       \*       \*

In 1947 I was thirty-six. That was when the doors had opened again. The longed for, the deprived of, became daylight fact: return to Europe. The Europe so long held down in agony and chaos, feared lost to itself, possibly for ever, was still there. Not intact, far from it, yet its heart, France and Italy, *les patries de nos coeurs*, were essentially, triumphantly themselves. Paris. Chartres. Venice. Rome . . . A shattered nave, a fractured bridge here and there brought home the miracle. One responded with a delirious sense of freedom and renewal. I was able to spend the summer between Normandy, Paris and Touraine: *les amis retrouvés*; and after this—immense privilege—autumn and winter in Italy: first Venice then Florence: in a Lungarno hotel, unheated (one bought logs in the street for the evening fire in a small grate), then Capri where the chief magnet had been Norman Douglas also just returned from exile. The euphoria, the daily intoxication of that year and indeed much of the decade which followed has become part of my actual being, my substance, not just a memory to be played with or left fallow. Joy, like grief, can enter the bones.

\*      \*      \*

Early post-war Italy was glorious. One embraced the people for whom the springs of

12

life were flowing again; they were at one with the staggering beauty of what there was to see, *everywhere*, dawdling in the sun, the sweet air, the new near quiet. Petrol was scarce, the Vespas and rattling trams were joyful toys, their noise another attribute of being alive. I was where I wanted to be, for ever of course, and I hung on. For the rest, I was on my own, on and off that was, partially escaped or trying to escape from a multilateral entanglement (easily classified thus later on, not in the least easy then); I had no possessions, no fixed address, let alone a home of any kind.

Yes, I hung on. I was where I wanted to be. Tenaciously, frivolously; perhaps sensibly. Following what may have been the logic of my life? The here and now were good, deserved or not. Parallel to the euphoria of these Italian days ran the disturbing awareness of their fugitive nature. Materially, and morally, my position might be seen as unsustainable. For a long time I had written nothing; on my own terms *I was nothing*. I still hoped that I would be a writer and arrogantly refused to consider any alternative aim. (How this must have irritated and antagonized some of my friends.) As for the question of talent or no talent— which *I* could not answer—I was in the position of the postulant standing empty-handed at the gate: admittance to be adjudicated by superiors.

Not empty-handed altogether. I had spent

13

the year before my return to Europe travelling over the Mesa of Mexico, a country chosen for being innocent of contemporary events. There, one warm night, on the terrace of an hacienda, lying on a deckchair under the sub-tropical sky, emptier, so much vaster than that of our hemisphere, alien and mysterious to my Western mind, on that night looking at that sky, seized by a sense of transience and infinity, the concept of a book had come to me. Abstract, ecstatic, eloquent though speechless: an apparition clear and complex moving unseen within myself.

From then on the book I wanted to write— all guns ablaze—was about Mexico: the oldest country of the New World, the Mexico of the frightful history and the paradoxical present, of the Aztecs and the Conquest, of the Inquisition, the silver rush, the civil wars, the Hapsburg Empire *al altro lado del mar*, on the other side of the sea, of Diaz the modernizing dictator who tried to re-create a Monte Carlo, of Madame Calderon de la Barca, of D. H. Lawrence and Graham Greene, of my experiences, my traveller's tales, of the strangeness, the remoteness, the unending luminous landscapes, the violence, the absurdity: allegro and panic.

Between the conception and the execution there falls the shadow. First came the getting out of Mexico (back to the *right* side of the sea). Foreigners are apt to get stuck—oh those

14

Anglo-American enclaves: it's the climate, the cheapness of living, the throngs of servants (rumour had got through about people now doing their own washing-up in England). For us—I had a lovable, super-naturally erudite, born anti-traveller for companion—it was a matter of distances and preposterous often perilous transport. Eventually the return to Europe. Part jubilant for me, part traumatic. By the time I realized that actual writing was now or never—rumination and scant notes have to lead somewhere—I also had to take in other facts. There was no longer any money at all. What I had lived on—scraps earned and saved by translating, cooking, language lessons—was spent. No family to bail me out. The reasonable, the honourable thing to do was to go and find a way to earn my keep. Ah, but this would have meant leaving Italy, living in England. So there I was, an aspiring *English* writer drawn—not the first to be so—to live 'abroad'. However in those pre-European Union days, foreigners were not allowed to work in Italy (nor France for that matter), even seeking a *permesso di soggiorno* as a self-supporting visitor was tricky enough; if it was not a matter of *douceurs* or the right connections, the system was a haphazard mix of bureaucratic niggling, whim and presumed impressions—the concierge's view at the not *too* shabby hotel, the standing of the shop one had bought a shirt from, accounts paid or not,

15

the foreigner's perceived comportment: decorous, decently dressed, altogether *signorile* (who says that England holds the monopoly in class society?), a pleasant image was preferred though a few brawlers did find favour. And when sooner or later the permit was granted, a scrap of poor paper to keep folded in one's pocket, it was valid only for three months already part-expired. Soon again the would-be resident had to get out of the country. A nip across the French border, a stay for a couple of days then back again, would usually do; followed by filling another set of forms (photographs enclosed). A cinch if one was, say, staying on the Ligurian coast, not so if one had taken a villa on the Bay of Naples or on Capri. Some of us sporadically followed the rigmarole, others didn't bother, taking their chances on a sudden call for *documenti*. Those who drove cars were most exposed to a uniformed minion's excited cry, *'Deve partire!' 'You've got to leave!'* I had it shouted once and it pulverized me. Having a permit, having one's papers in order, has been a dominant nightmare for a very large number of human beings for a very long time. I was far too scared to seek paid employment, however camouflaged.

A dilemma? An excuse? Did I really want to hold down a job (qualifications?) and write at weekends and at night as the disciplined and ascetic did? I did not. Today I am amazed by

16

my light-heartedness—where *were* the boot-straps? I had no plan, envisaged no solution. It came, unthought of, unsought for: Allanah Harper, a pre-war friend then, a friend, at the ultimate count, for more than a half-century, made over a part of her income to me for three years—'So that you can get on with your Mexican book'. This lease of life and work came from an act of generosity, affection, trust, that should not be forgotten, which I rejoice in making public now. She herself was not well off and the money going to me seriously clipped her financial wings. She told me later that she had set up a banker's order because she couldn't have borne paying out money herself quarter after quarter. Being able to talk about it in that way is another measure of her generosity; seldom financial arrangements run as smoothly.

We were in the late 1940s, a time of crippling restrictions: Exchange Control, at its most severe. Was it five pounds or ten shillings one was allowed to take out of the UK? It gradually eased as decades of time went on (though we should remember that all controls over movements of funds were only abolished by Mrs Thatcher in 1979). Then, the regular cheques care of a Roman bank were legitimate as Allanah, the donor, not being a British resident at the time, was entitled to hold offshore funds.

And so, sent off with a rough injunction

about non-writing writers from a recent and incisive friend, Martha Gellhorn, in a brooding summer on the island of Ischia, I was able to get down to writing.

## CHAPTER TWO

*Post-war Ischia: struggle into a page— Resurgence of a past—1920s by an Italian lake, an old scandal in the Kaiser's Germany—South of France, 1930s: acts of kindness—Flight from Ischia*

That beginning was as hard as any before, and after. I can still feel myself pacing the stifling room in the small hours of the afternoon, the sun on the flat roof of the guest-bungalow, struggling to sort out the disordered flood of words, approaching, then again avoiding, the inert stack of pages: the surprise of my putting down as by dictation a line of what I suppose Ernest Hemingway meant by *one true sentence*, 'All you have to do,' he tells us, 'is to write one true sentence, and then go on from there.'

Begin a story, a working day, a book . . . I have not the absurd pretension to link my struggles with those of such a master, I bring him in because what he knew about the sources and the act of writing is of acute relevance to anyone who aspires to write, *write*

18

*true*, as he would put it. Another of his precepts has been much before me—later on when I had managed a proper working life, not then—'I always worked until I had something done and I always stopped when I knew what was going to happen next. *That way I could be sure of going on the next day.*' It *is* fatal to exhaust the well . . . In my case there was still the doubt whether the well was there. What had come up was a declarative sentence, eschewing Mexico altogether, about a railway station in New York. It surprised me but it felt *right*, and it did allow me to go on . . .

That sentence, and the lines of dialogue which followed, was not changed by a word or comma from that day in July 1949 . . . not on the morning after, nor on proofs, reprints, switched publishers, paperbacks: Grand Central Station and the Baths of Caracalla, so alien, so apparently out of context with my subject, remain immutably on page one.

All that was still far from my mind during those weeks on Ischia; what mattered was that the book was moving and with it the discovery that I was writing in a voice unlike the one I had assumed before. My inner ear no longer echoed the cadences of Aldous Huxley.

So what had changed in that long interval of discouragement backed by idleness? Other company, other voices. *Time.*

There had been the separation from the two people I owe most to, who educated me morally, intellectually, whose conduct and many of whose beliefs are still a basis of my thoughts and actions (or so I hope). Aldous and his beloved wife Maria had left Europe in the spring of 1937. *Sine die.*

It was not the actual presence of Aldous which had cast that unsuitable spell on my attempted style. *His books remained.* I still read his new ones. (He published about three every two years.) They were in the full flush of his change from literary man and sceptic to preacher and to guru. I was not able to sympathize with the ways by which he had come, from despair and irony about the nature of the human destiny, to despair *and* practising compassion. I even had the presumption of writing a mildly demurring review of *Grey Eminence,* his religious and political history of le père Joseph, the Capuchin monk who became Richelieu's right-hand man and, for the greater glory and supremacy of France, one of the most important links 'in the long chain of crime and madness which binds the present world to its past'. (Aldous wrote me a very nice, rather sad letter about that review, referring to his own unease in 'a purely human world'. But then he was, among so many other things, an extremely nice man.)

There had not been much change really in my own reading; still a good deal of French: nineteenth-century poetry, Mallarmé, Rimbaud, Baudelaire, Paul Valéry; dipping into Pascal, the aphorists; Flaubert rather than Dickens or Trollope; Stendhal's *Le Rouge et le Noir* every year from page one to the end and its unfailing shock; Colette . . . The English writers re-read for pleasure (and, I now presume, for emulation) were Evelyn Waugh, Cyril Connolly, early Ivy Compton-Burnett. *The New Statesman*, faithfully subscribed to.

Now lately I had happened to be exposed to racy, unrelentingly demotic verbal American in that lovely gravelly voice of my new friend Martha. We had met in Rome where she was trying first steps towards adopting an Italian infant. Everyone fell for Martha at first sight: the brightest, most honourable and virtuous being one had ever met, one told oneself, and who moreover kept one high on laughter. He felt he had found the Virgin Mary, said Hemingway (by then an ex-husband) and could not forgive her for turning out a—very superior—College Girl. Over the years some of us shared that experience: from awed respect to disillusion: to judgement. Others did not. Martha's was a very complex nature. I owe her a good deal in one way and another; and it may well have been that it was her dazzlingly robust verbal style which provided the final kick that set my writing free.

\*     \*     \*

Ischi—the fact and circumstances of my

staying there, staying with *whom*—were an awkward and humiliating experience I was not up to handling. *That* was Martha's doing again. Martha, the intrepid frontline war-reporter who had covered the Spanish Civil War from Madrid, the Finnish Winter War, the Italian Campaign up to Cassino, who had landed—a stowaway—in Normandy on D-Day plus one. Well, she and I one fine morning had found ourselves on one of her meteoric forays from Rome (twenty-four hours and 'Let's get the hell out of here') strolling about Piazza on Ischia when she suddenly said, 'By Golly! Don't look round—there's the Baronessa—as they call her—the Kraut who was in with Ciano and Franco and all . . . I can't believe it, how dare she show her face? She must be one of the wickedest women in Europe.'

My God, I thought, it can't be! But it was.

I did not have to turn round, she walked up to us, made straight for me and said, 'Billi.'

I did not, as I wished, turn to stone. It was me indeed whom she was addressing (Martha had melted into the background), and the name she used was one I was no longer called by, a childhood name known only to what was left of early friends. And that was precisely it. She was a family friend, a friend and hero of my childhood and youth. My mother, her elder by half a generation, had been much attached to her. She was amusing in a dry understated way as well as entirely self-possessed and

22

extremely bright. My younger self she had twisted round her little finger. I vaguely knew that she had tried to elope once or twice with some unsuitable chap. We had not met for what must be fifteen years, nor did I *really* know what she had been up to. I knew *where* she had been—*en poste* on the wrong side. She had finally married: a man a good deal older than herself, a German diplomat, one of the 'old school', who had hung on or stuck it out after 1933 when Hitler came to power. That was enough for me. I cut all contact. Symbolically only, because *she* was at her embassy while *we,* my mother and her young Italian husband, were living in the south of France. But so was *her* mother, a gentle elderly lady (who had been outstandingly kind to me in difficult situations in my youth), whom I also promptly stupidly cut, a resident of the fishing village where my decorator stepfather had happened to do up a house for her a few years earlier.

Now, here, the daughter (not the mother) stood in front of me. She was cool and long; tall and slim like Martha, only more so: she was very tall. The hair, too, was fair, the features handsome. She gave me an affectionate if a tinge ironic smile. 'Billi,' she said, 'what are you doing here?'

She took me in with one amused glance. 'You look a bit shabby,' she said. Another mocking smile. 'I suppose that comes from having been on the winning side.'

*She* was impeccably turned out—white silk chemisier, a gold chain, plain but heavy, perfectly cut pleated skirt, polished Greek sandals: an elegance associated more with Italian than German women of her class.

'Issa . . .' I said in a strangled voice.

Her name was Isabella, her married name Isabella von N., Baroness N. No one had ever called her Isa or Bella; it was always Issa—short I, sharp S, which sounded both harder and smarter. It suited her.

'*We* live here,' she said. 'We have a house near Porto. Just finished building. It's rather beautiful. You must come and see us. Where are you staying?'

I said, 'In a *pensione* . . . I think . . .'

'Not divulging your address to *me*? On this island? Don't be absurd.'

Actually, I had no idea whether Martha thought of taking rooms at the Pensione Bella Vista or Mezza Luna, and fell into the trap of trying to explain this.

Issa lost interest. 'What's been happening to one's old friends? Where's Jacko? I hear she had a tough time . . . And Doris? That was bad, very bad . . .'

(Jacko was my sister, my half-sister; Doris, a girl who had been a little in our lives. Those three—Issa, Jacko, Doris—some ten years older than myself, had shared a brief *jeunesse dorée*. Their circumstances, not unequal,

24

became stridently more so. Their ways diverged. If the Berlin of the 1920s had been a less ambiguous, a less doomed place, they might have kept on meeting at the same dances.)

'Poor fool, Doris . . . but if you will mess about with Communists at the wrong time . . . *We* could do nothing for her in Paris.'

I felt that she wanted me to say, 'Did you try?' I kept silent.

Doing something in Paris meant Paris under the Occupation, having pull with the *Kommandantur,* the Gestapo.

'Little Billi, don't be so contemptuous—I know every thought you are thinking—you never were a realist, neither you nor your mother. (Whom I loved dearly.)' I knew that this was true and felt another kind of pang. 'It doesn't bear imagining what trouble she would have got herself into, she didn't know when not to sink. Idealists never do. For women like her, an early death is not a bad thing. Anyway, history is cruel to individuals, so individuals must learn to take evasive action with the means at hand. Because I shut up at a time one had to shut up, I was able to do a few things . . . things you would have approved of —yes, *in Paris* and elsewhere. Billi, few things are ever really quite black or white . . .'

'Some are,' I said through clenched teeth.

'I saved two or three Jews.' And into my continued silence, 'Did *you*? I happened to

25

have some influence and I used it. You would rather have had me sitting in cafés with the refugees.'

*     *     *

When at last I was able to join Martha again, I found her in a bar. She was keeping a Martini cold for me. 'I thought you'd need it.'

Martha had been reporting Dachau when it was liberated. To her *all* Germans were contemptible, untouchable. (A feeling I was not far from sharing at that time.) Now I expected to be dismissed for not having spat and run. Anyway, deeply, secretly, I felt myself to be dismissable because of my own origins, discarded however early. (The fact that Martha, too, happened to be of German or part-German origin was something we were hardly able to mention to ourselves, let alone to each other. Hers was more remote, her father having left the Kaiser's Reich in disgust at the end of the nineteenth century. Lucky Martha was a born American.)

I sat down and buried my head in my hands.

'It's true then? The Kraut Baronessa knows you?'

I groaned.

'I was watching: she seemed to look delighted to see you but she didn't attempt to shake hands.'

'Nor kiss me on both checks—she's far too

26

clever. She told me I looked shabby.'

'Which she does *not! Les signes extérieurs de richesse* . . . That outfit must have cost a packet.'

Martha's own clothes, too, looked simple, impeccable and becoming. They were mainly department store, not, on principle, upper-Fifth-Avenue.

'Not the chain,' I said. 'It did not cost her a packet. The gold chain was a present. From the Generalissimo.'

'No! Tell—tell everything she said. What did she sound like?'

'Cheerfully aggressive.'

'Attack being the best defence?'

'Oh I don't think she saw any need of defence,' I said, 'she made it clear how paltry an adversary I was. She just enjoyed her own effrontery. She was awfully good at it, you should have heard her. She pitied me for not having done well, for being hard up (she got that at once). She made a joke about my cap, but *that* was good-natured and quite genuine.'

'I bet it was,' said Martha.

The cap—I had taken it off—was a kind of fisherman's cap, blue denim with an elongated cardboard shield, long and narrow like a large bird's beak. I wore it at an angle against the slanting sun; the cardboard peak had begun to split. I was aware that Martha did not really like being seen with me in public in that cap.

'And all the time I was feeling embarrassed,'

I said, 'not because I was not cutting *bella figura* in her eyes—that I found nicely ironic—I was embarrassed because I was judging her—inevitably, stonily . . . I was judging an old friend. We were each feeling superior. Of course she didn't see it in that way at all.'

'Obtuseness?'

'She's not obtuse.'

'Natural arrogance?'

'Acquired arrogance, possibly. Issa was always good at getting up a front. She often had to.'

'Issa—?'

How else could I address her now? Even in my mind.

'I knew her when I was a child in Italy—she was a very young woman then—she must be in her fifties now, it doesn't show much—she and her mother used to stay with us in the summers, that was before we moved to France, a long time, a very long time before she married or even thought of marrying her ambassador.'

'Did she mention him now?'

'Not directly.'

'She's supposed to have been his grey eminence,' Martha said who seemed to know much more about it all than I did. 'Not that I ever saw them—they must have been representing Germany in Burgos then, I guess, while we were still fighting in Madrid. Not so *grey*, I can see now. She looks the kind of woman men fall for, young men, old men, the woman men do things for.'

'Yes,' I said. I had seen it; over and over again. 'But that was on a private scale.'

'Franco was supposed to have eaten out of her hand.'

'That's what she just told me.'

'Did she now!'

'She said, "Franco listened to us and Hitler didn't like it".'

'*Boy,* this is riveting stuff.'

'She played quite a part—as it might be seen some day, she said—in keeping Spain neutral. A razor's edge operation. Which came off. She also told me that she was actually *with* Ciano on September 3rd 1939—in Rome, in his office, the private room behind his office, the two of them alone, with her persuading him to persuade his father-in-law to put off joining Germany in the war. You think any of this *can* be true?'

'One heard she was very thick with Ciano.'

I groaned again. 'Was she trying to tell me that she—they, she and her ambassador husband, were covertly trying to work *against* Germany, against *German* victory? Why else delay Italy's entry, keep Spain out of the war?'

'Next thing she'll tell you she never was a Nazi.'

'She wouldn't. She's much too proud for that kind of cringery. Besides, I'm sure she wasn't. A Nazi.'

29

Now Martha groaned.

'There appears to be another twist to her story,' I said. 'They were *recalled*. Did you know that? Recalled to Berlin. In '42, I think. She said, "We weren't the rats leaving the sinking ship, we were the rats pulled in to be drowned." As soon as their train was over the Spanish border, they were under guard, SS Guard—not in uniform, discreet: they were still treated as Their Excellencies. She caught on. He didn't. They still had a few hours, crossing Vichy France. She managed to get one of the SS officers to help them—she hinted how—at night she and her husband were able to slip off the train at some brief halt. She said they wore overcoats over their nightclothes. They managed to disappear, eventually crossed into Switzerland, asked for and remained there in asylum. The SS officer, she learned later, was arrested on arrival in Berlin (as they had been meant to be) and sentenced to death. "It cost him his head," she said.'

'She told you all this?'

'She said there was a good deal more— perhaps I should ghost her memoirs. She meant it. *God, forbid.*'

'*You*'ll never make a journalist,' Martha said severely. 'You've got to get it all out of her, you've got to ask questions.'

'Would *you*?'

'Damn sure I would. Don't you realize that

the Baronessa and her lot are all that's left for us now to learn what it was like, what they felt, what they said to each other? The big fish aren't here any more, the Nuremberg lot are dead or where you and I can't speak to them for a long long time. You *must* get hold of her again.'

'She asked me to lunch at their house tomorrow.'

'And you said No?'

'She didn't give me a chance to say Yes or No, she said over her shoulder, "Two fifteen for half past," and was off.'

*     *     *

You do know about her, don't you? Martha had said to me later on that day. *I did know about her.* Her forebears, her story were part of those echoes emanating from a past lived earlier than that of her parents' and mine, reaching back into the nineteenth century and beyond, and which had first come to my ears and mind when I was a young child, echoes conveyed by anecdote and innuendo about events and judgements of events that had remained unheeded through my youth and early middle age, until they surfaced possessive, persistent, clear as the instinctive material for my coming work. The sources of *A Legacy* (my first published novel) were the indiscretions of tutors and servants, the censures of nannies, the dinner-table talk of elderly members of a step-family-in-law, my own father's tales, polished and visual; my mother's talent for presenting private events in the light of literary and historical interpretation.

That stock of youthful memories then—not always only at third or second hand—included the Baronessa. It was what she was called (with operatic undertones) on Ischia where she became a familiar figure in the post-war years: admired, disliked, a little feared. Her actual title was indeed *Baronin*, and as an ex-ambassador's wife, she also had a right to *Your Excellency* and indeed her Italian household addressed her as *Eccellenza*. (I did go to the luncheon I was bid, badgered into it by friend Martha.)

Issa was still a Fräulein von Hahn and a guest in my mother's house, which that year happened to be a rented villa on Lake Garda, and I a child come over from England, where I was supposed to get educated, to spend the summer in Italy. When I arrived the Hahns, mother and daughter were already there, installed in the two nicest of the spare-rooms. Mine was not particularly nice. Children are or were apt to accept any fait accompli; this did not prevent them from having feelings. I, if anything, was pleased by the new presences: they made my mother laugh. This was reciprocal and the house was filled with the talk of those three women. Frau von Hahn was a tiny woman with a small face that must have been pretty but now appeared somewhat shrunk. She looked as if her person had at one point been compressed by a sense of necessary self-effacement, a physical response to a desire to occupy the smallest possible space. This feat, and what had prompted it, must have taken place in the past for the impression she now gave was of someone alert, good-humoured, even jolly, and quite ready to enjoy such good things as life in our company might offer. She was about ten years older than my mother (who had then reached her latish thirties) and looked more so. Her clothes were unobtrusive, though neither inexpensive nor unbecoming. Her daughter called her Mamoushka and we were encouraged to follow suit, which we did. *We* included Alessandro, the young stepfather my mother had quietly married a year or so before, and a few brothers of his—he came from a large family—all male and handsome. Mamoushka adored Issa, was devoted to my mother, and quite obviously under the thumb of both.

Issa, barely twenty, carried herself with nonchalant elegance and self-possession; she was, as I already said, tall and long-legged, with a well-shaped head and a clear matt skin that never looked pallid or heated; her features were fine. She was good-looking on any count. Some days, in some light, people would speak of her as beautiful. It might have been felt that she was too tall, too cool, too Nordic for the taste of Latin men. That this was not so was apparent from the comportment of the brothers over whom she towered. Men clustered around her. Seldom in vain. (A factor which played a perilous part in her subsequent resolve to maintain an acceptable position in conventional upper-class society.) At the nearby hotel there were hovering a number of admirers who had followed the Hahns into *villeggiatura* from Germany, young Siegfried figures, Herr von This and Freiherr von That, who matched Issa in tallness and blondness. If they were rivals, they were well-behaved ones, scrupulous toward each other and to the Italian competition—Issa saw to that. Tension in the air there was, but no overt duelling or serenading. Issa's mother, an innocent at heart, regarded the swarm as an inevitable and quite suitable homage to her unique daughter, and looked on with benign tolerance and a pinch of mockery. My mother, a good deal less innocent and as fond of Mamoushka as she was of Issa, contrived to be loyal to them both by protecting the ignorance of the one, and the other from being found out.

\*　　　\*　　　\*

Emma von Hahn's father, Issa's grandfather,

came from Huguenot stock, French Protestant 'asylum-seekers' who were able to settle in Prussia during the reign of Frederick the Great, where like so many of their skilled, industrious and upright kind, they prospered. The earlier generations were said to have been talented clock-makers; the real surge to wealth and power came with Issa's grandfather in the later half of the nineteenth century in the expansionist years following the Franco-Prussian war and the foundation of the Reich. The *Gründer Jahre.* Opportunities were immense and Issa's grandfather was in the forefront of those who seized them. In sober fact he became the founder of one of the new Germany's most prestigious financial institutions. He was a man of whom it was said that his ability and ruthlessness were equalled only by his probity. The patent of nobility—a *von* before the family name—was bestowed upon him by the Kaiser. (The first Wilhelm, proclaimed at Versailles in 1871, not his fatal grandson, Kaiser Bill.) He married early and like his Victorian contemporaries begot a prodigious family, fourteen or so live children, brought up in fear and trembling under an iron discipline (only such clichés serve); the males in due course were pushed into careers, none of them amounting to very much, the girls married off into impecunious aristocracy (army mostly and ancient, not patent). When his long-suffering wife died, the founder of this dynasty remarried almost at once. The new bride turned out a poor thing and produced only two daughters, Mamoushka and a sister, also married in due course into Prussian cavalry. Issa's father, a Captain von Hahn, called François by his women-folk, I dimly remember as a not unamiable shadow, tolerated by his wife and submissive to his daughter whom he adored. One of the things the entire family dreaded was their compulsory attendance at the patriarch's Sunday dinner. Issa's mother said that having a bath in the evening still filled her with a nameless dread because it recalled the baths she had dressing for dinner at her father's house.

There was something much much worse in that family's past, something that could not remain covered up and ballooned into a national scandal. It happened before the end of the century, more or less at the time of the ill-treatment and botched suicide of my own father's brother at a military school. These events—taking place long before I was born—have become part of my juvenile mythology. They have two traits in common: the suffering of children and the chaotic often malicious contradictions of public reaction.

The outline of the earlier event goes something like this: the youngest of Issa's grandfather's progeny had become unruly—two fractious boys rebelling against their régime. When they were found unmanageable, their father, an extremely busy man, engaged a new tutor. The tutor averred that he would not be able to tame these pupils unless he were left with them in isolation. And so it was arranged. He took the boys to a shooting lodge in the Harz Mountains. No servant, no neighbours. What came out at the trial later was that the man was a sadist. A sadist, not a paedophile. He did not what we now call abuse the boys. He tortured them. Rumours, in spite of the remoteness, reached a village or two. Letters—anonymous—were sent. The boys' father dispatched tame husbands of his grown-up daughters to investigate—officers all of them, later described as men of honour by the court. The tutor put up a good front. The boys were silent. This might have been ascribed to truculence. The delegation reported that although conditions were spartan, there was nothing really amiss. A few weeks later one of the boys was dead. The other recovered physically while his mind remained impaired. He was placed in a mental institution—well endowed, it was said, well run—where he remained for the rest of his life which was long. His half-sister, Issa's mother, recalled visiting him. (An apathetic ghost.) The tutor was convicted and sentenced to life imprisonment.

One of the features that had much inflamed public and press (by no means all uniform-dazzled militarists) was the obtuseness of the army officers' report on the situation at the shooting lodge. Hostility was directed not so much to the father, an ageing man, respected and remote, as to the drill-sergeants' mentality of the boys' young brothers-in-law. The sloth of the heart.

Of all the family clan it was Issa alone who stood up to her grandfather. She faced him, she said, without awe. He liked her. They respected each other. When she spoke of him it was with a kind of sardonic approval. He used to give her a good deal of money; though not always, and rarely as much as she had asked him for. She also managed to keep this, by all accounts excessively shrewd, man ignorant of much of what she was and did.

*     *     *

As it happened it rained hard during my first week on Lake Garda; rain in Italy, when it occurs, is felt as a miserable thing under which one cringes. I remember us being confined to the villa for most of the day, quite happily engaged in listening to Mamoushka's, Issa's and my mother's web of talk. The Hahns were sharp-witted, sharp observers, giving as good as they got. Mamoushka's and Issa's voices were not unlike: both had a slow dry drawl which in Mamoushka's case contained a chuckle, Issa's an ironic undertone; her voice was low with a trace of huskiness that must have been quite a factor in the attraction she incited. Issa and Alessandro played bridge, the table made up by a couple of the brothers who braved a short sprint under a huge umbrella from a nearby villa. The Siegfrieds were not on house-visiting terms with my mother, an attitude towards her daughter's suitors Mamoushka approved of. They came to the front door though—in oilskins, no umbrellas—to pick up Issa for a tramp along the shore. The lake had turned grey and agitated, churning like the sea. But we needed fresh air. There were dogs to walk. Hers were enormous beasts—a pair of them—of some ferocious breed, answering to belligerent names like Lucifer or Hercules. They came to heel for her. Ours were Japanese spaniels.

Then one morning shutters opened and the countryside, the lake, the sky were glistening, sun-buttered and blue. There was a landing stage some ten yards into the lake from which one could bathe. I loved water: as an infant I had wallowed, nanny-watched, under inches of North Sea; later I had stood in a brook near our land in Baden, later still I had paddled, unattended, off the Sorentian shores. But as yet I had not known what it was like to be out of one's depth. That fine morning Issa and myself, accompanied by the Siegfried of the day, waded into the lake. When I got out of my depth she grabbed me and tucked me under her arm and went on: 'My good girl,' she said, 'there's no need to teach you to swim. Everybody can. *You'll swim now.*' She made a sign to the Siegfried, who towered over *her*, he waded a few yards further out to the point where he could still just stand. Issa flung me over her shoulder then tossed me to him. The Siegfried caught me, tucked me under *his* arm, swam out a few paces, then let go and dropped me into the lake. For a long second I started to sink like a packet of lead, then I got moving, had surfaced, I was swimming, was swimming with much splash and no rhythm, swimming like a dog, paddling with hands and feet, making back towards Issa who caught me, hoisted me up—the water was buoyant—threw me in again. That time I struck out myself towards Siegfried: reached and was tossed back.

The giants were playing. They were strong, it was a good game. When it was over I felt radiant and smug.

'Issa, Issa, Issa, I can swim!'

'Don't think I gave you a swimming lesson, little girl,' she said. 'The lesson was—if you want to survive, you must swim, not sink.'

\*　　　\*　　　\*

So that—and much else—lay behind us in that post-war summer on Ischia three decades later when I found myself again under the same

40

roof with Issa. Martha had prevailed. I *had* gone, as bid, to lunch at the Baronessa's house: a beautiful house as she had said, beautifully run, run as a (very superior) *pensione.* The von N.s had kept their family silver and it would appear not much else. They took in paying guests, *moneyed* paying guests. *She* I should have said, not *they.* Her husband, an archetypal Foreign Office man in retreat— a level-mannered south German with nothing of Prussian astringency or Viennese charm about him, much older than Issa—kept to himself in some study, making an appearance at the dinner-table, giving nothing away. In that quarter, Martha's great plan of my extracting history was a washout.

'. . . the perfect solution for you, Syb,' she had said when I told her that the Baronessa had proposed my staying at their one-room guest bungalow between house and sea for the summer months: half price, 'family rates'. Which I could afford. Just. Which Martha knew. And which on Issa's part put me at once in my place of the poor relation come down in life. Martha's argument went like this, 'You'll be able to get down to work at last, you don't want to chat with the Krauts all day; and in the evenings you *do.* You have a go at them at *l'heure bleue,* Syb . . .' No one before or since has called me that; for Martha—always—short was best.) 'Make them talk about the small facts . . . You owe it to posterity . . .'

41

I had to concede. The austere isolation of the island, a cell to work in, with plenty of pacing space, ten feet from the sea, my present non-place in the world . . . Was this not a hint from fate? Martha had assured me that it was a moral thing to stay with the von N.s. But was it? Martha's construct—war criminals versus investigative journalist—was out of joint. They had served under the Hitler regime, whatever their private reservations, and only turned their backs on it when they themselves became prospective victims. Whatever he and she had done or failed to do, I now believe that Issa when ambassadress to Spain played or tried to play a part in keeping Franco neutral in the war, with a view perhaps that a tilt towards German defeat would mean a better chance for the survival of a civilized society (for herself to exist in). The von N.s ought to be left to the historians. As for me, I have to pass some judgement on myself, the emotional ineffectual opponent to Hitlerism from the winter of 1933 (of the Reichstag arson, the first concentration camps). I had had the luck to have lived away from any of that long before it had begun; that is to say, from childhood. I lived in Italy, in England, in France, free to indulge in being an early anti-Fascist. I had the luck of being brought up in frequent proximity with a fundamentally anti-nationalistic mother. And when the horrors had come close, German armies complete with Gestapo pouring into France, I fled. Self-preservation. How 'moral' was it ten years later to try playing mole at Issa's? As for my being an authentic journalist at that point . . . Issa, needless to say, caught on.

*      *      *

And when I was actually living in the von N.s' house, it proved indeed an untenable situation. Not that Issa allowed herself any sign to show that this might be so. Her effrontery was impermeable and also quite unacknowledged on her part. Derisive enormities simply did not exist. She continued to mock me—my aspirations, my convictions—subtly, lightly; on the whole I was treated with a kind of rough affection: there was too much good past behind us. She was still attached to the memory of my mother; *she* had gone straight for her goals, if without any of Issa's ruthlessness. I, still seen as my mother's daughter, lacked guts. For my part I had become beset with remorse about *Issa's* mother—also dead—Mamoushka whom I had treated with idealistic insolence in 1933. I had told her over the teacups—her teacups—that I could no longer have anything to do with her. What politics and principles can do to one! How harsh and blinkered, how self-righteous, how illiberal the young liberals! (Their elders too of course.) What part should that lady, a widow then, have played when her beloved daughter, married to a German diplomat, had chosen to remain *en poste* at Cairo? Should she have refused to receive her daughter? Declare herself publicly as anti-Hitler, turn refugee—never mind where the next passport was to come from? I did not stay for an answer as to what her own feelings were. All I knew of her in the next few years was that she was living in her villa, La Tranquille, a couple of miles away, sheltering for her part as *dame de compagnie* a White Russian exile and her feckless brood (1917—the victims of another of this century's catastrophes).

La Tranquille. That was the name the original builders had given to the shoddy mistral-rattled house on the edge of a promontory, a name Mamoushka had chosen not to change after my stepfather's transformation of the place into a charming, comfortable country abode, warm in winter, sea-open in the summers, her last port she called it. She had turned her back on her oppressed Prussian childhood and middle-age for more than reasons of climate. La Tranquille was cannonaded by the Italian army in 1943 or thereabouts. Long after I returned to the site which had been a part of my own youth—we lived there before and *during* the rebuilding—talks alone with my mother deep into the night about Flaubert and Baudelaire, war and peace: how to prevent the one, how to achieve the other . . . I thought of sailor parties amid the scaffolding when my mother was *not* there and the roof open to the sky. What I saw before me in the new peace were some square feet of Pompeii without grace or a retraceable past.

(Now, the 2000s now, there are other seekers: German literary tourists trying to recall the movements of their more eminent *émigrés* of the 1930s. Sanary, that is where those seekers go, Sanary-sur-mer, of which they write and film. In Mamoushka's days— before my break-off—that place in many ways had been a haven for me too. She had been good and generous standing by my mother during the difficult years, helping in many ways— friendship, company, money.

*    *    *

I was a minor with a little money of my own rationed by remote legal guardians who distrusted both my mother and my future prospects.

There was money behind me. (At that point, *before* I jeopardized it all when in a juvenile doctrinaire state of mind I believed it incumbent on me to tweak the tail of the great German state.) At my father's death, the château, a wedding present of my mother's arranged by her trustees, which she gave to him outright in a state of absent-minded generosity at their divorce, that château had been sold, together with his own art collection, and the proceeds left absolutely to his daughters, that is my half-sister and myself. She was at present going through her share like the hot knife through butter; mine was being sat upon by my—utterly honest—trustees.

I was welcome at Mamoushka's house for lunch or dinner, even tea (one seems to have eaten so many meals at that time). Her grandee, ex-grandee, companion, still open-hearted after years of buffeted existence, was a fine carefree cook, lavishly dabbling in Russian and French cuisines. There was vodka—how not?—with daily wines white or pink from respective cooperatives at St Cyr and Bandol on my recommendation. Sundays: Bordeaux. However, Mamoushka's big imaginative good deed had been to give me a job. Part time. (I was supposed to read for education which I did; I wanted to write which as often I did not.) Mamoushka made me her chauffeur. Complete with salary and chauffeur's cap. It had a wide brim shielding the sun when towards evening I would drive the two ladies with quietly paced care to Toulon to a restaurant or a guest performance at the theatre. To these I too would be invited. I was car-mad and had managed to pass the French driving test almost within hours of attaining the legal age—eighteen then—and speed-mad as well of course. This I curbed entirely for my passengers' nerves and safety. Gears moved as if floating in cream. To me the job was bliss. My own car was an old open Ford roadster, acquired on tick, a convoluted transaction, and I also snatched at the chance of driving any wheels on offer.

*      *      *

On Ischia echoes from the past and feelings about Issa present—revulsion, amusement, censure—got at me at unchosen moments as noises off. Quite strong, unavoidable, discarded. The pivot of my mind was Mexico, was my book, the fact of writing with sentences, now pages, under my belt. At the end of the working day, though, the situation obtruded.

One feature I found hard to take was the intangible insolence with which the paying guests were treated. Businessmen from the United States or Milan with aspiring wives, whose jewels did not share the simplicity and style of Issa's which, like all appurtenances of that household, were in accord with the august Mediterranean dignity of the environment. I saw the shock, quickly concealed, when arrived by the evening boat, groomed and changed, smiles at the ready, the newcomers appeared on the long terrace and saw the tables set out with gleaming linen, silver, china, the polished candelabras designed to shield candle light from the nocturnal breeze . . . *Separate tables.* They met—small glasses of Cinzano were passed standing—they met her faithful shadow, the middle-aged Englishwoman, a diplomat's widow (had there ever been a war with Germany?), who lived with the von N.s, adored Issa and took most of the running of the establishment off her shoulders—her slave in a word, although herself not without distinction or means. The guests met me. They met von N. emerging . . . Dinner was announced . . . Nothing was said. It had become quite clear that they, the guests, were to eat it by themselves served, correctly, by a poker-faced young manservant, a few yards from the top table. It was not what they had come for.

The attitude of the servants was ambiguous. They perhaps did not exactly love Issa, but she was served impeccably. Italians tend to respect and admire *figura*, the signs of wealth and position of their masters. The von N.s might have lost their original fortunes and forfeited a pension, but they certainly had retrieved some handsome possessions in the shape of objets d'art, gold, silks . . . I saw chestfuls . . .

It must have been in my third week that the episode of the grand piano occurred. Issa had consented to lend hers, the only such instrument on the island, and sorely needed, to a couple of young Jewish musicians from New

York. It was let at a serious price with some stiff insurance clauses in the agreement. We all witnessed the transport—by mule cart, boat and mule cart again—which had something of the nature of an early cinematographic comedy: Issa recorded every bump and scratch. Those young musicians, obvious homosexuals, were a degree further beyond the pale than the p.g.s. Something snapped for me. I would cope no longer with that cool inhumanity. Issa, in W. H. Auden's heart-piercing lines, was one who

*never heard*
*Of any world where*
*. . . one could weep because another wept.*

A footnote: Wystan Auden as it happened was staying up-island, at Forio. I believe they knew about each other's presence, the eccentric poet and the bad *baronessa*, who looked down on him and his court as queers and bohemians. Exactly as, I have to add, did Martha Gellhorn.

I did leave. How was it managed? I decided that *I* would try to be *furba* in the manner of that approved Italian concept of underhand and cunning. I wrote to a number of friends asking them to send me urgent requests for my presence elsewhere. Easier said than done, given the nature of the Italian postal service at about the nadir on places like that island.

There was also the matter of obtaining access to a post-box. (The Englishwoman was in charge of that.) I managed—*furba* becomes who *furba* does. Things were complicated by it being now mid-August and I could not be certain where plausible accomplices might be. I sent off a multiplicity of letters. For days nothing happened. Then, very publicly, a flurry of telegrams arrived almost on the hour, born by agitated messengers expecting tips.

'An old trick, that,' Issa said. '*I* used to have telegrams sent to myself when I wanted to get away from a place. You seem to have rather overdone it . . . Where do you say your distinguished presence is required?'

I did not do my explaining very lucidly. She did not ask to see the telegrams. I owed her another month's board, she said, but among family friends . . . She just laughed. She actually behaved very well. She realized I would not do for ghosting their memoirs.

*  *  *

I never saw her again in this world. On her death, some twenty years on, the family sent me an announcement—black borders, many names. Then her son wrote, a very nice short letter referring to his mother's and my youth. She had a son—I never met him. She had adored him, her one weakness; through him she became vulnerable because he would not always do as she would have him do. Career and girls. She had fears for him; he was said to have none of her toughness. When he wrote to me I was moved. I hope that I have not been too severe about her here. What do any of us know about one another? And what does a writer know? Writing, perhaps, breeds even more distortion and uncertainties. When I was a child I may have loved Issa most among my mother's friends. That was a long time ago in age and years. The ambiguity persists.

## CHAPTER THREE

*Capri—Rome—Work—Precarious joys—
Full stop—A childhood terror—My
anachronistic father: early 1900s,
marriages, one to my mother—A corner of
rural Germany*

I had caught the morning boat. A ride on that bay is seldom smooth and from Ischia it is long. Even so there were still some hours of hanging about the port before the afternoon boat for Capri was due to leave. And Capri was what I had decided on as the first stage of my escape. Two or three hours for an unaccompanied woman at Naples means a good deal of evading of pinches and stares, clutching of bag, keeping guard over luggage. I was too light-hearted to notice, as I wandered about, ate lunch at a trattoria—paper tablecloth, thick tumblers, glut of *pomodoro* on the pasta. I felt free as a bird.

Capri proved serendipitous. From the friends met on Piazza by purpose or chance on arising at dusk from the Marina by the funicular, to the white-washed room bare and cool in the backstreet pensione, to the work resumed there in clear mornings and after the steep noon-time scramble down to the sea and up again (no money to spend on a carrozza) through torrid afternoons, to reunion at sundown with friends, friends of a feather . . . Kenneth Macpherson; Islay Lyons; David, the sprightly young British vice-consul on leave; the Fitzgibbons, Constantine and Theodora; Norman: Norman Douglas, when disposed to see one (one always knew when not); the first drinks of the day, the slow late dinners in open air, under trellises of honeysuckle and jasmine. Some people ate well on Capri. Norman, known for his ado about it, thought he did. Capresi innkeepers gave him of their best. For the rest of us it was too often stringy *melanzane*, thick macaroni, undistinguished fish. Grapes, figs, green almonds were good. The local wine—famous, cherished—was I would say just drinkable. One drank . . . One talked . . . All in all, I had a good, a happy end of summer on that other island; in October, head high and conscious of that privilege, I

52

returned to Rome.

* * *

There I was lodged a few steps from the Piazza di Spagna at the Albergo d'Inghilterra, that perennial resort of the famous, the bohemian and the out-of-pocket. The lower-floor rooms tended to be funereal, lacking daylight, stuffed with pompous furniture, whereas the top ones were a-cackle with the fowls kept on balconies by the more domestic-minded inhabitants. Yet the establishment was still imbued with the shades of Byron, Henry James and the intermittent presences of Brian Howard, Tennessee Williams and Janet Flanner. All rooms, it was believed, were the same price. By what principle they were allotted, one did not find out, no flesh-and-blood person representing the management being visible. One stayed of course on good terms with the concierges. Returning at daybreak you would be handed your key with a discreet, a very discreet, smile of approval. Such good relations were not engendered by a mere tip. You did tip, adequately mostly, not extravagantly, at the end of a week or in receipt of a parcel or message; what mattered was human comportment: mutual good manners, some pleasant talk, warmth. It is this rapport which comes naturally to Italians, which makes one feel belonging for an instant to the brotherhood of man. I am not speaking of rogues, there are plenty of these, perhaps more than elsewhere, to be found in Italy. All the same, humanity, as I learned being minded by them in my childhood, is a rooted trait of the Italian people. It becomes feebler in those risen to the bourgeoisie and in some, by no means all, of the well-born or the very rich.

For no reason I could fathom I was treated extremely well by the invisible powers. I had a large room on the high floor just below the chicken attics, French-windows giving on to ochre-and-apricot façades of the side street, a huge almost square bed, my own bath, a well-swept fire-place and a marble-topped sideboard on which I kept the paraphernalia for my breakfast—an economy the albergo never commented on: my father's compact spirit-stove, kettle, egg-pan, caddy, handsomely crafted and neatly fitted into its original Edwardian pig-skin case. There stood also bottles for the friends who came before our going out to dinner. On offer I had brandy, *faute de mieux* Italian, acceptable with San Pellegrino water, a fiasco of light red Tuscan wine from the charcoal merchant's cave: *Carbone—Olio—*Vim, who plied his trade round the corner from the tremendously elegant and expensive boutiques and jewellers of the via della Croce. There was also proper English gin for martinis. Ice obtained by going down four flights bowl in hand to the exiguous bar below: a five-lira note—how grubby and worn they were—exchanged for a ladle of clinking cubes and up I climbed again.

I paid for that room at a weekly rate; the way I lived kept well within my resolve to make Allanah's money last beyond the arranged three years. They had given me a desk for my typewriter and papers. During the daytime hours I worked. Diurnal austerity. It has often stood me in good stead ever after.

The Mexican book took me in hand: I was discovering the scope of non-fiction fused with telling a story, or inventing one. A book on its course is like a rolling ball, to mix metaphors, gathering and losing moss. One day—lack of faith? misplaced ambition?—I decided to make it take a more academic turn. Surely unwise for someone whose entire education consisted of a few months each at a south-German village school and an Ursuline convent, followed by an irregular assortment of private tutors. Whatever knowledge I had acquired came from listening to my elders and betters and from reading. I suddenly felt that I ought to give some legitimacy to my Mexican impressions. Research! And here I was—a few streets away from that splendid Latin American Library at the Palazzo Antici Mattei. How felicitous, how tempting. *How presumptuous.* I never knew in what way some added learning would have affected that book—hubris was too quick. No sooner had I collected my sackful of fat tomes—the authorities took me *au sérieux*, a friend had lent me his jeep—than I was laid low. The reason was eye trouble which limited, often stopped, my reading. To creatures born in the North, drawn early and irreversibly to the South, the sun is not kind. I was exceptionally fair-skinned and although I never sunbathed there had been hours upon hours of floating on Mediterranean seas, days of high-summer motoring in open cars . . .

Now, quite suddenly I found difficulties with a page and I panicked. Of all my anxieties, and I am beset by them, from a delayed arrival to an unexpected doorbell, the worst are about doctors, illness, talk of illness, hospitals, and the very worst of these are anything to do with sight. When I was a small child (I must have been three or four) my mother was still with us, she and my father—*both* (unusual)—took me to a clinic in Freiburg to have my eyes examined. (I suffered, and still do, from some form of conjunctivitis.) I had no knowledge of what lay ahead but may have felt that something was amiss because my father insisted on giving me a good luncheon first. We had arrived from our country-place by horse-carriage and train, I recall a quiet, subdued, panelled room, lightly redolent of vapours of good hock. Afterwards, as we walked through the clinic door, I stood stock-still and howled, loudly, unstoppably, like a

56

dog under the moon.

*     *     *

The consequences of this incident reverberated. The attitudes of persons of authority towards myself were never the same again. Before that long moment of the fortissimo public howl (*public:* that's what got my father), I had been an easy, a naturally easy-mannered child, content, fearless, immersed in my games, captivated by food, generating my own interests, respectful of animals, affectionate towards my elders, loving my half-sister (a grown-up sixteen) with chivalrous devotion, never *noisy*. Such at least were the descriptions hurled at me after my fall.

What happened on that afternoon is a blur, a concourse of people running, agitated women in starched attires, men in white coats, rounding up on me. I was hurried across a vestibule, along corridors, into small rooms filled with disquieting objects. At one point I was up before the great panjandrum of European renown, Professor Achsel or Axel, whose name I came across doing research fifty years on. *He* was the man Aldous Huxley, aged eighteen, unable to remain at Eton, uncertain to be able to go to Oxford, was sent to see in Germany in 1912, a couple of years before my infantile débâcle. For me his role

57

was brief: lights shone into my face, a sentence pronounced. The most terrifying confrontation, vociferously insisted upon, was with a paediatrician, *a Kinderarzt*, a hard word *Arzt*, to me an executioner for children. Here all was open condemnation, angry tones, words loudly spoken above my head. Hysteria. *That child is hysterical.* Over-indulged . . . Change of regime . . . Corrective schooling . . . *Reform* . . . Shattered, my instincts were strong and clear: *liberty* was at stake, the good things I enjoyed.

Afterwards: the journey home. In tangible disgrace. My father mortified. This much I understood. Then and there.

\*　　　\*　　　\*

My father was not a man of the twentieth century. In assumptions and comportment he would have fitted better into the world of the more backward-looking *émigrés* after the French Revolution. In his own youth and a part of his middle age, Paris and the Monte-Carlo of the 1890s had been his intermittent playground between long stretches of isolation—he liked to sketch, he dabbled in esoteric subjects, he sought climatic warmth— inhabiting remote villas in unfashionable parts of the Mediterranean: on Corsica, in Spain. There—according to his tales which loomed large in my early childhood years among fruit-bearing trees, he could nurse his small gang of chimpanzees; then back to Offenbach, expensive mistresses and the ever futile systems of roulette. Back eventually also to the needed, though never actually looked out for, solvent marriage. He had to fall in love with the woman first. He *was* susceptible. Looks were essential, and so of course was perfect feminine behaviour. Whether by birth or training. The first kind one married. At one point my father's money, such as it can have been, was gone. One of several brothers, no primogeniture, parents dying early, family land ... Brief spells in one or two cavalry regiments (not cheap), eventual escape into what were for him the better worlds. So relatively late in life my father tied himself into two marriages. The first ended in death, TB, and left a small child, my half-sister; the second in divorce, leaving another young child, myself. My father's first wife had been an heiress, a real one, heavy rich Jewish Berlin until the great post-war inflation put a stop to that. My mother's family was well-off with strings attached by antiquated wills. There had also been money on my maternal grandfather's side, commercial interests in India where he spent part of the year. I never knew him. His wife, my grandmother, had thrown him out when something suddenly came to light: a dancer, quite a respectable affair, my mother would say. *She* took his side but was not

59

allowed to see him. Now that family was also Jewish, partly Jewish. I never learned *how* partly, nor through whom. Nobody cared much, or had to—happy days; they did not practise or talk much religion, though most of them must have been baptized at one time or another. Protestant baptism, unfêted, unobtrusive. What about, I sometimes ask myself, social anti-Semitism, prevalent then as much on the Continent as it was in England? Well, one doesn't have to read Proust to realize that wherever it was rampant, it was also patchy. There was a charmed Jew in every *faubourg*, every Jockey Club, at every royal court. Money? Yes, money counted, equally so did looks, chance, caprice. *We* also had had the other extreme: there was a much-mentioned, strictly orthodox great-grandfather who made a point of not eating with his numerous goyim friends. He called them so to their faces. *His* fortune held up for a while—making much bad blood among the various family branches—in fact, a share of it lasted a year or so into my own majority.

\*     \*     \*

At the time of my mother's marriage—pre-1910—there was enough left for the trustees to let her buy a country house for her husband. A château, a Schloss, as it was called in those parts: the Grand Duchy of Baden. It was a

60

manor house, architecturally respectable, with parkland, and a good deal larger than many of its namesakes at Bordeaux. All the same, a family seat it was not.

What was best about it for me were the stables, the vista of lawn and old trees, the grape vine on the south wall of the guest wing from which we vinified a small barrel each year (I was familiar early with the vapours of good hock), the apple orchard with a score of varieties for eating and strong cider, the kitchen garden growing strawberries and asparagus on sandy soil, sent off in the early morning, horse-drawn, to the markets of Breisach, Freiburg and Basel.

As to *why* we were where we were, in that south-west corner of Germany, a couple of hours' ride from the Swiss border, ten minutes' walk from Alsace, from *France*, yet still inside Germany, is something I am reluctant to go into again here. I am paying the price now for having folded a certain amount of actual fact into my novels—fact moulded to fit the shape of a particular narrative. My difficulties now that I have committed myself to writing what could be called fragments of autobiography are multiple. When I feel that I must repeat myself—to explain, to twitch the thread of chronology—I am afraid that I shall bore, even disgust the reader who may feel cheated; alternatively it would be presumptuous to assume that the reader has read the book, *the passage in question*, and that moreover he remembers what he read. If on the other hand I fail to jog the unremembered memory, I may cause lack of clarity or cohesion. Well, this is something I shall have to balance as I go along. So now I will say that it had to do with my father's dependence on the goodwill of his previous parents-in-law concerning his own young daughter to whom he was much attached, and who was of course *their* granddaughter, about whose health and proximity they were despotically concerned. Her mother's young death loomed large. I cannot recall a time without awe at the mention of words like Sanatorium or Consumption.

*     *     *

My parents' marriage, the first part of which they spent in southern Spain which they only left because of my impending and unwelcome birth, did not last partly because of my mother's habit of falling seriously in love with another man every few years. This might not have prevented a union on a durable base—my father in spite of many rigidities was of a tolerant nature—had it not all turned out to have been a mutual mistake, each having embarked on a false premiss. My mother—she made this clear to me, later, during the periods when I, adolescent, had become her companion—had hoped to get over a serious, previous attachment. My father, dazzled by looks, had failed to notice that his conquest was also intelligent, very intelligent, and worse. He read little besides sale-room catalogues and Sherlock Holmes. His interests were aesthetic. He was a collector, chasing handsome, well-crafted, sombre objects, pewter, china, bronze, as long as they were made well before 1700, and to the scale of his fluctuating finances. The new château's function was to house and display his acquisitions. Except for my mother's graceful things of a much later period, light-heartedly arranged in her two drawing-rooms, we lived in a museum. There was a Renaissance wardrobe and a Gothic prie-dieu in what passed as my nursery. And this at a time when my mother began to discover and love the French Impressionists. To confuse matters further, my parents shared a civilized surface; his easy manners covering reticence and formality, hers animation, sparkle, an effortless handling of situations. They liked telling stories, anecdotal versus analytical; one *recalled*, the other tried to rearrange the world.

That 'previous attachment' of my mother's, in plain words a love affair between a married man—a painter of some stature—and a young girl of good family was not a thing one got away with. (I repeat: pre-1910.) My mother *had* a way of getting away with. She paid later.

63

The attachment came to an end because the wife was making gestures towards suicide. There had been talk about an open window. The lovers honourably made the joint decision to separate and kept to it. My mother went to Paris; met my father, got engaged. She intended to enter a new life and milieu. She soon realized, but not soon enough, that it would not do for her; at the point of girding herself to break off the engagement, a family crime occurred in a German garrison town. An horrendous front-page item: my father's elder brother, the colonel of his regiment, had been shot dead by his wife's lover, a captain in the same regiment, and with her connivance. She eventually was sentenced to death; the lover succeeded in hanging himself in prison. These events unleashed intense public reactions, they gave grist (goings-on in the Army élite!) to the not inconsiderable anti-militarist factions as well as to an anti-Semitic populace—the press falling upon my father's connections: Jewish parents-in-law wallowing in their opulence. The Kaiser's establishment hardly knew where and how to cover up; there was a full-blown political scandal, not the first of that reign, nor the last. My father was both aloof and shaken: there was no place for such things in what may have been his private universe. My mother decided that she must stand by him. And she did.

*　　　*　　　*

One thing never clear to me—tales varied—
was whether they got married in Berlin
Cathedral, *the* official RC strong-hold in the
*terra infidelibus* of Protestant Prussia, or
privately in one of the in-laws' drawing-rooms
by an amenable Jesuit. What is certain is that
my mother had to convert, as had her
predecessor; my father was not in the least a
religious man but a Catholic was 'what one
was'. We had fourteen—or was it sixteen?—
unadulterated generations behind us. No
mixed marriages. A social thing. How unlike
dear England.

*　　　*　　　*

There was one domain my parents had
counted as common ground. *Both liked to eat
well.* My father was a connoisseur, he knew
what food ought to be, when and how it should
be bought, cooked, presented. He was able to
cook himself. He had made friends with the
chefs of the epoch, sat in their clattering
kitchens, shared their imperial pints of
champagne provided to keep them cool, drunk
from the bottle in full combat: lifted by left
hand, the right carrying on with spoon or
chopper. Then he went home, simplified, took
the glazes out of the sauces, tamed the
bastardizing profusion out of the grand-hotel

cuisine of the Edwardian era. He was on the right road early. The road to Escoffier's *'Faites simple'*, to Elizabeth David . . . The road insolently, vulgarly, clogged up now once more.

When we came to live on our own, my father was my first cooking master though I was hardly tall enough to reach a stove. He was one of many who followed, a genealogy of men and women, beloved friends, amateurs, near professionals, who taught me such principles and skills as I may have.

Now my mother, if she liked good things—she too, if much later, learned how to put hand to pot—often disagreed with the way my father held they must be done. She was apt to be *distraite* at table and did not take too seriously his axiom that two items, flour and water, ought to be rationed in a decent kitchen. While my mother was with us, we had a full complement of servants. All but one vanished when she left (leaving bricks and mortar but no money). The cook of the old regime was female and north German. Our chief manservant was French. Flour, like sugar and animal fats, never seems to be rationed in the north of anywhere. The cook, unlike the Frenchman, was on the mistress's side. There *were* sides. And so food, the one thing my parents had counted on for pleasant daily safety, turned out to be what they quarrelled about tenaciously and often. I can still hear the altercations about my mother's having ordered cauliflower covered in white sauce.

*     *     *

Now back to the day we returned from the visit to the Freiburg clinic. My father had always been well disposed towards me, much in the way he was to animals, wild or domestic. But I was not an animal and had shown that I did not know how to behave. There came a time full of menace spoken or unspoken. They had been impressed by the child executioner. He had drummed into them how wrong my previous upbringing must have been. The immediate tangible outcomes were only sessions with compresses dipped in a camomile solution, and the grated carrot substituted for my mid-morning chopped smoked ham on bread and butter.

*     *     *

I do not hold with the belief become so prevalent these days that any traumatic or so-called incident in childhood exercises a fatal hold on future life. Anyway, my *mauvais moment* had been self-inflicted. (Whatever its origins.) I daresay it was mishandled. A distrust—mutual—had been created; it surfaced on occasions in the after years. While my father was alive, it expressed itself in an

67

anxiety about me which perhaps, after all, I inherited from him. I have also seldom been quite unafraid of my mother who was capable of random tyrannical moods. Barks indeed, not bites. But it is barks that induce shock. When I was already eighteen or nineteen, she would threaten to throw me to the wolves in consequence of some misdeed or other. I often behaved not well in terms of conventional morality. (Not that she knew the half of it.) The wolves were of course the bureaucratic eminences, my legal guardians, who loomed large and far away. My bugbears like doctors. Against them she was often my ally.

# CHAPTER FOUR

*Paris 1949—50, winter/spring—Friends—
Young American talents—Head in sand—
Solutions?*

When I had become aware in Rome that I could not read a printed page with ease, my age was no longer four, it was nearer twice nineteen. I did not howl. Yet something was wrong. I was alone. What should I do? What did I do? Nothing. I stopped trying. Stopped work. Presumably stopped thinking. I find this incomprehensible now.

I hung on for some weeks. It rained a good

deal as it can in the Roman winter, heavy rain falling on huge umbrellas tangling perilously above the slim strips of pavements. I did not tell anyone. I had company, good company, if not real friends as yet. So I fled to France where people I was much attached to happened to be living. Did I tell *them? Not at once.* 'Good advice' was what I felt I must ward off, sure though that it would be given in due time. Side-tracked as long as possible.

I cannot account for the kind of secret hibernation of those months that year. I can recall in detail where and how I lived: how I got through the days, the evenings, the nights. Agreeably much of the time. So apparently no hauntings, no guilt; nor sprint of words to keep the Mexican book alive. I shut out any notion of medical help. Why the conviction that there was nothing to be done? I don't think I was even badly frightened. *And I did not ask myself what was to become of me.*

Others might. In Paris there was my guardian-angel friend, Allanah Harper; there was E: Esther Murphy, the companion of my Mexican travels, the woman with the passion for oratory, history, politics, and no aptitude whatsoever for domestic life. Suitably, she had married in turn first John Strachey, the socialist MP and one-time British Minister of Food, then Chester Arthur III, grandson of the American president of that name. 1881—1885. (Oh, the amount of White House lore I have absorbed!) And there was Pierre Mimerel, my first French mentor, the elder and better of my early youth, the brotherly, and ultimately the paternal friend. He lived with a second wife in Touraine on a wine estate, where I stayed for weeks on end, alternating with a room at the Hôtel des Saints-Pères on a corner of the Boulevard Saint-Germain. One or all of these friends, sooner or later, would find me out.

The days ran along through that winter ... I must have been good at staving off inquiries. One source of diversions (incurious) was a nest of young American writers, some already in limelight, some not at all, squatting at another small hotel off the other side of the boulevard in the rue de l'Université: Jane Bowles, Truman Capote, Carson MacCullers with companions and one elder and better, Eudora Welty. Allanah and I spent many of our evenings in their lair. We called them the nail-biters, because this was what they did, sitting in a row in one of their hotel bedrooms when we had assembled, clutching a glass or a toothmug, for a session, always too long, of pre-dinner drinking, biting their fingernails in despair over world affairs. How right they were. Allanah and I shared many of their views if not their habits, were captivated by their writings, deplored their drinking—bad stuff mostly, and too much of it—Allanah on principle, I for the delay of dinner. We were much attached to Jane Bowles, an angelic, witty, suicidal imp, with a profile that recalled Rimbaud.

Dinner achieved, bill shared more or less fairly, at some bistro, some of us would end up at the Café de Flore, or the Deux Magots while others, when these shut by 2 a.m., would disappear on foot towards Montparnasse.

That much for the evenings. In the daytime I slept late, walked streets for hours, went to afternoon concerts (never to a film of course), treating music as the opportunistic amateur consumer that I am.

E. began to notice the aimlessness of my existence and its cause, reacting mainly with a wringing of hands. Being fatalistic as well as unpractical, she rather easily fell for my farrago—'There *is* no diagnosis for this kind of case . . .' 'Reading specs would be of no use at all . . .' (That assertion turned out to be the one thing I was right about.) Pierre Mimerel was French rationality and intellect personified, a Cartesian by every turn of his well-educated mind. This included, logically or not, a cynical view of the Faculté de Médecine: stoicism was his own comportment, one did not go out of the way to seek relief from opinionated medicos. Moreover he did not take my later and later literary vocation very seriously; perhaps I had already read too much for my own good. During the early phase of our acquaintance, he had dubbed me, '*Dix-sept ans: Je Sais Tout*', the title of a youth-magazine

71

of the day, *Seventeen: And I Know It All.*

*       *       *

There was another threat. Living, *practising*, in the rue Bonaparte footsteps from my temporary abode at the Saints-Pères, there was Jeanne Neveux—then married to the playwright Georges Neveux—Aldous Huxley's sister-in-law, recent convert to and proselytizer of the Bates System, *The Art of Seeing* (Huxley's book written in gratitude for the remarkable improvement of his own sight). It was unthinkable for me to be in Paris without seeing Jeanne. She was Maria Huxley's cherished sister, linked to her by the long spontaneous, vivid, ill-typed letters Maria wrote at night—Aldous asleep—from the unfathomably remote house in the Californian desert with the intention of leaving a record of Aldous's life. (Maria was fluent in three languages and colloquial in two or three more; she could not spell in any.) I was fond of Jeanne—straightforward in speech and action, robust, forging her own road; unconventional, yes, but without any of the extravaganzas and style that marked the other three Nys sisters (Nys: their maiden name), Belgian though they were. Jeanne had nothing of Maria's visionary, subtle and fantastic nature, nor the fragile health, subdued every hour of the day, laying down her life to serve gracefully, lightly, those she loved. Aldous—*who needed it*—first and last.

Of course I went to see Jeanne. And inevitably was shown the Bates Sorcery Chamber—blackboards, cut-outs, beads, balls, cardboard fans . . .

*       *       *

In the end the most effective lever in undoing my serene inertia was Allanah. Allanah, fully as eccentric, in quite different ways, as E, vague, indecisive, weak when pursuing her own ends, was capable of acting at times, acting with quick forceful, focused precision in order to rescue or direct, indeed change, the future of a friend or anyone she saw neglected, underrated and in need of help. Her interventions were often effective, always in a right direction; she saw aptitude or talent in the lame duck where no one had looked before, and although her own main interest was in literature, or rather poetry and poetic literature (Rilke, Virginia Woolf, Edith Sitwell when Allanah was still a schoolgirl and Edith exposed to ridicule by Noël Coward). Her range of rescues and launchings covered a variety of fields: refugees stuck in menial work, prisoners of conscience, gypsies, battery hens, dogs too fierce or too submissive, dogs in quarantine . . .

*And unpublished writers.* I was still living on

the money she had made over to me at that barren time. What happened, out of a hat it seemed, went somewhat like this: Allanah had gone to England to see her mother, shortly afterwards I found myself stepping out of the night-ferry at Victoria Station. Allanah met me and the next stop was an NHS surgery. The appointment had been made. Now? 'Yes now, we have twenty minutes to get there.' I neither consented nor collapsed. Just went. I was seen by a woman who was vaguely and not very interestedly puzzled. Allanah paid little attention to the inconclusive outcome as she had a second appointment up her sleeve. After lunch. It was the weekend, Friday afternoon. Off to Harley Street to an Hungarian of some reputation who had done wonders for a mutual friend. An intelligent, unstuffy middle-aged man (I went to see him more than once in the course of time) who advised me to have a cocktail whenever I felt strain. He did say cocktail, not a drink. He seemed to have no objection to a third consultation with the Corbetts, who were then practising the Bates System in England and had been the teachers of Jeanne Neveux. I was booked with them for the Monday. I found two kind and serious elderly women and left with a few tips that have been useful to me ever after. (Write on green paper, not white: less glare. Never read or copy looking down on a flat surface: hold the page or book at an angle. Never stare . . .')

74

*Glare* . . . Back in Paris, Allanah having led me for good measure to a very eminent old man, le professeur . . . who radiated humanity and reason. And at that point by the convergence of opinions, a definition of my trouble was beginning to emerge. *Glare*—strong light, sun . . . I had the wrong kind of skin. Photophobia . . . Nervous tension . . . (The wrong kind of nature as well?) From then on, slowly, not at once, everything got better.

## CHAPTER FIVE

*A well-loved friend transferred from fiction—France: his first world war, his 1920s—Marriage—Oriane—Enter a young fool—Ditto the fool's sister*

In the late spring I planned return to Rome. Conveyed, I hoped, helter-skelter by the Pierre Mimerels in Allanah's very new, very small 5CH Renault, lent to us—ex-Paris—for five and a half days. Cars were hard to come by, petrol ruinously expensive; Pierre's only car in running order at the time was a very old, very large Rolls-Royce. Allanah must have been mad to part from her vulnerable little treasure, making it travel all the way to Rome and back. The stipulated five and a half days' return was because of a *concert spirituel* at the church of Saint-Sulpice a few streets away from her hotel, she wanted to attend on Friday next. *I* would have argued; Pierre refused to consider so ungrateful a response. *We* were mad to accept. The Mimerels wanted to see Rome and indeed Pisa and Florence on the way, to none of which they had been. I was enchanted by the prospect of their company and, like all of us in our younger days, would put up with any discomfort rather than *not* go by car.

I have written about Pierre Mimerel before: he appears in three of my novels. In two of them as the same fictional character, a writer of social philosophy, a man of perhaps too rigid principles. In the third novel he reappears, still under a fictional name, in nearer biographical form. Simone has not yet been heard of; instead we have a semi-biographical display of his first wife Oriane, who—semi-*auto*biographically—put me through a good many hoops.

The real-life Pierre, my elder by a decade, though immensely advanced in wisdom, calm and serene resignation, was not a dry man nor an over-educated theoretician; he was a sportsman, a practitioner of many skills, a man whose daily life was animated by laughter, humour, irony, with mishaps turned into hilarious stories: being with him entailed constant teases, often at one's own expense. He also happened to be born one of the very best amateur drivers I ever sat next to. Driving motor cars in my young days was an activity passionately pursued. Pierre's double at the wheel was surprisingly Maria Huxley: they equalled each other in speed, safety, grace. Both were more than competent mechanics.

Maria drove one of Signor Bugatti's snorting monsters (to their creator's amazement). Hers was scarlet, with the long linear bonnet beautiful to our eyes in that decade which had fallen for cubism and much that it implied; the passenger seat had been specially designed at the Turin Works to accommodate Aldous's grasshopper legs. Maria was the first woman to hold an Italian driving licence. One remarkable thing about her crossing continents in racing cars was her physical fragility. And so was Pierre Mimerel: fragile. After his three elder brothers had been killed by 1917, he though under military age went into the trenches. He returned seriously ill and remained so for several years. This was the reason why he was sent to live in a warm climate; first Biarritz, then the south of France. It was that fragility which prevented him from becoming the tennis player they thought he was going to be. His friends and early partners had been Borotra, Brugnon, Cochet, Lacoste, the Four Musketeers. At the start of their first summer of play, Pierre won every set. He was slightly older, had the tennis eye and mind; by autumn they had overtaken him, he was unable to win a single game. (He did become a very good, quite highly placed, French player; his mental agility had remained, if not his stamina.)

*     *     *

Now forward to the planning of our Italian jaunt. We decided that we would have to set off pre-dawn on the first of our allotted mornings. To get Allanah's car, the Mimerels would have to come north to Paris the evening before, which meant a night at an hotel. The well brought-up French do not have the habit of the well brought-up British of asking their friends to 'put them up' on such occasions. It is called being given a bed and entails no obligations on the guest. The other day *(our* day: in the 2000s) I happened to come across a comment made *circa* 1905 by a pillar of New York society in one of Edith Wharton's novels, 'Lady Cressida', the pillar said, 'is coming over—you know the English: they never go to hotels!' Well, the Mimerels who did, and paid for their hotels, were not well off. I may have been misleading by mentioning the old and large Rolls-Royce. They were too generous, quixotic, too *unbusinesslike*, to cope with the demands of friends and neighbours, let alone succeed in any commercial enterprise. Unfortunately, commercial enterprise was what Pierre frequently had to let himself in for. Of prosperous if by no means opulent family, he was the descendant of a long line of *magistrats*, civil servants holding high judicial office since the reign of Louis XIV, a class of men of rigorous financial probity. Pierre's *lycée* had been Condorcet until he was swallowed into the Great War. Afterwards, when up to a point recovered, he was educated at Polytechnique, one of the *grandes écoles* which could mean and did in his case a wide acquisition of technical skills as well as intellectual and administrative knowledge. However, during the post-war years, his diminished health ruled out any official or sedentary career. Hence the stabs at commercial enterprise . . . The first, by choice not chance, and little gain in view, was in publishing. Pierre happily joined the firm of Bernard Grasset, the hope and home of new young literature. Too soon it became clear that this entailed Paris, an office, an indoor life. His connection—his friendship—with Grasset endured for many decades, yet at the beginning of what might well have become a partnership, the frail young man alight with insights and ideas was chased away by a (detested and determined) conclave of doctors into warmth and open air. His parents were persuaded to consent, remaining formidable shadows in his life.

Formidable, not because of his father's being the holder of an eminent position in the

French judicature, they were formidable in their stoicism and their grief—the loss of their three elder sons and the stony readiness to sacrifice their last. Pierre had enlisted as a volunteer. Encouraged? Persuaded? *Pushed?* His father was a liberal man, an agnostic, a Dreyfusard . . . We knew of the icy dislike Pierre bore his mother: a rigid Catholic, fanatical xenophobe, unshakably *anti-Dreyfusarde*. In the long years with him—Pierre lived into his nineties—I, his two wives and his large devoted entourage were still aware of the tragedy and the conflicts of his younger life. For his part, it remained unspoken.

Letting a survivor be the heir was not seen to be right. Pierre was expected to make his own way: to work, or rather to have an 'occupation'—sparingly helped along by his father—that could be pursued in a mild climate and mainly out of doors. So at one point he had found himself exercising his talents as a hands-on mechanic in running a garage at a small fishing port in the south of France. Garage Excelsior (the name bestowed on it by the former—bankrupt—owner) was a large and airy workshop in which the vehicles owned by anyone who knew Pierre—and everyone in that village knew everyone—were being magnificently serviced. On account more often than not. I, while under-age, was allowed to draw petrol on credit and thus able to run a car. In due course the sheer space of the Garage Excelsior had inspired Pierre to set up a bus line to link his village and others such with the great naval port of Toulon. The service was conducted open-handedly and with panache. The buses looked somewhat home-made and up to a point they were: put together from diverse obsolete parts. They *ran*. Pierre had contrived an intricate timetable—not an easy matter in pre-computer days—using the system, he said, of the French National Railways. The resulting schedule admirably served work-men, shoppers, office girls and a public eager for the cinematographic offerings of Toulon. The bus line was much enjoyed. It went into liquidation even before the reprieve of 1938 presaged the end of an epoch and that kind of life.

\*   \*   \*

The war. In the long years when the perennial deeds of human courage, crime and madness were committed the world over in an unfathomable crescendo, much depended on where and what one was—the accidents of place, age, race. Germany? Poland? Soviet Russia? Japan? England, the England of Dunkirk and the Blitz? One may well have considered France the least fatal option. Quantitatively. In terms of danger, misery, losses, fewer men and women were tortured, deported, dispossessed, frozen to death; fewer were killed, fewer cities destroyed. There was hunger, severe hunger, though not to the point of terminal starvation. France was inflicted with another kind of suffering: moral dubieties, divisions. A man in Pierre Mimerel's circumstances—turned forty, without political allegiances, without so obviously a trace of the 'wrong blood', was only moderately likely to become a victim or a combatant. In a measure he had his choices or what one might call predispositions. He had been conditioned to be revolted by the physical realities of war and to distrust arguments and emotions in favour of the justice or efficacy of waging it. Although quintessentially if unselfconsciously French, he was no nationalist and innocent of chauvinism of any kind. His choice of friends was cosmopolitan.

Pierre had long despaired of the human race at large whose hope for a better world, he held, could be realized only by the rule of a moral and intellectual élite, drafted, for a limited stint, not elected. (*Quis custodiet . . . ?*) There were other factors in his make-up such as a spontaneous readiness to spring to the assistance of anyone in need. This in wartime entails dangers. One must add that he happened to have known Charles de Gaulle quite well at school where the two boys heartily detested one another.

So how did Pierre fare in the war?

82

That he survived we know. He did not join the Free French; he did not seek to make his way to Carlton Gardens, London; he did not join the Resistance at home; nor did he express approval or enter into any contact with the Vichy régime. A lack of engagement that made him look compromised to many sides. The winter of the Phoney War—with the future both so perilous and so blank—he spent with Simone, who had recently and decidedly come into his life for good, on a viticultural property in Provence owned by friends with whom she was learning to make wine, having given up a city job for Pierre's sake. The vintner friends were Jews and were wisely making arrangements for a withdrawal—one did not quite speak yet of an escape—to Algeria. When the débâcle came in the spring of 1940, the German armies streaming into France, Pierre's first and still legitimate wife, stuck with her parents who had already fled from further north, claimed her husband's protection. Dutifully, painfully, uncertain of their chances of reunion, he left Simone, who then took charge of her friends' estate: they had got away in time. He managed to make his way in the direction opposite to that in which what appeared to be the entire population pressed to go, and so was able to find and conduct Oriane and his in-laws through the exodus from Paris. They, as everybody else on those roads at that time in that excruciating crawl, came under fire, took cover in ditches, saw much grief and horrors, passed endless days of tedium, noise, discomforts, punctuated by spurts of acute fear. They succeeded in reaching the Unoccupied Zone and, eventually, the Mediterranean coast. There, once safely installed—safely for the time being—in the house, the spacious white cubistic structure in a calm olive grove the Mimerels had had built a few years ago— Pierre left them. It was not the end of his marriage: *that* had begun at its beginning; it was one more stage in the never entirely accomplished ending of that bond.

The beginning, some fifteen years ago, had been sought for and applauded by families and friends. They came from a compatible, if by no means parallel milieu; they shared the disillusionment of the young of the inter-war years, their thrust towards freedom from old ethos, stale ideas, bearing children (cannon-fodder!), towards pleasures unconnected with careers or duty—*Les Fêtes*, *Le Sport*, *Le Grand Air*, New Art. The Jazz Age of the upper-class French as I see it now—as I was told about, read about, having been both too young and not belonging to have lived it: I would never have been asked to *Le Bal du Comte d'Orgel*— that brief age, in that coterie, had in my imagination talent, verve, fastidiousness and style. The Paris smart and young shared some of the tastes—hoaxes, dressing-up, parties in unlikely places—of their contemporary English counterparts, while eschewing their excesses. One might worship the circus, Joséphine Baker, fast cars, Suzanne Lenglen, but one retained one's manners. One did not dream of smashing up one's host's apartment, one tried to pay one's way, and one certainly did not get drunk. Indeed, guzzling of any kind, the venerable and classless French creed of good living, was dismissed as gross and out of date.

In their set, young Pierre and young Oriane were symbols, leaders. Their great good looks, their stance of pages hanging about the corner of a Florentine Renaissance canvas, the way they moved, insubstantial, epicene, displayed a kinship with each other, a common provenance. Yet they were not related. People said they were made for each other, but what prompted this was that they looked so much alike, not feature by feature but as types, figures cut out from the same fashion plates. Which is not the same as *being* alike. For them, *fatally* not the same.

That *faux jumeaux* image of the first *ménage* Mimerel, the false twin-image was ubiquitous. *I* saw them—before they ever saw me, a year or more before we actually met—saw them on the sea front, on a beach, passing in an open car: hatless, hair streaming in the wind, profiles finely, austerely carved; saw them leave a dingy cinema hall after a Buster

Keaton film, gliding by lightly like cats' shadows. To me they were apparitions. My mother, a cool observer, would refer to them as the Heavenly Twins—she did it to annoy, irritated as she was by my admiration and curiosity, the latter shared by half of the inhabitants. That was at the time of the Mimerels' first descents on Sanary, our village port.

*     *     *

Pierre and Oriane got married to each other because they were expected to. Oriane in her fashion loved Pierre; she often betrayed him, would have humiliated him, had he not been uniquely impermeable to humiliation. She leaned on him, sought his attention and his services through decades, to his frustration and Simone's. However one looks at it, all was not her fault. In spite of various levels of appearances, they were crassly unsuited to each other: in character, in moral outlook, in temperament. Above all in temperament. Pierre was quietly affectionate, emotionally chaste, yet capable once he had reached maturity of deep emotion. Oriane, assertive, restless, volatile, quick to set up drama where she found none, had required from the onset of their married life a strong husband with definite demands and the will to get them met. Capable of ruthlessness, she would have respected one greater than her own; determined to dominate, she might have flourished under a more powerful domination. She was bright, very bright, well educated, having made, as they say, *des études brillantes.* (Without an end in view.) She could organize, had taste, visual taste, instinctive and acquired, welcoming with ease Braque, Derain, Juan Gris, Dufy and others before and after, to whose canvases Pierre's mother would have liked to have taken the sharp point of her umbrella while *her* parents had the portrait of their cherished only daughter done by Kissling who made her look what to some degree she was: an essence of the modernity of the day. Quick-minded, she had no abstract or speculative intelligence, nor much innate moral sense, indeed Oriane felt quite pleased whenever she succeeded in pulling off a bit of cheating, some little lie, some small meanness or unnecessary complication. Work, a job absorbing her (considerable) abilities, might have been salvation: born a stretch further into the twentieth century, she might have become an efficient and successful executive; instead she got herself, and others, into a good deal of mischief. Serious mischief, impairing her own stability and health.

There was one terrain on which she need not have been defeated: as it happened— another facet of the twin pattern—Oriane matched, more than matched, her husband's tennis talent. Indeed for a short period she was a sparring partner of the Divine Suzanne. It all came to naught by one of Oriane's provocative involvements. The international tennis world proved more tough than herself.

\*   \*   \*

I realize that in trying to write as—truthfully as I see it—about my dear Pierre's first wife, I have been using a fictional name, one I once used in fiction. What is the instinct that prevents me (in another country . . . after all that time . . .) from lifting one veil off her identity? Names have a curious potency: without this camouflage, I should not have had the detachment nor the candour. I am writing about a friend; I am writing about a woman whose life might have been a splendid one and instead got stranded in make-believe, singleness (despite a string of lovers, for show often, more than real), unfulfilment. She did not succeed in wrecking her husband's life, she *remained* in it. As she did in mine.

We became friends after I was well out of my adolescence, and I remained fond of her, if at times exasperated. When I was very young, I exasperated *her.* I was madly in love, she strung me along. I was made a component of her suite—a poor thing, wrong sex and all, but her own. I carried her market baskets (squashing in my ardour cream cheeses under

88

melons), walking one step behind her aspirant-in-chief, a handsome scowling young man who was trying to become a painter (the *amant en titre*, the locals said; Pierre said nothing at all; then and ever after). I was taking it deeply—as one does at seventeen . . . First real love, one says to oneself. *How I bored her: such adoration!* (Well, she could look beautiful.) On occasions she treated me quite roughly; public contempt she was best at . . . I was asking for it. Goose is who goose does.

*     *     *

During the last decade before the war, when I was in my twenties, Oriane in her thirties, we saw a good deal of each other, with increasing equality. Oriane had become an affectionate friend and a help in hard times. Inevitably she quarrelled sooner or later with the women friends she elected to induce into her circle. I was property whom she flattered by trying to draw into accompliceship—meaning my help in covering up her more and more unfortunate Bovarisms with men of varied provenance. She needed to live on the edge of scandal; something in Pierre, he *had* his core of iron, forced her into keeping up a minimum of appearances. This put me into an untenable position: if I let myself be charmed into, say, backing up an alibi, I was betraying—shielding?—Pierre; if I refused, I was betraying her.

It was never a question of *telling*. One could not, in any circumstance, impart to Pierre something he did not regard as fit for him to hear.

I was frivolous enough to be amused, even pleasantly alarmed, by the daring and elaboration of the schemes Oriane devised to set up alibis. It was not just her own husband she had to keep account of, her preferred protagonists were themselves attached (generally to wives). Oriane might have done well applying her mind to writing Feydeau farces. All in all it was not a happy situation. Little that was going on was of substance and she was beginning to diversify her undertakings. She *had* unstable health. Her 'nerves' were much to blame. There were interesting cures and providers of cures to be found for which her parents happily paid. Pierre meanwhile, maintaining his public support, was not only nursing a cool distaste but, one felt, reaching out towards a saner, richer, more balanced existence for himself. He was coming out of the arrest of emotional and sexual maturity caused by his war-time experiences as a boy. Neither he nor Oriane had been quite aware of that delay which I now believe was disastrous not only for the marriage but for Oriane: many of her troubles came from the discrepancy in the time-scale of their individual developments. She might never have been wholly satisfied by any role below that of Cleopatra, but she would not have been driven into her desperate search for such a role.

*     *     *

When I wrote of my tenacious hanging on to where I wanted to be, Rome, without prospects, possessions, nor home to return to, did I indicate that I had no family, no family to fall back on? (My mother had hardly ever been in that category.) I did have a sister—for much of my life—a half-sister. Nearly grown-up at the time of my birth, she had been good to me, a loving and sensible rock whenever she was available, which became uncertain due to her escapades—seen flirting with young officers in cake-shops, leading to punitive months in a convent, and not much later to her own early marriage.

Jacko—Maximiliana Henrietta by her baptismal names no one ever used—was the child of my father's first marriage to the poor little rich girl, daughter of the Jewish plutocrats ensconced in Berlin, who died so very young of TB.

Of course Jacko's health was an acute worry to everyone: to her grandparents who cried wolf, pampered, watched; to her father, my father in due course, who was not allowed to take her on his travels and became reduced to living within his in-laws' country. This most unworldly of *hommes du monde* became much attached to the young thing and she to him. When little Jacko did travel, it was with her grandparents and their own sheets on the train to some sedate and pompous spa. Dull it may have been but catch Jacko at any stage not to find something to amuse her and enjoy. She was a flirt, a giving flirt, as soon as she was old enough to smile. Soon after came a propensity to dance and sing. To dance-bands on the gramophone, the tunes she warbled from bath to night were—goodness knows from where she picked them up—the latest hits.

By the time she was fifteen it began to be assumed that Jacko had 'a voice'. My mother, who meanwhile had come into her life, thought of ways to help her towards a musical career. She was very fond of her stepdaughter (at that time). As marriage had forced the chores of maternity on her, a bright, attractive, if definitely *un*intellectual, adolescent was more rewarding than a small inquiring child. She explained this to me rationally. 'Let us see', she told me, 'how you develop.'

I saw her point. My mother's ever fluent talk, impassioned and detached, addressed to whomever might be there to hear, ignited a part of my consciousness for life. What I received from her as soon as I was old enough to feel, well before I was old enough to think, was an impregnation of her own lucid

compassion for the suffering and brutality of—
I cannot put it lower here—the Human
Condition: poverty, violence, disease, the ever-
lurking blows of nature and of fate, the
immutable fortuitous inhumanity of man to
man and beast. Early in my own existence,
much of this became relevant and acute. I was
three years old in the summer of 1914.

Then, around us and all over the articulate
world, events were trumpeted about by rulers,
authorities, newspapers and masses as Just
Causes, Victories, Heroic Defences while my
mother spoke to us of wounding, maiming,
death and devastation. This awareness I owe
to her (an awareness counterpointed by my
penchant for the sybaritic, the epicurean, the
romantic, for the sane and sunlit side of life);
as I owe her for a sustained attachment to
books, to painting, to baroque churches and
Palladian façades, in short to great works of
art. I did not require, it did not occur to me to
require—or to miss—a one-to-one attention
or affection from my mother; what I minded
was that her position gave her power which she
exercised thoughtlessly if seldom. There were
few bridges between her ideals and her private
conduct. As for the needs of my own
childhood, I had Jacko who gave me love and
the fundamental early disciplines—'Don't tell
lies', 'Have you washed your hands?', *'No, you
can't have that'.*

Jacko and my mother got on splendidly:

93

elder and younger sister. Men were attracted to them; rarely to both, though it happened. There was a theatre critic, eminent and feared, a Casanova kind of man, who took my mother to rehearsals of Ibsen and Shaw, talking to her as an equal *and* a beautiful woman, and then walked my sister in the public gardens treating her as what she was, a very attractive, very alive young creature.

There was not a niggle of jealousy: my mother was too assured of her own supremacy; Jacko's ungrudging, unsuspicious, live-and-let-live nature was innocent of the green-eyed monster and its near twin, envy. She would suffer from *chagrin d'amour*, which is not the same. Not the same at all.

Meanwhile there were Jacko's musical intentions to deal with. My mother, uninterested in music herself, brought off an audition with Madame Schnabel, no less. (It may not be remembered that Arthur Schnabel the great pianist's wife, Therese, was a singing teacher of no mean renown in her time.) Insanely spoilt by her grandparents, Jacko was seen as a precocious, frivolous member of the Berlin *jeunesse dorée*, so the outcome of Madame Schnabel's audition came as a surprise. The verdict was indeed there was a voice, a warm light mezzo in the making. For the concert hall. Mme S. was smug and proud of her discovery, ready, indeed eager to begin training a new Lieder singer. Jacko was disgusted. Her aim throughout had been grand opera. She heard herself as Carmen; Mme S. heard Schumann, Wolf and Brahms. Jacko proposed making do with operetta. Mme S. remained adamant—Lieder or nothing. Jacko said she had no *feeling* for 'that kind of drama'. Mme S said that feeling was indeed the essence. And so it came to nothing.

Jacko never quite gave up the vision of herself as Carmen. Disappointed she was, but she did not repine—there were so many good things in life, now and to come. Even during her banishment to the convent there had been a young *curé* with tender eyes.

She went on confidently bawling snatches of cabaret songs, into middle-age, into old age (unacknowledged if noticed at all); some found this cheerful: noise was a part of her presence; it exasperated me. When the wireless came in, Jacko must have been one of the first fans of Radio Luxembourg.

*    *    *

They need not have worried about Jacko's health. It was radiant. It withstood not only the forty cigarettes a day year in year out, but an existence often confronted with grief, precariousness and loss the rich little rich girl had not been prepared for. She lived through these unbroken, with elegance, having what was needed—vitality, courage, strength, combined, unfortunately, with a lack of moral sense as far as world affairs and money were concerned. Her understanding of individual human needs *was* instinctive *and moral.* Perhaps not an unusual feminine combination?

*　　　*　　　*

Jacko, as one may have deduced by now, had looks. No classic features, instead a charming cat-like face with an upturned nose; straight dark hair; a dark healthy skin, monkey-brown, she had come by in the many summers of her later life in Italy and France, wherever she found sun, sand, salt . . .

Add to this a figure envied in and out of fashion, not tall, not short, with long well-shaped legs, wide shoulders, a small waist without—not due to any particular attention on her part—an extra ounce of fat.

My sister's appetites for the sensual good things of life did well by her. She ate like a horse, a discriminating horse (wish she'd been that in her choice of men) who tucked with abandon into any honest food on hand. One of the treats she gave me when I was a child was brown bread and butter: the butter unsalted, firm and cold, a half-inch on the slice of strong farm bread. Yet she had been weaned on—oh those grandparents sunk in upholstery and their own corpulence! a Germano-Edwardian version of French *haute cuisine:* more truffles, more *foie gras*, more cream, more aspic than are allowed by the sense of fitness and measure of true French food. Jacko herself became a serious cook, with a definitive French accent and an extravagant touch of her own.

*       *       *

Was she, my sister, my brave and happy-natured sister, 'family to fall back on' in post-war Europe, I in Rome, she in Paris: both about penniless by then? She was not. Which I am not going into yet. This passage is going to be about a happy, sane, insouciant episode: Jacko's brief, or not so brief encounter with Pierre Mimerel.

*       *       *

It was in the south of France, in the Thirties. I, grown up, was living in my mother's house. By then much had gone wrong. We needed help. I wrote to my sister, who came. She was currently living in Paris, getting detached from her present husband without telling why. We feared that he was up to no good, though not to what extent, nor Jacko's part, if any. Her loyalty to him was firm.

Jacko's first marriage, so obstinately got into at eighteen to a middle-aged man of intellectual distinction and human inadequacy had been a web of incongruities; her second to that young charmer with the radiant looks she had run away with was a disaster of lifelong consequences. At the point she came to stay with us, she and my mother had been estranged for a long time, each alienated by the other's course. Another lost past.

Jacko took to Sanary joyfully. The south of France! I took her to meet my friends the Mimerels. Pierre took to *her*. For the first time in his life, he was interested in a woman as a woman. (Not that he had ever been, for all his graceful looks, attracted in the slightest by a man or boy. There was no homosexual element in Pierre.) He liked, he sought the company of women; the company, no more. Now he fell in love. Not with a pretty young girl, not with the proverbial experienced older woman, but with a woman (experienced, yes) of his own age (their mid-thirties), even-tempered, sensual, sane. She responded, liked him (never conceiving any real idea of his character and mental weight), lightly fell in love. Pierre did not mind 'lightly', he entered that new world with nearly as much ease as Jacko; *ease* not detachment: Pierre, overnight as they say, was a man. He had lost that whiff of insubstantiality, of a shadow too perfect to be real. In more prosaic terms, he and Jacko were enjoying a happy, equal, affair: a love affair. Pierre never looked back. There followed two or three more women—all with dark hair and skins—all good experiences, leaving their beneficent mark. What opened then was the way to permanence, love, peace—the way to Simone.

My frivolous, life-enhancing sister had been the right thing at the right time.

## CHAPTER SIX

*Back again in post-World War II—Pierre* retrouvé—*A wine state—Private unhappiness: tough luck and a mixed cast*

I am aware how far I have reversed—some twenty pages of written words, many years in time—from the spring of 1950 and the southbound start of our little outing, the Mimerels' and mine, Paris—Rome; and how much further still from this book's starting-point, my compass fix, to which I am aiming to return after giving more answers to the questions posed on page one: 'Who was I? What was I? What had I arrived at? From where?' Not that such thoughts had touched my mind on that luminous high-summer day by Lake Geneva; there I had walked immune, a seeing traveller, borne by euphoria. It is *now*, fifty years gone, that I am attempting to give some account of the life of a fairly nonconformist individual in a variety of twentieth-century oases. An account by an amalgam of fragments. The relation of the single man or woman to history is that of victim or of escapee—and in that huge context which turn of the roulette-wheel determines the overlapping elements of circumstances, heredity and chance? As for me, I would consider myself largely and gratefully—an escapee. *As such I owe.* To what, to whom?

Events, we know, are inevitably preceded by a myriad of other events. To give sense and sequence to the recollection of anything one has in person felt and lived, one needs second-hand foundations, expositions, prior events not experienced but guessed at, heard of, cobbled together, *judged.* Or so I find it.

Writing, when it follows its own, often unlooked for, commands, is a queer and puzzling business. And this must be why I shall find myself so often in retreat from that day in Switzerland.

\*     \*     \*

I do not need to say very much about how Pierre Mimerel got through the Second World War. For him and Simone—by then immutably concordant, rocks of strength to one another—it went more or less predictably by their odds. For a time they had gone on tending the vineyard property of their absent Jewish friends, safeguarding what they could. When, after the Occupation of the whole of France, their own position became too exposed, they managed to withdraw in time to a mountain sheep-farm in a remote part of the Savoie. And there they remained more or less for the duration. Occasionally they put themselves at risk: a man—friend or stranger—on their doorstep needing concealment, shelter, a plan for moving on. No one was quizzed or turned away. Beside some painstakingly grown vegetables—seeds were hard to come by—the good meat they were able to produce and the deplorable rationed bread—part sawdust and rats' droppings—there was nothing to eat. An egg was a rare treat, butter an obsessive dream. They had firewood to chop for the winters. It was an existence without most normal pursuits or reliable news, though untouched as it turned out by military action from land or air. A healthy life in its way. There is much tough outdoor work on a mutton farm.

As for Oriane. Her parents had been able to return to Paris after the Pétain armistice. She remained in her own house, looking after a Dutch refugee, a painter with false papers, and is said to have fronted occupying soldiery and Vichy police with considerable cheek.

The worst that happened to Pierre was the destruction of his family home, the thirteenth-century castle of austere beauty in the depth of the Ardèche. It happened twenty-four hours *after* the German surrender of May 1945. A fortified stronghold, the castle had been held by members of the Résistance, the FFI (Forces Françaises de l'Intérieur), and blown up in frustrated rage by retreating Germans.

Two years later (when I had returned to Europe from the other side of the sea by converted troop ship) I had no idea where and how to find Pierre; nor had I met Simone. Pierre spoke to me of her on the day he and I said goodbye on the Mediterranean waterfront. It was September and the war had come. I foresaw return to England, he was about to join the woman he implied was going to be the companion of his life. She came from Normandy; he spoke of how splendid she looked sailing in a sharp wind. 'You would love to see her on a boat,' he said. I vaguely tried to imagine Pierre, who could not and had never learnt to swim. He said that *'physiquement elle est un peu comme ta soeur'. Physically*, I noted, a bit like my sister, *not* in other ways. Pierre glowed with hope. All the same it was a dismal day, that of our parting on that quay; one knew it would be long. It turned out to be seven and a half years.

What one also did not know was that one would not be able to receive letters from or write to Occupied France, and that when this would become possible again, one often *did not write*. The gap, in every sense, had been too great.

*     *     *

Almost at once on my first return to Paris, I saw Oriane. A telephone call to her parents, still alive, still there, and so was she: Paris was now her base, the house at Sanary sold. Pierre? She was evasive. 'You will not like', she said, 'the woman he is with now. And nor', that came out knife-sharp, 'will *she* accept you. And what *she* doesn't accept, he . . .'

A few days later, when I got back after lunch to the Hôtel des Saints-Pères where I had put up, the small hotel at Saint-Germain-des-Prés favoured in pre-war times by some of the Bloomsburies, referring to it as the Holy-Fathers, there was Pierre sitting in one of the stiff armchairs in the narrow ante-room. He was wearing riding breeches and a hacking jacket. He stood up to embrace me. He had filled out; he looked robust, no longer an ephebean cut-out but a man of authority such as you might see in a portrait by Clouet. They were living in the Loire now, he said. 'I've come to take you there on the four-o'clock train, Simone will meet us at Tours.' 'But . . .' I said. 'Oriane . . .' I said. 'Go and pack a bag,' Pierre said.

Simone met us.

*     *     *

It was their second summer as owners of the handsome manor house that had served as hunting lodge to the Château de Chenonceaux in the 1600s. For the Mimerels as for so many others at the end of the war there had been no continuity to slide back into. The Midi, both had loved? Too much for too long had happened at Sanary, too many shadows remained: Oriane's, and Oriane's all too public exploits; and later the years of bitter rifts among the population—as where not in France at those times?—which hurt more if you had known every name, every house, every face. That was a lost past to which they sought no return.

Pierre's parents had died and for the first time he was financially his own man. A share of the inheritance had come to him: one quarter exactly of the whole. The lost brothers' parts went to charity and an only niece. Pierre's own part was not insubstantial.

During the guardianship on their exiled friends' vineyard, he and Simone had become competent wine-makers and later in their sheep-farming fastness they had acquired a taste for agricultural life. Now Les Coudrais, the well preserved, sensibly sized house in the heart of a flourishing wine estate complete with farm, farm buildings and land, was for sale. The price matched their resources. (Probably just.) They bought it.

They had no previous ties with that part of France, knew no one, had no recollections other than high-summer drives through broad calm river landscapes.

By the time of my first stay, they might have lived there for ever.

In the shed, the wine of their first vintage was being nursed in barrels large and small; underground, wines of many previous years were dozing in stacked rows of casks. Human life on the estate was well tempered, calm, content—steady work at varying pace according to the season, light-hearted leisure: over some undemanding card game—*belote* or *chasse-coeur*—in the evening. On Sunday mornings we went riding the work-horses who shared our unserious pleasure. Pierre acted as his own *régisseur* and *maître de chai;* Simone, besides running the accounts and order office, worked hands-on in vineyard and cellar. As did the farmer, the farmer's nephew and the farmer's wife who also saw to the cooking at the main house. (We ate well: an easy return to pre-war French regional plenty thanks to pigs, poultry, orchard, kitchen garden.) Girls from the village rolled in on their *vélos* as needs arose. Wine-making at whatever scale, though exacting constant vigilance at all stages, is not labour intensive at all times; only at the vintage, hordes of old hands, students, casuals from anywhere have to be called in at exactly the right date, kept engaged, entertained, hugely fed. Simone led the main picking line, setting the pace. A tough job for all. And they did it.

I was caught from that very first stay at their house by a sense of harmony, of shared belonging. The farmers, Jean and Elise, had worked on that land, on that edge of their village, since their grandparents' days. They were *tourangeaux. Settled.* The Mimerels were strangers from unknown parts. And such they had remained more or less to the hybrid population of the French Mediterranean coast. *Les Mimerels—Pierre—Oriane*—were perceived as unfathomable birds, affluent (apparently), suave in their ways, made of an alien clay. *Super-Parisians?* They puzzled; were gaped at, talked about. At close quarters, Pierre could inspire awe and for those who worked for him reluctant acknowledgement of his abilities. There were few thanks, however, for his quixotic business ways. He was often duped.

Now in the enclosed, traditional territory of mid-France, the arrival of *Les Mimerels—Pierre—Simone*—had struck gold. Human gold. There came trust, respect, mutual affection. All growing fast. I became aware of the strength and inevitability of the bond between Pierre and the young woman, the wife I had not yet met—she moved towards him from the car she had been standing by, swift, light, intent as we stepped out of the station. Then came the welcome that included me, the

106

ease of the half-hour drive that followed, the welcome we received on entering the house.

That first stay at Les Coudrais went on week after summer week (the very hot dry summer of 1947 which had come after the unconquerable cold of the winter before) without a counting of days or dates. I had brought with me little beyond a change of shirts and linen slacks; oh, the washing and ironing that must have gone on in Elise's and Simone's hidden domains. The Mimerels even inflated their insane hospitality by asking E., left stranded at the Hôtel des Saints-Pères. She came, she stayed, she spellbound her hosts and Elise—who waited at table—with her broad evocations of French and American history delivered in an oratorial voice in near-flawless French with a heavy, not disagreeable accent, while she vaguely stirred about the *noisette de porc aux pruneaux* congealing on her plate, and the luncheon hour—such was the courtesy of that place—became unreasonably prolonged. And when E.'s rather touching appreciation of her hosts' acceptance of herself became felt, the hosts went a step further and asked some of her friends to weekends. They came. Graceful and charmed. Noel Murphy, Liedersinger, the widow of E.'s elder brother, who had fought in France in the First World War; Janet Flanner, back again doing her weekly 'Letter from Paris' for the *New Yorker*, sharp-minded, researching. 'How was it possible that *white* wine was made from *red* grapes?' Irritably, I knew: 'Elementary, my dear Watson.' Pierre took over: patiently, at length. And throughout we drank a goodly amount of our wines, much red, some white, a little rosé—*Appellation Touraine,* all excellent —to hand on an ancient contraption by the dining-room table made of in-built cylindrical stone-lined holes, some shallow, some deep to keep each bottle at the wanted degree of coolness.

And did I bask in what was here on offer? The civilized simplicity, the accompaniment of laughter to the steady theme of daily work, the ease and dignity of human contact in that house, the blessedness of living at the heart of a great uncrowded landscape? I floated rather than basked, fell in with the routines of the present, best-uncounted days. My own life was too much in disarray: I was as unhappy as perhaps I have ever been. The vision I had had in Mexico of the book to write had faded, was nowhere. For good?

After a universal cataclysm, return into a previous world is apt to be convulsive. In my case it was, as well as geographical and material, deeply and privately emotional. (As well as entirely unexpected.) No sooner had I set foot again in Europe—we had landed at Cherbourg—than I and others were dragged into a labyrinth of re-found, new-found old and future loves. One might describe what followed (I have no wish to do so, and never fully shall) as a kind of disordered game of chess; those with supporting roles: confidants, best friends, ever quick to take or switch sides, were more apt to see it as a comedy teetering toward vaudeville, with a cast as shifting as that of a French government. The distribution was unhelpful to begin with; the number of the main players was uneven, precluding any smooth solution. Always someone left out. And so there was pain, betrayals, grand renunciations as well as pettiness, attempted suicides, notes left on dressing-tables: some good behaviour and much bad.

For my own part, I did not come out of it well.

\*      \*      \*

That 'world of telegrams and anger' lasted for the best part of two years. With consequences well beyond. Friendships were mended; none of the original patterns of relationships remained. Outsiders stepped in: one solution was achieved by a sudden and improbable marriage which ultimately may have contributed to the early ending of a life, another by an even more improbable emigration to the United States. For the rest, the venues shifted between Normandy, Paris and Rome. (Oh, the dashes through Alpine tunnels by inadequate cars, the wagon-lit journey where an unexpected individual on the platform stepped onto the already moving train.)

Today there are no survivors of the episode except myself.

The Mimerels were entirely out of it. Whatever they became aware of was not mentioned. *Pas devant . . .* It had been thus in the pre-war years of Oriane's quasi-public enormities (she, by the way, had no connection whatsoever with my current imbroglio); there was a chaste austerity about Pierre—*and* Simone, who was, not merely *became*, so like him—which precluded some matters from being taken seriously or discussed. Pierre had already begun his habit of addressing me as *'ma fille'*, and indeed there are things one does not talk about to one's parents.

*     *     *

Balance returned eventually, and with it flickers of the Mexican book. I had been exhilarated—possessed—by Rome when I was spending time there—contentedly—on my own. It was after Martha Gellhorn (promptly worshipped as the incarnation of courage and honour) had lashed my conscience into actual writing against the forces of self-doubt and sloth. Never wholly conquered. And so after Ischia, which proved so fruitful and disconcerting, had come the slice of time with the book in prosperous progress, cut off by the disaster that seemed to have afflicted my sight and the eventual flight to France, finding friends, rescue and eventual improvement.

We are back again in 1949—50, the winter turning toward spring. As usual—and in contrast to the life of the American nail-biters, touching and doomed, of Saint-Germain-des-Prés—I spent some time in Touraine: Pierre and Simone appeared more established than ever. I was disquietened though by some of the phenomena that had been evident in the days of the bus company and the Garage Excelsior. So much given; so little received. The vineyard seemed flourishing, their wine as well regarded as ever. The estate had kept its old clients, there were almost too many new ones. There were also a few somewhat opulent changes. Handsomely designed new labels; new suppliers for the very best oak for the barrels; the very best corks from Spain (cork still in short supply); experiments with a device for drying raindrops off the grapes at harvest times, not always proving their worth in gold. The real trouble was that Pierre did not seem to like selling: when clients rolled into the yard in their cars and vans to pick up their orders, he could not forbear to slip in a bottle of *marc* or eau-de-vie *de cerises*, some sample of an older vintage or a neatly presented threesome of *rouge/ blanc/rosé*—these people after all were friends, or had come a long way: surely they must stay for lunch. And as for sending out reminders for a bill . . .

## CHAPTER SEVEN

*Three friends' little outing*

So in due course in the pre-dawn light of a fine Sunday morning in May, we were rolling along unobstructed the near-empty Boulevard Raspail, reached the *quatorzième* at Denfert-Rochereau, turned into the Avenue du Général Leclerc towards la Porte d'Orléans— before us *la Route* . . . How often have I done this, before and since, setting out for the south, driving—all leisure and speed? The experience has entered spirit and bone . . .

> Peeling off the kilometers . . . sizzling down the long black liquid reaches of the Nationale Sept, the plane trees going sha-sha-sha . . . through the open window, the windscreen yellowing with crushed midges . . . with the Michelin beside [us] . . .

(That was Cyril Connolly: his words are more potent than I would be able to make mine. Seldom have I resisted quoting at least one passage by him per book.)

112

Our journey this time was not quite like that, the lyrical quality turned out hard to maintain. We were still in a decade before motor traffic glut and ubiquitous autoroutes, but we were also in the decade when cars had been getting worn down and new ones rashly built of poor stuff. Allanah Harper's little new Renault was not the happiest piece of *nouvelle construction.* Engine in the back, boot in front, a perilous distribution of weight, counterbalanced in our case by having filled the front space to the gunwales with bags—that space was not designed for the stocking of neat luggage—bulging with *my* belongings, which were books and the rudiments of clothes. Ourselves we had disposed into a living-space meant for four. Well, we were three. So two in front, one in the back in turns: we were going to share the driving in shifts—long shifts if we were to make Paris—Rome—Paris in five and a half days, with the proper stops for sights at Pisa and at Florence. This meant that we had to get to Rome by the second day's night, however late. The back-seat space was shared with the ingeniously encased spare-wheel, an encumbrance to which we had added overnight necessities, such as sponge-bags, changes of linen, sweaters, as well as basic sustenance: ham, Gruyère, hard-boiled eggs, a few apples from Les Coudrais. There could be no question of stopping at any of the *lieux gastronomiques* we were going to pass, nor for a snack at a café or a picnic by the side of the road, only a darting for bread and Evian water in one of the numerous main streets— animated as the morning got alive—we had to pass through. We would eat in the car as we bowled along. (We had our clasp-knives, mine a Swiss-Army, and well-laundered kitchen towels for our laps.) Our spirits were high and the day was as fine as its dawn had promised. The shock, noise and all, was so instant—that kind always is—that there was no time to feel fear. *A blow-out.* Fortunately it had been Pierre's turn at the wheel—within seconds we were stationary, upright, on a safe edge. Next steps went smoothly: we found tools, jack and all, strapped beneath a seat, changed wheels, pushed the dead one, dusty, greasy, limp, into its case. What next? Wasn't that tyre, *all* the tyres, supposed to be new or as good as? Allanah had only had the car for a few weeks . . . The tyres were new all right, it was the quality that was at fault—ersatz. Pierre refused to go on without a sound spare wheel. Repairs, if feasible, would take too long. So get, buy, *find* another—tyres, new or second-hand, were in short supply. The right size? Those small Renaults *were* for export and few of them yet about in France. Well, we could only try. Moreover, it was Sunday.

Gingerly we went on, driving without a *roue de secours.* We were still only somewhere north of the town of Sens. Then we did find a garage

114

open and willing to sell us another brand-new spare. Black market. We moved on again, we had lost time: it could have been worse. We'd make up for it.

Less than two hours and less than another hundred kilometres on, bang—another blow-out. This time a front wheel. Simone had been driving. She, too, coped well. *They* saw the farcical as well as the disastrous side of the situation. This *was* a ridiculous enterprise. For me, the thing to do was to live up to the Mimerel spirit. So once more we went through the rigmarole—aggravated now by the approach of the sacred hour of the French: *le déjeuner.* When we did get to the point of paying for another 'new' tyre, Pierre turned to us: what do we have by way of money? Simone said she was carrying some francs, she had faced the bank . . . not for much, it didn't seem a good idea at this moment to involve the manager . . . Quite. I piped up. I had brought dollars. (Allanah's generous arrangement— nearing its end now . . . Curious how Allanah had come to underwrite this journey in one way or another.) Dollars, exchange controls being still in full swing, seemed a good way of being able to pay one's way beyond the border. There was certain to be a market for them whenever one had to draw purse. How many lire we could expect, how long these dollars would have to last me, I didn't know; at the moment we were still quite a way from Italy.

Pierre told us that two blow-outs in one morning might well be a coincidence and not necessarily an indication of an impending serial repetition. Silently, I dredged up two lines by Racine (correctly?):

*Seigneur! Trop de soucis entraînent trop de
    soins,
Je ne veux point prévoir les malheurs de si
    loin . . .*

Alas such was not my way. Anxious apprehension was the unbridled response to any possible future misfortune. I took my turn in the driver's seat, they folded their kitchen towels over their laps, began peeling eggs, cutting bread, hand-feeding me a length of ham sandwich at the wheel. We were rolling along at quite a good clip.

Our forced delays, Pierre told us, must never reach Allanah's ears. It would belittle her kind deed: she loved her car and had a high opinion of it; moreover she might, God forbid, feel that *she* ought to pay for those *new* new tyres.

Could *we* pay for any more if . . .? Simone said; none of us as yet had owned to any exact amount of cash in hand.

My mind conjured up the winery in the Loire, the account's office, the invoices . . . Firmly I switched it back to Racine.

In the event Pierre proved right. No more

burst tyres, not as much as a puncture—the car performed impeccably (within its limits). All the way.

*     *     *

We got to Lyon, we crossed Lyon, Pierre navigating, we passed Vienne-sur-Rhône and the gates of La Pyramide, the three-star-four fourchettes—Michelin restaurant . . . There we would have liked to eat oh, their cervelas, their unique white house wine, le Condrieu. (La Pyramide—chez Point in those lean, restricted post-war years, was one of the handful of restaurants declared *Monument National* by the government—that is, exempt of all rationing restraints.)

By mid-afternoon we were well beyond Valence: *in the Midi* . . . One sniffed the air, breathed the herbal wind . . . (Why did we ever give up living there?) Somewhere south of Orange, we saw another imposing *hostellerie*, a terrace open to a flowering garden. A sudden need to be still, to stretch, of a sustenance presented other than to monkeys in a cage. Enough of counting minutes. We stopped. The place was silent, empty, we were swiftly, elegantly served—not a tea *à l'anglaise*, just some China tea and a few *sablés* presented in fine porcelain on an immaculate cloth. It was what we had needed, reposeful if short.

The bill was extortionate. I protested. They

were indignant: did we realize where this was
. . .? Their stars . . . (They had stars all right.)
Pierre just drew his portefeuille. We left, I
marching out, head high . . . Halfway down the
garden path, I realized that I was without my
shoulder-bag (dollars and all . . .). But already
the young woman receptionist came running
after us swinging my bag, all charm and smiles.
I thanked her. Pierre grinned, enchanted.

*     *     *

It was a good way still, down from Avignon,
Aix-en-Provence, through back-country—one
glimpse of that austere fragment, the basilica
at Saint-Maximin-la-Sainte Baume, Brignoles:
another crowded market town to pass through,
down the coast by Fréjus, then on to the long
pull along the Côte d'Azur: Cannes, Juan,
Nice, Monte-Carlo, Menton, Ventimiglia,
where we crossed the border into the Italian
Riviera. Somewhere by the Ligurian, we saw
an albergo still lit . . . We stopped. We called it
a day. I forget where it was on that string of
fishing ports, shipyards and small resorts on
the Gulf of Genoa . . . Pietra Ligure it may
have been, or Spotorno. *Quien sabe?* Whoever
they were, they were welcoming, kind and
helpful beyond any call of duty. If it was not
yet midnight, it was not far from it. At what
hour had we risen to our alarm clocks on that
morning?

Yes, they could give us rooms. A *matrimonio*, a double-bedded one plus a single. *Prego. Subito. Not* subito, we said, not at once—we needed something to eat. We were led straight to a table under leaves—it was still balmy. Little beads of light switched on. One could hear the sea. Bottles of wine and Pellegrino water appeared. Was it *antipasti* we'd like? *Salume*, some ham? No; it was something hot we craved. Bowls of chicken broth with floating leaves were brought while solid food was being cooked—*not* warmed up—somewhere indoors. I would like to be able to say that it was the local dish, now much abused, *trenette*, those long, matchstick-shaped strands creamed with a basil pesto, or that some fish had just come in; again I cannot remember beyond that it had been honest Italian family food, and that we, reanimated now, devoured it happily. We liked the nameless red wine.

Somewhat abruptly *il padrone* appeared— we had been served by family, an assortment of boys and middle-aged women. He looked puzzled, a shade offended. Had we been pulling his leg? In his hand was a passport and a length of form. A stiff blue passport.

Indeed, on arriving at the reception desk when we were allotted rooms, there had been the call for *documents*: standard procedure in every hotel or *pensione*. Passports were usually held overnight and the information they contained patiently transcribed on to a form ultimately lodged at the Questura, a branch of provincial police. Earlier Pierre, when he saw to our crossing of the Franco-Italian border, had collected our three passports with the car papers. For all I knew they were still in his briefcase. I had heard him say casually that as we intended leaving before daylight, well before the Questura opened, there should be no need for all that trouble, surely one of our passports would do. I did not pay much attention but gathered this was agreed.

Now *it padrone* plonked down the form: Pierre put on a pair of very small spectacles. *La fiche*, the form which he now began to read in the pretty dim light, was long and the questions it asked were in three languages: Italian

French (idiomatic)—English (not quite so). Answers it required had been culled, as it became evident at once, from *my* passport.

NAME ... MAIDEN NAME ... FATHER'S NAME ... MOTHER'S NAME ...

| | |
|---|---|
| PLACE OF BIRTH | L'Allemagne |
| NATIONALITY | Britannique |
| PASSPORT AUTHORITY | Issued by British Consulate at Guadalajara, Mexico |
| DOMICILE | None (in French) Sans |

                     domicile

Both sounded sinister.

PROFESSION                    Femme de
                                       lettres

    Oh dear! That was Aldous. On a journey long ago, he had liked the tease of it—it was old-fashioned even then—and put it on his form advising me to get into the habit. I did. Less untrue than WRITER.

    And so it went on. That inquisitorial piece of paper exacted more answers than the passport had provided. Pierre, trying to control his mirth, while *il padrone*, not appeased, muttered   *Mexico*?   And   went   on supplementaries:

RELIGION
Agnostic? I muttered; Pierre, turning conventional, squashed that.
                                 Catholique
MEANS OF TRANSPORT    Automobile
REGISTERED               En Grande-
                                 Bretagne

Even the secrets of the poor Renault: exported, then re-imported of course.

DRIVING-LICENCE         Prefecture a
                                   Draguignan,

DESTINATION . . .

And so it went on. All true, Pierre said to *il padrone*, who finally went, still shaking his head.

When he had gone, I said, 'So that is what I am . . . So that's what it looks like.'

Something in my tone perhaps a Mimerel joke too far—prompted Pierre to say, very gently, '*Mon petit*, I had never looked into your passport . . . I had no idea . . .'

Simone tried, 'It does seem a bit . . .' Then, resolutely, she said, 'Pierre, tell Sybille.'

'Why I gave them her passport instead of one of ours?'

'Pierre did not mean to tease you.'

He said, 'To avoid scandal. Simone and I are not married. *Voilà.*'

Shaken out of self-regard, I said '*You!*' Then, 'Ten years, it must be twelve . . .'

'Simone and I have been living as man and wife ever since we went into the Savoie hills during the war. Nobody, including our families, knows we are not legally that. A quick, quiet war marriage is what they believe.'

In a neutral voice Simone said: '*Oriane n'a pas voulu.*'

'Oriane did not want what?'

'They had agreed, she and Pierre, to divorce on grounds of his desertion. Every time it came to the point, she refused to be served with the papers. He tried many times. It's been going on for years. We think that she may give in.'

But why, I said, why desertion? 'Surely there were other grounds . . . Oriane, after all God, when I think of it—the *evidence*—Oriane was so blatant.'

Simone said, *'Pierre n'a pas voulu.'*

I bowed my head. In honour of what Pierre was, of what Simone allowed him to be, in grief for the damage done. Whatever could happen in future, it must be too late for them to have a daughter, a son.

'So when we travel, it has to be in my maiden name.'

Later, when we kissed each other good night outside the doors of our bedrooms—theirs the *matrimoniale*—Pierre said, 'In France nobody raises an eyebrow . . . But *here:* the Vatican invigilates the police and the police invigilate the hotel trade. One avoids causing trouble.'

In a lighter mood, Simone said, 'It's not true that no one knows—my parents *don't.* Jean and Elise do. Oriane told them.'

Jean and Elise, the farmer couple at Les Coudrais . . . ?

'As you well know, Oriane comes to stay with us from time to time, Pierre thinks she needs support. He runs her money affairs. So when Elise took in the breakfast tray to her one morning, Oriane said, "I am the real Madame Mimerel, you know!" Elise told me, and she told Jean and they never ever told anyone else!'

'*Des braves gens!*' Pierre said. 'Good people.'

\*        \*        \*

We did leave at first light and we drove through Genoa and over the Bracco pass and we saw the adorable trio, the Duomo, the Battisterio, the Tower at Pisa dropped down on their rectangle of grass as by the hand of God, and in Florence we stood in the Piazza della Signoria and in the Cappella Medici and trotted at pace through the Uffizi, the Pitti and the Bargello, and after nightfall we entered Rome by the via Flaminio through the Porta del Popolo.

*Part Two*

Junctions

# CHAPTER EIGHT

*Rome, 1950s—Nocturnal glory—Mornings after—Serendipities: the Gendels . . . ? The FitzGibbons . . . ?—A home-making à l'italienne—The Gendels take a hand*

And now so here I was in my old room ottant'otto, 88, on the fourth floor of the Albergo d'Inghilterra, alone after thirty-six timeless, near-sleepless, lightstruck hours of movement and splendour. I had wanted to put before my friends a display, necessarily in compressed form, of some of the greatest artefacts the human world had created in the last two thousand wars. In this I succeeded. Among my more recent local acquaintance were two Americans, two very brave, very difficult men, who had spent the war in Italy underground. One of them, Peter Tompkins, a young, newly married US Army officer who had been parachuted after the Anzio landing beyond the American lines where he led a perilous existence as a wanted man contriving daily, hourly, against the odds to pass himself off as an Italian inhabitant for what turned out to be month after month until the liberation of Rome by the Allies. His survival had left him farouche, both resourceful and immature, thin-nerved, contemptuously unreliable about money, affectionately protective to women, obstinately inclined towards esoteric pursuits. His compatriot, Donald Downes, middle-aged, full of knowledge, given to rages, an Epicurean, very good company when he chose to, had no less dangerously spent his Italian war as an agent of an American organization less open than the Army. Both men spoke Italian like Italians; both had chosen to stay on and live in Rome. Rome had gone into their blood. As it was beginning to get into mine.

Each owned a jeep and *drove* it. Drove it at times like a fury unleashed. And of course they had come. They picked us up late on our first night outside the Inghilterra, lit with ardour and wine, each astride his vehicle. Of course they were rivals, unadmitted if obvious. It was decided that we would hunt in pairs, leading or chasing by instinct and whim. For the first turn Peter took Simone; Pierre and I went with Donald; later we would swap. It was a moonless night, the Spanish steps, the trees on the far-off Pincian, the streets were in shadow, sharp-lined not dark—we raced down the Corso in less than minutes, suddenly roared upwards, rose like an aircraft on take-off: up! a slamming of brakes, a dead halt—we were on the top of the Campidoglio, the Capitol hill, a room-sized space, façades and the central equestrian statue brilliantly floodlit, leaving us breathless, stunned by beauty, perfection, surprise. Seconds and off again diving—a flash

128

of Trojan's Column—into the nocturnal penumbra of Roma Papale: fronts of Palazzo Doria, Palazzo Farnese, via Botteghe Oscure and on with unabated speed, now in tandem, now abreast, towards the Pantheon—it was a jubilee year, it was the beginning of summer: the grandest, the most august, the most playful monuments were illuminated, *lumière* from some unheard source, silent theatre, expanse of cinematographic images of architectural miracles that were of solid stone. A pause in Piazza Navona, in the peace of night, the thick of human hordes abed, a stroll along the live fountains: nymphs and tritons, the movement of water, the sound of water, and *light.* On . . . over the Tiber, over Bernini's bridge, saints and angels flaunting their extravagant gestures the magical dimensions light gives to water, light naturally bestows upon the baroque—we too flew on . . . and presently our ugly little crafts, dun-metalled constructs of the century of mechanized warfare, stood like two specks of refuse in the empty vastness of Piazza San Pietro. Here, for all the elegance, beyond the worldly beauty of that circular enclosure, here beckoned other—further—intimations . . . We merely went our earthly way, the roller-coaster ecstasies of the night were not yet done, swinging up, swooping down one hill then another, we attained, we saw, we sped on— Foro Romano, Tempio di Vesta, San Gregorio, Baths of Caracalla, Il Colosseo, Teatro di

Marcello, San Giovanni in Laterano, Santa Maria Maggiore, Santa Maria in Cosmedin, up the Palatino, up the Quirinale, classical—imperial—ecclesiastical . . . On and on through the glorious jumble of Rome Piazza San Silvestro, Piazza Colonna . . . Dawn was breaking . . . the floodlighting already off as we reached the fountain of Trevi. We threw our coins. Soon after we were done, were back, parted, sank into sleep both dream-ridden and deep.

\*       \*       \*

Late mid-morning our showmen reappeared. We stepped out into bright sunshine and began what evolved into a long, slow day of uncounted hours. They had decided on no galleries, no museums, the time to be given to street life, to markets, the countryside . . . We sought, though, stopping for cappuccino on the way, the Villa Julia for that essential Etruscan link, the Apollo of Veï. By high noon we trundled along the Via Appia Antica, found a trattoria acceptable to both men and there we sat shelling and eating mounds of new *fave*, broad beans, patron vegetable of Rome, you made a wish over the first ones; we ordered, sent back, grudgingly accepted, drank, mezzo-litro after mezzo-litro of wine, Pierre and Simone shocked and amused by our imperious ways (I had adopted them too); the

130

comedy of rejection, promises, protests between padrone, waiters and guests. '*A mano!*' we roared. San Daniele ham had to be cut, transparently thin *by hand*. Why was the mozzarella di buffalo not dripping? Those artichokes must not be *cold* which does *not* mean they have to be steaming . . . All the same we ate well, drank tolerably, were happy, chewing the cud as it were of our phantasmagoric night. We watched a sunset. For dinner we went to Trastevere. That *was* street life all right, populace and tourists. Pierre and Simone began to realize that Italian food could be taken seriously. Our American friends considered them as under their wings; there was an accolade and for them that was enough. The Mimerels were elated, impressed, and knew how to show it. What I saw was how observant they also were and how amused. Here too we sat for a long while in animated peace (punctuated inevitably by bouts of fairly atrocious music).

\*     \*     \*

We left well after midnight. Goodbyes in the stuffy salotto of the hotel. When I woke, late again in the morning, they were gone. In a corner of my room stood two high wobbly stacks of books: the books we had carried in the front belly of the Renault on our journey Paris—Rome.

Time to take stock? I took time. First: catch up on sleep. Then the post. Small piles of it, delivered over the months, turned up in odd drawers and pigeon-holes of the concierge's lodge. Nothing of much moment. Then the day-porter inquired whether I had seen yet the young couple who came by quite often asking about my return. What couple? Americans, he thought; they had left a letter by hand. I shuffled through those piles once more and indeed found an unstamped envelope. The note it contained turned out to be from someone I had known reasonably well in New York when I was living there in the war years, Rosalind Constable, English and a successful journalist already then, a bright light of the *Life/Time* establishment, hard-working, hard-playing, all of which she had been quite openly aware that I was not. We used to meet in the middle-distance, as it were, in a milieu—native and refugee—of writers, painters, patrons and editors of political and literary reviews thrown together by world events. Rosalind's note to me turned out to be a letter of introduction. Young people she knew . . . a married couple . . . They were setting out for Italy . . . He had got a Fulbright Scholarship . . . Their first time in Europe . . . She did not know them very well but thought that we were just up each other's street, he being seriously intellectual (for serious I read uppity and did not take it for a compliment) . . . So would I perhaps, etc . . . That letter of introduction had been lying about for weeks. Out of compunction I sent a note to their lodgings asking them for a drink the next evening. A drink in the Inghilterra's social quarters, the dusky and quite pretentious salotto—gilt and stuffed chairs, next to the small bar. They came. Their names were Gendel, Milton and Evelyn Gendel. They were slim, dark, with fine-cut Slavic faces, and they looked exactly what they were: second-generation Ashkenazi Americans, New-Yorker-Americans. The resemblance to each other was generic, though not literal, they might well have been a brother and a sister rather than man and wife. Gendel brother stood out as intelligent all right, in a laid-back, laconic, self-assured, non-show-off way. The sister was eager, charming and quite openly in search of what he had already coolly taken in: art, erudition, Europe in a word. He had served in the Pacific during the war as an interpreter, I gathered, having previously studied oriental languages as well as architecture and zoology, most of which appeared to be still among his prevalent interests. (He spoke in a tone of near-affection of a one-time acquisition of a reptile. 'A snake,' she said, *sotto voce* far from happy.) *Her* chief enthusiasms were for opera and the glamour of the literary life. He would have preferred to win his scholarship for China; she had longed for Paris, perceived by her as a Proustian stage. Now nevertheless they had fallen for Rome. He to the point of having continued to live there (in and out of three marriages), *is* living there, *now*, this day as I am writing. He had married young, before America's entry into the war Evelyn had barely left college—married early enough for Milton to stimulate her European longings by obtaining a toehold for her on the fringes of that André Breton, Max Ernst, Peggy Guggenheim, *Partisan Review*, avant-garde milieu into which he already had an entrée. So when one day Evelyn Gendel all radiant with the news of their scholarship to Europe ran into Rosalind Constable travelling on the same Madison Avenue bus oh, how the wheels of chance do operate—Rosalind, a mere acquaintance, touched by such enthusiasm offered a letter of introduction, kindly, if mocking: 'I know just the kind of "intellectual friend" in Rome for you and Milton' . . . Evelyn, who in her turn did not think much of the kind of journalism Rosalind was currently engaged in, was more than eager to accept the letter to the unknown quantity of 'highbrow' that was me.

I liked the Gendels that first evening. We went on to dinner—at Toto's, via della Croce, where I often ate. Friends, Italians, Americans, joined us. Conversation flowed. Milton amusing, brief, detached; Evelyn chattered. Happily, disarmingly. Yes, I did like the Gendels well enough. But. They were *young.* The gap between their mid-twenties and my late thirties was too great. In my friendships, in my love affairs, I had always sought my elders . . . Having hardly ever been to school, I had but little knowledge of or commerce with coevals, my very sister being near fifteen at my birth; so a ten-years' seniority was about the minimum qualification for any intimate relationship for me. I would run into Evelyn and Milton now and then, that was inevitable among the foreign colony in the Rome of those days; we would inevitably talk about the glories to be seen—they were alert to these, and I would introduce them as occasion arose to such literati—few enough—I had the chance to know. And that was that.

As it turned out, it was not this that had been in the minds of the gods on the occasion of the meeting between Rosalind Constable and Evelyn Gendel on that Madison Avenue bus. Within the next forty-eight hours after that first meeting one or two things concurred. I buckled down to assess the realities of my material situation. Existence. The books we had transported from France were still stacked high against the wall; I was still compelled, or thought I was, to ration my reading; I still had to wear some very dark glasses when I ventured out into the Italian midday sun. Indeed I had been advised to avoid outdoor daylight, so my outdoor life was mainly nocturnal. And I had not taken up my own book yet at all. When could I? When must I? How long would it take to get into what I saw as the life I had wanted from my youth? Then I had aimed to write in French and to write like Stendhal; later it had been English and Aldous Huxley. Now behind me were the many desultory years of false starts and failure, hedonism, sloth and doubt. How long had I still got? It came down to how long money could be made to last. One thing was certain: I must leave the Inghilterra, find somewhere cheaper to stay.

At exactly that point of my cogitations the FitzGibbons, Constantine and Theodora, entered into my life again. They were to do this from time to time at different stages in our futures, acting as precipitants, for better *and* for worse, of where I was going to live next. We had seen a certain amount of each other on Capri, where Constantine was collecting material for a biography of his kinsman, Norman Douglas. A biography he soon decided not to write: Douglas's complexities and contradictions, he found, could be tackled only by a man of the world cum scholar of very mature years. What young Constantine nevertheless produced was a long, remarkably good essay on Norman which originally appeared in *Encounter.* I re-read it recently. Yes: *Constantine FitzGibbons.* Who himself became in due course a brilliant and original writer, civilized, versatile, on the side of the angels. Do we have to be reminded also—he died relatively early—of *When the kissing had to stop, The Shirt of Nessus,* the BBC documentary of *The Blitz,* the *Life of Dylan Thomas*?

At the Italian time I am writing about, Constantine and Theodora—a first marriage for each of them—though devoted to each other, were known for the frequency and ferocity of their public quarrels. Oh, the spilled wine, the insults, the broken glasses, the shouts, the dashing out of restaurants and bars ... They were farouche to each other like wild beasts; next time one met them, all was sunshine. Or perhaps not at all. Days after my return from France, I found that they had been living for some months in Rome. And fed up with it, they said, couldn't wait to leave. They were in a flat, the lease had still some months to run. The landlady aged, hostile, hard— wouldn't let them go unless they could produce someone reliable and *quiet* to move in and pay the rent. Which was cheap. Perhaps *I* ...? Quite possibly, I said.

'It's not quite a flat,' they said, 'more a sort of hut on top of an office building on Piazza di Spagna.'

'On *Piazza di Spagna*,' I said.

'Nothing works very well, but it's got a marble bath.'

They took me to see it. The building, five storeys high, was nearly opposite the Spanish Steps, and apparently contained commercial offices only, which meant, as I was to discover later, that no living being dwelt there during the night. We climbed five flights of solid stone, past impeccably kept office doors, and thence a short dusty stretch of wooden steps and emerged upon a roof. A *very large roof*, with a profusion of tangled greenery struggling out of a variety of semi-broken tubs and urns. The view was staggering: we were standing face to face, at almost touching distance from the over-life-sized head of Santa Maria Immaculata on the top of her great column in the square.

It was the roof, the very same roof, Constantine explained, on which the first great Italian post-war film, Rossellini's *Roma, Città Aperta* had been made.

Where, I asked after I had ceased to be stunned, is the flat? And indeed part hidden by the creepers, the climbers and the urns, there stood a longish kind of shed cobbled together, it would seem, from tarred paper and packing-case wood. It had windows and a fragile front door. The inside was a pleasing surprise (if one discounted the evidence of Theodora's house-keeping): an L-shaped studio of good size, white walls, superior

138

garden furniture—bamboo and striped canvas, a (potentially) neat little Italian kitchen *and* the marble bath.

Moving day seems to have come upon me almost immediately. The FitzGibbons were keen to be off, the harridan accepted me as their substitute, I had added my name to the lease, vaguely took in a paragraph about paying for damages and repairs, handed over a month's rent. It did not turn out a smooth day. For one thing it happened to be a holiday, not a religious one, a public holiday of the kind Italy had set up so many—I forget whether it was to commemorate the victory over the Austrians in 1918 or the surrender to the Allies in 1943—anyway, working Rome appeared to have closed down. This happened not to matter too much at first as Theodora was found still lingering over the aftermath of a spaghetti luncheon in the early hours of the afternoon. (Constantine had already *evaporated*, the term Norman Douglas used for any opportune departure.) A waiter from the Inghilterra had laid on a handcart for my pile of books and the rest of my belongings, with a boy to push and haul the lot up to the threshold of my new abode. When at last we gained entry, the sight was not encouraging. It went beyond disorder. Nothing looked clean, nothing looked safe to sit, let alone to sleep on. I was and am addicted to a certain Spartan neatness: how could I move in here, how could

I *sleep* in here? I could see no way of coping with the apparent mess and I panicked. There was a telephone. I called up everyone I could think of, quite recent friends though some of them were. Half had gone to the seaside—on that fine warm day; to those at home I wailed my plight: it was hopeless. No, no, they said, they'd come, they'd bring their brother-in-law, they'd bring their maid, get hold of the gardener, dig out an upholsterer, a carpenter, never mind if their workshops were closed. Within the hour we were a crowd. Smartly dressed Italian women (equipped with aprons), Italian workmen with their buckets, spades and tools game for a bit of theatre. Scrubbing, rapid and efficient, soon got on indoors; what was spectacular was the work-space improvised on a corner of the historic roof—they cleared away some of the most obtrusive plants and set up a work-bench on which a mattress was being gutted and remade from scratch, pillows turned inside out; another man was hammering away on chair legs while I was hovering on the edge of a deck-chair bleating inanities. 'How can I ever thank you enough . . . ?' 'Do you think this can really be made all right?' Everyone else was soothing and high-spirited—goodness, how efficient (domestically) Italians can be, how helpful, how *generous.* Someone went down the five flights into the piazza and brought up a large jug of frothy ice-cold lemonade. And not long after sundown, there was a neat, clean, habitable living-space—studio? refuge? hut?—under the sky. The women were hanging up my clothes in cupboards that had acquired hangers and hooks, someone else was helping me fit books into a case a carpenter had knocked together . . . All done, they cried: you can move in, you *have* moved in, but before, we must all go out now and have some dinner and celebrate. It was at this point that I looked up and saw that arrived among us were the Gendels. Milton and Evelyn.

Dusk was setting in and before I could greet them (sent on, I suppose, by the Inghilterra?), somebody turned a switch. There came some sharks and a crackle, more switches were tried: more flashes, a plop or two and lamp-bulbs here and there flickered into uncertain light. Seems to work all right, they said, when there rose a strong American voice. 'She's not to move in here, not tonight! This set-up is a joke . . . Illegal . . .' It was Milton speaking. It was only the second time that we had met and I had judged him a cool man, composed, detached. Now he sounded alarmed, determined and aggrieved, '. . . we're talking e-l-e-c-t-r-i-c-i-t-y . . . No city regulations would allow . . .' I realized that the time had come for me to take a part again in the events.

'We are not,' I said, 'in New York City.'

My Italian friends, twittering again, concurred. Stern Milton was not easily fobbed

141

off—the *perils* to me: something had to be *done*. Not tonight: we *were* a crowd so eventually we won. Victorious, animated, we all trooped off down into evening Rome, had dinner, laughed a good deal, drank a good deal, reasonably so: we were *not* New York, NY. The next thing I remember of that long day was being in bed, alone, flown with wine, drifting towards sleep in cool, smooth clean sheets—cotton surely? Egyptian cotton? a moving-in present? a loan?—vaguely wondering whether what the Gendels had said about their coming to redo the electrical installation could be true, vaguely perturbed by the prospect of walking up in that empty silent building on my own in future nights, past all those polished brass plates of 'International Ltd' companies on the doors of offices empty of all human life, and then the last image floating through my mind of a large jagged piece of marble in that bathtub.

\*     \*     \*

The Gendels did turn up next day. With coils, plugs, wire and on his part a good deal of manual expertise, with her acting the alert apprentice. In less than a week they managed to create a simple, safe, efficient system of electric light indoors, then set their minds to dreaming up a charming and discreet display on the roof itself, giving a nocturnal lease of life to the vegetation, illuminating the *plein air* dinners I could now begin to eat out here at night.

Inevitably all this took some time and when it was done I still seemed to see the Gendels practically every day. Evelyn would drop in at the siesta hours reading to me, bring manuals teaching to touch-type, typing without eye-strain, typing practically without using one's eyes at all? Milton took us to chamber music concerts; soon they began to join me on my after-dinner walks, having come to share my passion for Rome at night, and so we went, to and fro, accompanying each other home, first in one way, then in the other, and around again, often well into dawn. The advent of the Gendels in Italy did more than change the electric installation they had found so perilous, it changed my life.

## CHAPTER NINE

*Rome continues—A working writer's days:*
*industry, eloquent mind, night walks—*
*Fear—A farcical situation—An act of*
*charity—'All's well . . .'*

And how did it all begin? Slowly, imperceptibly, improbably . . . I had found courage to look at my dormant Mexican typescript; then feeling a need not of an outside opinion—not yet!—but an outside voice, I asked Evelyn to read me my chapter one aloud: *The Bath of Caracalla* opening. She did not read it well and her boredom with the text was evident. Asked, she said she just didn't know what to make of it, just did not know. Amused rather than dismayed, I quizzed her about what she had read and liked among contemporary English writers. She came up with Proust and James.

For my part, I did what Martha Gellhorn— returned to live outside Rome with her newly-adopted baby son—took for granted: I bit a nail, sat down before my pages and the typewriter every morning. I worked, and it worked. Soon I never lacked that 'one true first sentence' at the start of the writing day, and at other hours there might swim across my mind, too swiftly often to catch and hold, fragments of words, of dialogue and thoughts. My eye trouble had led me to the way in which I am best able to write, that is, without previous notes, reference books, without research. (Hence no doubt the mistakes I make then and now.) The book I had in hand was emerging as a traveller's tale: a Don Otavio part actually encountered, part made up.

After the morning's shift, I laid out a simple Italian lunch on a card-table outside in the shade—it became very hot under the tarred paper roof during day-hours—tomatoes, an egg or two, salami, fruit, a large glass of water from one of the live springs in the Roman hills. Most domestic dwellings in the city had drinking water laid on by way of a very small tap, fixed between the normal-sized hot and cold, this tap we also drew for our coffee or a soup, it dispensed a measured trickle—one pint per minute—of still mineral water. In our district it was *acqua di Trevi* from the source that fed the Trevi Fountain. The taste was exquisite.

As soon as the heat of the day had abated, I went out on the roof again, preferably alone, to do some rough gardening. I took great pleasure in trying to tame some of those exuberant climbers, to give them shape, direction, support; above all water them. *Not* from the *acqua di Trevi.* Later, at the hour when the Roman sky loses its colour for ten minutes or so before flaming up again with the sunset, and the swifts begin their flight over in formation, I sat watching, fiasco and glass to hand. Dinner with friends later, nearer ten p.m. than nine . . . I had also taken to eating on my own on the roof. I enjoyed those evenings sitting amidst my private *son et lumière.* There was sound when *la Radio Italiana* decided to lay on an opera, which was often, and what I had cooked for myself was never less than acceptable. The Gendels—who occasionally came to pick me up for our late-evening

145

walks—seemed over-taken with mirth finding me *à table* formally set with hot plate, first course, main course and the right-sized spoon for every grain of Parmesan.

*     *     *

My part sybaritic, part Spartan existence on that roof gave me a few nasty jolts. It had been my habit after a night out to walk back late and insouciantly alone. The streets were mostly empty and always without threat, even offering occasionally some spectacle of a joyous kind. Once having just left, as prudence required on the break of dawn, an apartment in the respectable Via Veneto quarter after a fond farewell with an entrusted key and cheerfully on my way, I saw a young man astride the sill of an open first-floor window of a house I was passing; he raised an arm to blow a kiss into the darkness of the room behind, turned, swung over his other leg, lightly sprang down unto the pavement below, landed upright and jauntingly marched on humming a tune. All in a matter of seconds. I had a glimpse of his smiling face.

A smile that felt rather like the one on mine.

Ah, but those late returns took place in my Inghilterra days when all I had to meet might be a night porter's smirk. Braving the walk up to my Piazza di Spagna roof became a different matter. I soon tried to arrange going out at night only with a friend or friends who would see me home; this did not always necessarily turn out to be someone willing to see me all the way upstairs. Milton G. always did; to others it might not even occur. It was a strenuous chore and if I could cope with spending the night in that isolated flimsy structure, I should also be able to get myself there on my own. Or so was the reasoning. I accepted chivalrous offers but did not ask for one, not right in any case if my companion happened to be a woman. Yet I *was* afraid of the climb up and apprehension grew as the time approached.

One night . . . I had made it, had turned the loose little lock and was about to undress when I saw brief sparks of light outside the front window, sparks that might have come from a touching of wires or the striking of a match, followed by the faint sound of a series of crackles . . . Then nothing. No footsteps. Darkness outside. Silence. I was very frightened.

I spent the rest of the night fully dressed on the wide studio bed. Beside me I had laid a slim sword-stick—an elegant object that might once have belonged to my father, one of those things one finds turning up (from where and how?) in the course of existence—fully aware of the absurdity of this protection. Yet I hung on to it, touching it, between dozings off.

Morning. With it daylight and rationality. I ventured outside. No signs of any kind. No spent match, no cigarette stub, plants undisturbed. Could the sparks have been produced by some flaw in the dabbling with an obsolete circuit? I settled—what else?—to the daily routine. But day, inevitably, is followed by nightfall, and from then on I found it harder to control my unease at its approach. Living by myself the way I did had become, in today's jargon, a problem.

Once returning—solo—I was struck by panic to the degree of seeking out a telephone box and calling Peter Tompkins—of the winged jeep—it was after midnight: neither he nor his wife were asleep. Peter said at once that he would come. They lived in Via Margutta, a short walk away. I waited standing rather foolishly by the front door of my building. After he had seen me up and in, he told me not to ask him to do so again.

'If you can't get yourself to coping with this on your own, you won't be able to go on staying there. That lease has got some time to run still, hasn't it?'

It had.

Some nights on—we were well into June by then—I was home and dry, undressed, asleep, I had a waking dream so tactile, so solid, so physically solid that I was sure I was awake and what I saw in front of me was *here* and *there*: round a table in the middle of the room, very upright, sat four tall silent men in tail-coats and white ties, playing cards—bridge, I knew, not poker—they did not make a sound, they did not look at me. I could not see their faces, only their straight backs and black formal clothes and not for a moment did I doubt that they were *real*. Real ghosts? Or real intruders? It is hard to convey how menacing they were, and how frightening . . . I cannot tell how long it took—ten minutes? seconds?—for the scene to dissolve itself, and for me to believe that I had not been, but was becoming now, awake.

* * *

Later that week Milton came to tell me that Evelyn was not well. Some gastric upset, food-poisoning, probably. Public food in Rome at any level is usually fresh and healthy; foreigners, however, particularly those from non-Mediterranean countries, are apt to misuse it—too much of this, too little of that, unsuitable combinations at irregular hours. Slabs of spit-roast pork spiked with rosemary off a street-cart, an ice-cream cone a little later. They think they know best when often they don't.

The Gendels were living in a rented room somewhere near the Forum, a splendid view, bed, no breakfast . . . Evelyn felt too weak to go out. So what were they doing about food? Oh, she couldn't even think of eating, Milton told me. Had they seen a doctor? No. He'd been to the chemist, she did not get better and was feeling a bit scared. A doctor? Well, not out of the telephone book. This was where my Italian network came in. I got on to an omniscient friend of mine, Natalia Danesi Murray, a woman of radiant vitality whose great lifespan encompassed liaisons from d'Annunzio to Janet Flanner, who told me one must always go for the best, in no time at all arranged for a rather prestigious man to see Evelyn, a *professore* who had been one of the king of Italy's consultants (when the king was king). Natalia said that he was good, very good, and we had better listen to him. The prestigious *professore* went out to see his patient and afterwards required a talk with the husband. And would there be a responsible female about? Both Evelyn's and Milton's mothers being in New York, it was I who went along in that role. He saw Milton and me in his consulting rooms and had this to say: what your signora has now is not serious but as she has a delicate gastric system . . . He saw no need to overwhelm us with medical terms but if not looked after now, a disposition to be nipped in the bud, as it were, it could become serious, or at the least a nuisance, in later life. So: it should be treated *now*. By the simplest of means; he believed in these. They needed no more than some patience and conscientiousness. But where were they to be found? Public hospitals in Rome were useless for the present case. A private clinic then. They are *very* expensive. He looked Milton in the eye, who said, 'We have no money at present other than from my scholarship.'

'A Fulbright, Mr Gendel, a most honourable achievement. No clinic. They're robbers anyway. Can you cook, Mr Gendel?' The *professore* did not pause for an answer. 'Can this lady cook?'

I said I thought I could.

'What I shall be prescribing is a régime, a simple régime of rest and suitable food. Not a *diet*—not food forbidden, but the right food meticulously prepared. And see that it is taken. And much sleep, some fresh air—have you got a balcony?—a little reading, a little music . . . Three weeks, twenty-one-days, should do it: achieve a present cure, avoid future aftermaths. Are you willing to undertake this?'

I said that of course I would.

'I assume you have a suitable place for your friend to stay in.'

It could be made so, I said bravely, thinking of the Italian network. Then I had to add: It happens to be five flights up. No lift.'

'That should not present too grave a difficulty: a good chair and a couple of strong young men.'

The consultation ended with the *professore* giving me very detailed, oral and written instructions.

And so it came to pass. The very next day. The network worked. An acceptable camp-bed for Evelyn had been installed in the L-wing of the studio. I had got up early to go to market (provided with a generous purse from Milton)—I would have to do this every day: only the freshest of provisions would do for the régime. The strong young men had delivered their burden; the first meal was cooked—there were to be three identical ones per day. Evelyn looked settled and unscared. Milton had arranged to call on us at *l'heure bleue.*

A routine was established. Evelyn slept well and late. In the afternoon hours she transferred on to a deckchair outdoors in the shade, reading a little, talking a little, reading to me when I was available which was sporadic. It seemed as if I were cooking most of the day, the *professore*'s régime being exacting if simple. It consisted of four items: lightly poached white meat of chicken, from a lean young fowl dressed every morning by an excellent butcher; a small helping of plain white rice steamed without any seasoning whatsoever to the right consistency; a mound of scrubbed, washed and then instantly grated raw carrots sprinkled with a fingertip's worth of finely chopped parsley; followed by a bowl of peeled, cored, stewed and puréed apples sweetened with a hint of honey. The identical sequences prepared anew three times a day—nothing ever to be served left over or warmed up—at roughly four hours' interval. Quantities to be increased gradually. Nothing else whatsoever: no bread, no biscuits, no fats, no sweets. Liquids were lime-blossom tea in the morning, jugs of Trevi water, cool not iced, flavoured with slices of lemon.

At noon a small boy would appear dragging half a block of ice wrapped in sacking. This kept fairly well in the insulated wooden box of modest dimension we were glad to have in our kitchens in those days. It adequately cooled wine and water.

Evelyn's mother sent a pressure cooker from America by sea. It arrived too late, and would have been small use for the cooking in hand. Having a sense of obligation towards it, the cooker came with me on all the moves that followed, until many years on it found itself outclassed by the Aga in the rented wing of a manor house in Dorset.

Evelyn began to eat quite willingly and soon with some enjoyment, not seeming to mind or even notice the monotony. She was turning out a charming guest, and I was able to do a certain amount of writing-thinking during the hours of kitchen chores. What *I* minded was the loss of solitude—essential to the cashing in of writing-thoughts. And I have always liked to do my gardening on my own. By sundown Milton would arrive bearing gin, English gin. I chipped ice. The swifts—I thought of them as swallows, genus *hirando* rather than mere *apodidae*—began their over-flight, Evelyn would sit up and the three of us talk agreeably. Later on, Milton would take me out for a *dîner en ville* at some good place, his way of giving pleasure in return for looking after his wife. I had got to appreciate his conversational quick wit and take; he was not too young after all, just himself and ageless. He was disappointed by what he had met of Roman intellectual life, the Elena Croce and Botteghe Scure circles, he found them provincial, he said. He could talk on a more equal basis with his fellow American, Donald Downes, but Donald had to be first in all things and moreover was too prone to rages. If Milton himself was arrogant, and I am not certain that he was, his way of showing it was quiet. Evelyn meanwhile was content to remain behind on her own: early bed and sleep. The place, perhaps due to the new domesticity, had lost some of its spookiness.

Shortly before the end of the prescribed twenty-one days, Evelyn was able to get up and go to see her *professore*. He was pleased with her. She would be All Right. Finish the three weeks, he told her, then think no more about it. 'Eat what you like, eat as much or as little as you like, but learn to *know* what you like. *Culinary discrimination.* It's a good guide to health. Your friend here'—I had come along—

'will be some help.'

She did turn out to be All Right, in unremarked good health that is. (At least for the next twenty-five years.)

*　　　*　　　*

So presently Evelyn returned to their quarters by the Forum and I to attempts at sustained work, and the tending of those exuberant climbers, looking forward to cultivating peacefully *mon jardin*.

Thus a few days passed. Then the Gendels sent a note suggesting that we go to an afternoon concert of baroque music on the Sunday next. It was the beginning of the period in which sounds of Monteverdi and Vivaldi could be heard pouring forth from many an open window. We decided it would be agreeable to precede our treat with a quiet leisurely luncheon in the shade of a tiny trellised trattoria in a side street round my corner. This we did. When the time came to be on our way to the Accademia Santa Cecilia, I remembered that I had left some washing hanging out—Rome's ubiquitous habit—and ought to retrieve it now before the evening dew made it damp. Evelyn offered to come with me. We left Milton at the Café Greco. Up on the roof, Evelyn and I were facing each other across the washing-line folding pillowcases, kitchen towels, when I heard her

clearly enunciate what I call the three fatal
words. Most of us have heard or spoken them
at one time or another, rashly or deliberately,
gravely or lightly, acceptably or rejectably,
meant for the moment, meant for ever. Now I
did not believe what I had heard. I looked at
Evelyn, pulling down another piece of
washing. She looked at me. The way she did
forced me to say something. I did so in a
soothing now-now sort of way, as one might to
a cat wanting to get at one's plate. Another
look, more silence. Which made me speak
more seriously. *What* was she talking about?
No answer. She left it at the three fatal words;
Milton was waiting below; Santa Cecilia
concerts began relatively on time. I took the
washing indoors, we made our way downstairs.
Disconcerted, I became aware that I was
feeling slightly flattered.

The three of us spent an equable evening.
They saw me home; Milton escorted me
upstairs. All was as if the incident on the roof
had not occurred. Next morning I worked. At
the gardening stage of the day, trowel in hand,
thoughts shaping ways, I found Evelyn
standing beside me accompanied by the
inevitable urchin carrying a sizeable suitcase.

'I've come to live with you. I left Milton.'

It was high summer in Italy yet the scenario
struck me as that of the maiden, infant in
shawl, coming in from the snow.

First reaction: I must—gently, firmly—shut

her out again. This, I tried to say, is the caprice of a disloyal child—no one is allowed to be as young, as naïve, as wilful . . .

She took it calmly. She knew what she was doing . . . She was devoted to Milton, wished the best for him . . . It was their being married which wasn't right, they'd gone into it, fondly, mistakenly, too early . . . *She* was not what he needed now: a bright, affectionate, admiring student to run about with . . . He would eventually come to see it . . . 'I have for some time and more clearly during the weeks when I was up here resting so much.'

'You told him all that? Now? This afternoon? What did *he* say?'

She didn't really know—when he came in she had already packed. So she said that she was leaving him and when he didn't seem to understand, she walked through the door.

I did the equivalent of tearing out my hair.

Of course she had left him in no doubt that she would no longer live on his money (which he had been generous with); she had left all he had given her for this month; she had even emptied their common marketing purse.

Oh my God! I envisaged the wad of lira notes on the dressing-table.

It was dollars, she said.

The suitcase boy had vanished, I noticed it then. 'I tipped him,' she said, 'I had kept a lira note. It must have been quite large. Was I wrong?'

Wrong! You have to go back. Now. At once. Did you tell Milton *where* you were going?

Oh yes. I told him I wanted to live with you.

Without telling *me*!

Again calmly, sweetly, she said, 'It's going to be all right. One knows such things. We are going to live together and we shall be very happy.'

*     *     *

How could it solve itself, this sudden, this preposterous situation which held the seeds of so much disruption, strife, probably grief for all of us? I *had* become fond of Evelyn, I realized, as I had of Milton, but to *that* degree . . . What did I do? What should I have done? I tried to persuade her, to order her to go back. Too late, she said. If I made her leave, she would cable her parents (who could ill afford it) to send the money for a return passage to America. They, the parents, had been inalienably married for some thirty years. Their shock?

Something took over in me, it may have been the shade of my father, he had been a chivalrous man, and instinct made me feel that chivalry must be the guiding line now. I did not send the stray back into the snow. Instead I went and started lighting one of the charcoal burners in the kitchen. I was going to cook us some supper and it was damn well not going to be poached chicken.

*     *     *

Many attachments have improbable beginnings, this one for me was the most abrupt; it also turned out one of the happiest, due mainly to Evelyn's innate goodness and serenity of nature which were essentially hers, however one may view that streak of naïve obstinacy she occasionally displayed. When I speak of happiness, I can speak for myself only.

Milton and Evelyn's eventual divorce was civilized and constructive. He had wanted children—she decidedly not—and when his opportunity came, she took every step she could to help him seize it without delay. Milton's abilities and talents became recognized early. He was taken up, taken in, by two prestigious coteries, one Italian, one English, the latter of great social and literary distinction (bang into something like Evelvn's wildest Proustian dreams: she was able to see the irony of it with humour, good humour; he taking it coolly in his stride).

Milton married again twice, once into the English and, after the death of that wife, into the Italian aristocracy.

In our later, much later, years, Milton a few times did me the honour, gave me the pleasure, of coming to see me in my London flat. There he noticed on my chimney-piece the copy he had sent me of one of his Roman photographs from his American Academy exhibition in the eighties. It shows a fountain—god and dolphin—taken in Roma Papale a foot or two from his home. It had been up on that shelf, centre front among the invitations and the cards, for a long time. Still is.

On a later visit, he had to leave early as a very grand, or should I call it stately, car was about to draw up at the door in my side street to take him for the weekend at an august place indeed. What is it like, I asked, to stay there? What *are* they like to stay with?

He said, oh quite cosy.

Milton, I said, what do *you* feel you are?

'A New Yorker,' he said, 'a New Yorker abroad.'

## CHAPTER TEN

*A week in the present: September 2001—
Returns: Germany—
A small child's 1914 war—Revolutions—A
country life patched up—Education: get
thee out of a nunnery—Bolted: my
mother—Eclipse of spirit—My ruthless
move*

160

A week ago, a very long week ago, I tried to begin this chapter with a reflection on the nature, the precariousness and cost of an individual's private well-being, let alone happiness. Mass happiness is something else and although it can engender a sense of solidarity and belonging, the solidarity most often is one of combativeness, aggression, envy. It precedes and celebrates, uprisings, revolution, war. It can also be a bonding fraternity of loss and fear. The week I am writing in is that after September 11th 2001.

Another turning of the screws of horror, suffering and pity, of man's inhumanity to man, has occurred. How will it end? How can it end? Very little has changed in our nature since we first set out from the caves, stones and cudgels on hand; infinitely much has changed about the means by which we are able physically and spiritually to torment and kill. And there are more and more of us, more to envy, more to disagree with, more to hate, fear, destroy. *We have overrun the earth, exploited nature, disregarded other forms of life.*

Now more than ever we exist in the world of Matthew Arnold's closing lines of 'Dover Beach', the world

*. . . which seems*
*To lie before us like a land of dreams,*
*So various, so beautiful, so new,*
*Hath really neither joy, nor love, nor light,*

161

*Nor certitude, nor peace, nor help for pain;*
*And we are here as on a darkling plain*
*Swept with confused alarms of struggle and*
*  flight,*
*Where ignorant armies clash by night.*

In Germany during the First World War, when I was a child of four or five, my mother told me in very simple terms what war meant: people killing and maiming each other; this war should not be; no war should ever be, war was a barbaric way to obtain one's ends however just they might appear. 'Fighting for one's country', as the young were taught, if often selfless and brave as well as intoxicating, was inevitably a fight of one part of humanity against another; on all sides there was innocence and guilt, and *ignorance.* 'My country right or wrong' was always *wrong.* One might love a place, feel belonging, one must not love 'a nation'. In a mature world, my mother said, there would be no nations, only differing places, with different people living together with different customs. 'Mummy, are there such places?' I remember having asked at some point, which must have reminded her that she was addressing a four-year-old. Her answer was something like: not yet, one hopes that lessons may be learned after this war. More hesitantly she added that something (for home consumption at least) had been achieved in America (to which she had not been),

162

meaning of course the United States.

That talk took place one year or so before the American entry into that war.

My mother's lesson struck; as fast as the other one did for so many: *pro patria—dulce et decorum est* . . . Mine was reinforced by the reality I saw on trains and railway platforms: wounded soldiers, stained bandages, missing limbs, sights made indelible in my future consciousness by a couple of dreams surrealist in their terror. Even now these images with their unaltered climax of fear are recalled by me.

Today the realities of distress are transmitted in the raw, instantaneously as they occur, received again and again by all; nightmarish in themselves, they are the stuff of which future individual nightmares are made. And retained.

\*     \*     \*

Those long slow journeys across Germany from south to north with hours immobile in iron-grey, dimmed-out stations, were made by us, my mother, my sister, a nanny and me, because we evacuated ourselves in 1915 from our château—a short walk from the French frontier—to safety in my father's ex-in-laws' house in Berlin. *And* travelled back again, that time from even further north, the Baltic sea-coast where my mother liked to stay, in

November 1918, in the thick of the sailors' mutiny at the outbreak of the German Revolution. At one point we were marched out of the train at Schwerin, the capital of the duchy of Mecklenburg, and corralled in the lounge of an hotel on the main square, and here the sailors with their banners and slogans were mutinying all right. The authorities, officers or police, a handful, were trying to disperse them. There was shooting and much noise. Our fellow passengers shouted that we were being machine-gunned. The windows giving on to that square were broad and high. Most of us were crouching on the floor. Not so my mother: she stood up to look. The sailors, she said firmly, were right to mutiny—it was time, the Kaiser's régime was rotten. My mother had spontaneous physical courage (not inherited by me). I crept after her, for one or two cautious looks. The people in the lounge were too concerned with the shooting to take notice of my mother's revolutionary stance. The shooting must have stopped by nightfall. Whoever was in charge did not judge it safe for us to leave. The bedrooms were full up, so we all slept on the floor. After day-break, another train, another journey, more incidents. As chance had it, we made home base, unharmed we returned to our corner of the comparatively tranquil south, found my father, my sister, quite a few servants, no more horses, no livestock, offspring of cats run wild, fallen trees in the park, nettles high on the drive, the house intact, contents undisturbed, dusted, my father's collection in museum-order, and thus for a brief spell of time, on a diminishing scale, a *Vie de Château* resumed.

And this, in a nutshell, was an early pattern of what the phases of my future life were going to be—intermittent brushes with the catastrophic events of the century and a largely unharmed continuance of my existence as an individual, freer than many. By the grace of chance.

Survivors pay with their conscience. Some have paid to the end of their own road. Those who have got off lightly paid perhaps too little (because there never can be enough?). I feel I am one of those.

*     *     *

By the beginning of the early post-war period the spurts of the German Revolution petered out, became modulated, legitimized in the Weimar Republic—divided, imperilled, hopeful; the centres of catastrophe had moved to Russia, civil war and to what became the Soviet Union. First cognizance of that world event came to me in the simple terms of being shaken awake at night by a young German housemaid. We were still living under the sheltering roof of the substantial Berlin town house, months before our own homecoming.

The news had been given out in the servants' hall to the underling by the senior retainers—a crumb thrown from the evening paper. The family, unreachable anyway, were likely to be still at table. Need to communicate drove the girl upstairs. Emerging from sleep, I heard, 'The Russians have surrendered to Germany . . . The war in Russia is over . . .!' 'I'm so glad,' I said. 'I hope your fiancé will be safe now.' The girl knelt down by my high bed and hugged me. You are a good child, she said, a kind child. At moments now when I am in distress about the many things which in the course of my life I said or left unsaid, or did or left undone, a recall of that night, so very far away in time, is consoling. Through that child's quick impulse I may have been accorded a grain, a very small grain, of absolution.

\*       \*       \*

During the first two or three years of our country life regained, news and comments of events global, national and local came to me erratically. One prime source, my discursive mother, was not often available to me, a growing child regarded as rather forward by some and not so by her. I had reached the boring stage, she found. For one thing I was beginning to express opinions of my own. There was animal welfare: when I inherited our land—heartless brat—lawn would be turned into fields where calves would safely drink their mothers' milk for ever; the human race could do with cider. Butchers? Well, butchers might sell game. Then there was religion: the village girls who now came in to work for us (post-war: no more trained parlourmaid and of course no butler, no coachman) had gleefully informed me that so far I had been 'brought up godless'. Quite true, despite being a cradle Catholic, baptized and all. I did not like what I was being made to hear—mortal sin, hell fire, finicky Church commandments. So I took against religion, simple as that: disliked it, didn't believe it, didn't want to. My mother was not interested in the subject nor in my views about it. It must have been beginning to show that I had as yet had little that could be called even a semi-formal education. My father hadn't thought about it, my mother vaguely held that any child of hers would somehow pick it up. In fact, I could read, having picked it up quite easily and early. How? I only recall that one day during the war I saw a newspaper lying by me on the floor, I read a headline and went on . . . Just like that. Nobody showed surprise. What they all forgot about was to get someone to teach me how to *write*. Unlike Bill the Lizard, I did not even have a slate; I was in fact quite backward in many ways, I can see that now, although I'm not sure whether I was actually unable to write 'The cat sat on the mat' or the

German equivalent thereof. If I could, it must have been pretty illegible; engraved in my memory is the hushed scandal I caused at the first attempt at schooling I was briefly submitted to at the age of eight or nine. Someone must have persuaded my parents—a minion of some Ministry of Education?—so one morning I found myself a day pupil—supposed to commute by bicycle and slow train—at the Ursulines convent in the nearby university town. The nuns were gently dictatorial, I only saw their habits and the crucifixes, and was petrified. There seemed to have been some uncertainty—I had no scholastic record, and eventually I was put on a back-bench in a roomful of what seemed to me much bigger girls. Years on, I was struck by a film at an American natural history museum displaying graphs of animals' sight. The screen showed what a hen placed in an alien chicken coop saw, or surmised she saw, which was a flock of birds each twice her own size when in fact each established fowl was in weight and height her equal. This phenomenon was called 'psychological sight' which was supposed to revert to 'factual sight' in due course when the newcomer had sorted out her true position. Perhaps my own passage as a pupil of the learned nuns—they *were* learned: that establishment, as we grasped eventually, had an international reputation—was too brief: my schoolmates continued to appear to me revoltingly grown-up. Some in dress as well. (The only garment *I* respected was my own Red-Indian suit, already somewhat shrunk and *not* allowed on that alarming day.) In the front row lounged a group which today, with factual sight, I would describe as dark and slim, indeed future beauties. One or two of them appeared to be wearing earrings! They were the Latin-American contingent. Rich. (One soon came to hear such things.) A more clod-hoppery lot turned out to be the daughters of our landed-gentry neighbours. Most of these, like ourselves, were the new poor, or relatively poor. There also emerged a half dozen or so town children from professional or artisan families—*they* showed up very bright. The Ursulines, having their own way of dealing with politics and class, knew where to find them and were quick to offer free places. Scholarship material was not abundant in that Catholic backwater of newly republican Germany. Twenty years on, many of these nuns and their priests showed much courage and self-sacrifice standing up to the Nazi regime with all that opposition entailed. My hostile self, which had turned its back on anything German a long time before (the seeds for this were military events in the Kaiser's pre-1914 reign, central to my first mature novel) is still capable of surges of affection and pride in figures of the past such as our archbishop, Karl of Baden.

None of that yet on the horizon on the day I sat at the back of the class juggling apprehensiveness with curiosity. The class was, I gathered, in the thick of some classical poetry or history lesson, the future night-club goers and the pony-grooming clan taking little part, while a flabby-looking child, undeterred by the closed faces around her, spoke easily. In *Hoch Deutsch*, proper official German. The native aristocracy communicated in attenuated Baden patois—more or less like me, the Latinos in alternate snatches of French and German in attractive foreign tones. The engine-driver's daughter—that is what the plump girl was: how interesting for her—talked fascinatingly. Carried away, I too broke into speech. I too had dreamed about the walls of Troy. Nuns and Miss Plump took note. We were slipping into a discussion. Surprise and approval were in the air. I drank it up. So far, so good. Then came a recess. Another nun took charge. She banged a gavel and in a strong voice called '*Diktat*'—pens and copy books were presented right and left like small arms. Versailles, I vaguely wondered, the Treaty? *Diktat*—my mother's friends defined it as something which had always been inflicted by the victors as deserved and always been rejected by the losers as unjust. Peace treaties, almost inevitably, sooner or later, led into the next war. I sat back and pricked up my ears. But no . . . Hands (still kindly) slid lined pages

on desks, the nun began to speak slow words—
*we were supposed to write them down.* Heads
bent. I froze.

And so did everybody else.

When the full facts were out (this child
cannot write at all), they swarmed around me,
black cloth billowing about unseen feet—
humming to each other in distress. What
mattered, mattered vastly, was not my shame
but their reputation, their universal *renommée.*
That holy house sent its alumnae forth into the
world to bear witness not merely to the Faith
but to the elegance and perfection of the
calligraphy they had been schooled in. Their
dilemma now was this: by their Rule, I had
become an integral part of the establishment,
my contribution apparent in the record of the
entire class. A blot. A huge blot on the
collective whole. What could be done? What
would they do?

Teach me to write. From scratch.

Well, they tried. At once. Day after day I
was whisked off into a discreet little study on
an upper floor. Were they in time? Was it too
late? It takes years to train a fine hand. (For
which I did not show the slightest disposition.)
When I had managed to remember and
roughly reproduce the necessary letters, and
ceased to be classifiable as analphabetic, the
situation became worse as I had to be
readmitted to the team, take part in all written
exercises, including the dictation.

171

They might have sent me packing, asked my parents to withdraw me—or whatever was the form, but this too proved not to be quite simple. The nuns were both too charitable and too worldly for any crude dismissal. Their recruitments were selected according to three alternative *desiderata*—money, scholastic promise, family standing. Regard was shown to the workman parent of academic talent, to the Brazilian *haciendero* and to my father for that matter. And so the situation dragged . . .

Meanwhile I carried on in a mixed kind of limbo, embarrassed by my semi-secret writing lessons—stopped often on my way to the attic study by some younger nun: we never set foot anywhere without being supervised. 'Where are you off to, child?' An hour later I would be entranced by the magic of a verbal lesson, my parents' travelled lives had given me an anticipatory interest in geography, I also knew some bits about odd historical events, the elephants' crossing of the Alps, the retreat from Moscow . . . The rest I learned quite happily and fast. Thus: sole brief sweet moments of success.

The other feat that elated me in my new school life was the early morning—a pre-light start—bicycle ride to the railway station on my own. All of five kilometres. Pack of ham sandwiches and clutch of books strapped on. Seen off into the saddle as it were by my father in person, a very early riser. I was exhorted to be careful. The road, life, the world, were full of dangers. I felt contemptuous of such views. I took a few years to realize that I had inherited them. Then, in those dawns, I only strained to be off . . . Once out of sight, cold with the speed of my own wind, there was a hill, a serious hill, the *Krotzinger Buck* in native speak, between us and the country station. The joy of riding downhill fast as fast with both my hands—point of honour—off the handle bars! I was observed once or twice by peasants working in the fields, observed and reported. (The German populace had a tendency to spy on and denounce their neighbours.)

My father seemed to become aware that something was amiss between me and that convent and was furious with the institution. On the lines of 'Any daughter of mine . . . The nuns would speak of him to me as 'your dear papa', I don't recall them ever mentioning my mother, or her existence. I believe she was already quite often away at that period; I mean she went somewhere on her own, went and came back. Not much yet was made of this at home; perhaps those nuns knew more about how things stood. I don't recall my mother being much involved or commenting on my convent schooling. Nor do I know how it was all eventually resolved. It just came to an end. One week I was given a medal, a silver cross hung on a chain, the *Ehrenkreuz*, awarded for the best conduct plus performance of the week, worn publicly upon one's pinafore for six schooldays (as a non-boarder I was encouraged to take it home for showing off) and surrendered for good on Saturday afternoon.

What was that due to? My eloquence about Hannibal and Napoleon? Or to the good old maxim of charity-cum-worldliness? My father seemed quite pleased. The following week—with me *sans* cross of honour—passed routinely. The week after, I did not go. I had not been withdrawn, I had not been expelled, I was just back home.

Discussions, thoughts, of further education appeared shelved.

\*         \*         \*

One aspect of this episode marked me for life. My scrawl. It fell too far short of their standards, so the nuns had not made any effort to improve it. And no one subsequently attempted to raise it to a more customary level of legibility. It was assumed by village school (another brief and none too fortunate experience), by a miscellany of private tutors at varying localities and times, that this would be no longer necessary. I had become too old: 'Surely that girl can write.'

Well, she could not. Not properly. A handicap for any writer. I learned to type. Never *very* well, but quick enough to follow thought; and I am pleased to think that I have typed the final version, the one they print from, of nearly all my books (a process giving one more of a chance to catch a *longueur* or a limping cadence). I have been much attached to all my typewriters, borrowed, given, bought—all portables, always with me, travelling, in hotels, at home (me impersonating an American reporter or more reverently young Aldous typing in the dark on a small Remington on his knees). My own first was a Remington also, a fine model in near-mint condition, given me by my young stepfather at a moment of great mutual desperation; later came Allanah Harper's old and very steady Royal, followed on retirement by two identical bespoke Hermes, bought myself—I *had* become a kind of reporter—one to be kept on in France, the other in London. They were equipped with a few special keys: keys for round brackets, for editorial brackets, keys for single and for double quotes, for dashes of varying lengths, for French accents, a key for a $ sign. (Cost: a half-crown—2/6s. per key, then.) Now, for the last few years that is, the writer actually has to *write.* Arthritis has undone me, I can no longer tap those keys, or any other keyboards. (Dictation is out, I only command words in solitude, or by voice.) Writing slow-hand is all I can do: the scrawl is back; not improved. Hard to read for me, impenetrable to anyone else, except for one devoted, generous, clever, literate and literary friend, travelling from another country on weekends. Then, together, we decode the insect's traces on my pale green pages (less glare) to be borne away and made visible by a version of my now defunct machines.

*     *     *

The uncertainties which appear to have been at the basis of so many happenings in my life inevitably affect attempts at recalling them in intelligible order. September 2001 has just led me backwards into 1914–18, into my own infancy, the rigours and forbearances of monastic education and my short unpropitious experiences thereof. Yet I don't want to go on from there, I still want to interrupt the account of my post-war Roman years, by writing first about a previous adolescence. How do I transfer the misfit schoolgirl brought up at the edge of a slowly disintegrating family situation to the modest fishing village on the French Mediterranean coast with the girl having turned meanwhile into apprentice, disciple, near-equal in a complex human world? In life it took a good part of the Years-Between-Two-Wars. The snag is that I already wrote about those sections of my youth in a published novel. ('An Unsentimental Education' is the subtitle.) The events in that book did happen, they were *true* in fact and essence, but they

176

were presented in a form suited to a novel, not a record. Going over the same ground again, it will come out differently, and not just because—sadly—most of the dramatis personae are dead, but because one's view of actions, people, the view of oneself, perhaps the very memory of it all, changes perspectives. That book ended in the summer of 1930, which still leaves me now with the second half of the inter-war years to write about. All the same, I fear that some repetition, tangential, will have to come in, some rough résumé of the passage between my return from the Ursulines and my stepfather's leaving my mother for good at a quarter of an hour's notice. Let's make it brief.

\*     \*     \*

Well, up to then it was always my mother who left the man. She was still with us in the early years of our country life, resumed quite normally for a while, friends to stay, meals served, tea daily under a vast tree with animals trotting up to seek out my father. (Yes, he did lift his hat to the donkey, when they met on a walk in the park.) My mother travelled a certain amount, I had a vague notion as to where and with whom. I believe that she took me with her a few times; that must have been when she missed trains or went to the wrong platform to meet the stranger (who always tipped me, and often had something interesting to say: I heard early about Picasso and Klee, and became vainglorious because the village children, whom I slipped out to meet, had not). Then one day when she had gone on her own she did not come back. Nobody talked about it to me. All the same the word Divorce was in the air and I knew that I was not supposed to hear.

The new reality must have been in place practically overnight. The servants gone. All but Lina, the pious elderly village woman, unmarried, leaf-thin, who worshipped my father and treated me (affectionately) as her kitchenmaid-cum-stableboy. The dining-room, the drawing-rooms, the Delft room, the library, the main kitchen and sculleries, my nursery and the guest wing were shut up, though most of them kept aired and pristine. What remained open were the two baronial halls, one on ground level, one first-floor, each with their pair of massive unlaid fireplaces and stuffed to the ceiling with gothic bric-à-brac. These *had* to be traversed to get up the broad stone stairs to reach the top floor to which we had retreated. There remained in use my father's suite and, separated from it by what had been my mother's large balconied white-and-gold Louis XVI bedroom bereft of furniture and icy cold in the long winters, was my sister's old room, now mine; and the morning room, east-facing, sunny, where we ate, the three of us. (Lina slept isolated in a little room off a passage leading to the guest wing.) Mademoiselle's room had been plausibly converted into a kitchen. It felt kitchen-like to me because it was there that I took my first steps in a long cookery life that began with my doing the dogs' dinners, trying hard to introduce some taste into stale country bread and scrappy scraps of meat, and went on from there. Lina and my father were my first mentors. Lina's cooking was execrable (my father told me often; never her). His would have been exquisite had he not lacked most ingredients and moreover been prevented from going near a wood-fired stove by bronchial asthma.

How loud his cough sounded nightly through the house! My mother was no longer there. My father's wife. Their marriage had long ceased to occupy their emotions, it had probably turned into sheer façade at the time of her Danish lover's death. (1915?–1916?) My father learned of it, the death—formally condoling like the man of the world which a part of him was—and must have known of the previous liaison. The Danish Lover (sounds like a film) was a writer, the Maupassant of the north he was called—a statue of him, life-size, is still to be seen at Copenhagen—and is almost entirely forgotten as a literary figure today, while he is still admired as an eminent newspaper editor and remembered for his looks and his success with women. 'He was one of the great loves of my life,' my mother told me, and I daresay had told my father as well. 'Your poor Mama,' friendly Danish colleagues have said to me, '*she* was not the only one.' His face is still familiar to me: she kept his photograph—often on her dressing-table: a profile, aquiline, alive with intelligence, and a slim hand holding a cigarette in a long holder. He died of smoking a hundred a day.

\*     \*     \*

The missing element in our new life was not spoken of. The village had never looked upon my mother as the mistress of the big house; she was an alien, not much liked—let alone understood, best ignored. The house remained. She who had bought it for him now simply let him keep it. No song and dance or lawyers being called in. No thought about money either. That, too, had been hers. She kept that (what was left of it: not very much). My father had none. Between not much and none there is a chasm. Overnight we were the new poor. All poverty is relative: we were the poor with possessions. From which my father could not bear to part. We turned ourselves into a no-cash economy. Produce and barter. There was the orchard with a great variety of apple-trees; there was the kitchen garden; there was wood from the park. We had some lawn ploughed up and planted potatoes (a couple of sackfuls went to the ploughman). There was plenty of poultry, and a nasty-tempered turkey cock. Our animals had such high regard for my father that they saw the rest of us, Lina and me and the postman, as some subspecies they might peck or scratch or kick at their pleasure. We reared pigs and sheep, two a year. (They cost apples or wood.) When the sheep were still lambs, they were given names by my father: Jacko and Billi. (Shall we have Billi for Easter?) When they were slaughtered, on our own ample premises, the visiting butcher received some cuts. We smoked most of the hams. Smoked leg of mutton *is* very good, not dissimilar in texture to Spanish Serrano. It was my father's idea; I've not come across it again. There was still some wine in the cellar, serious wines for our dinners *à trois.* Properly decanted. We also drank the small quantity of white wine, Baden wine, we grew ourselves. We could not afford to buy beer. I used to long for fizzy lemonade, stood me by Lina on rare occasions. We made plenty of cider, a little of it for lunch, the bulk a mainstay of our bartering income. It paid for the sound bread from the village baker, for butter, for milk, salt, candles and matches and the dreadful acorn coffee Lina required. (My sister, when she was able to—she, with her husband, was still resident in the Occupied Rhineland Zone—sent us packets of tea and peppercorns.) Essential services, too, such as digging, wood-felling, carting, chimney sweeping, could be exchanged for our produce; and so was straw for the pigs and some animal feed. So far so good.

To subsist even in a backward, slow-changing community, bereft as yet of the very notion of a cinema or wireless transmission, one needs a *little* cash. For stamps, not that we sent many letters; for the weekly local paper, indispensable for exchanges of goods; for taxes (oh, my poor father!); for the electricity bills. Before the war, the village had had no power laid on, the château generated its own. In the barn, by a resident Italian electrician. The man was a ruffian and a socialist (of the ranting kind)—who antagonized the husbands of the younger peasant women. However, chandeliers were ablaze and our stable was a clean well-lighted place. Not so now: a municipal authority provided, so there were the bills and the dread before the arrival of the bills. Lina and I were exhorted to switch on as seldom and as late in the day as might he contrived. The theory being that what costs most is the distance the current has to travel to reach a house. So no casual fingers on the switches, no flicking-on for an instant a light in the cellar. (I used to be sent down there for wine.) After nightfall there would be lit lamps in my father's sitting-room—as well as a warm stove handsomely tiled—and a ceiling light in the kitchen. On other territory we would grope our way or resort to candles; awkward this, as it meant carrying out a task candlestick in one hand.

*      *      *

Beyond our walls, the background to it all was the raging inflation undoing peoples' lives. The facts of the great German post-war inflation and its ultimate consequences are history, yet when we now talk of and fear devaluation, the scale of its catastrophic course then is no longer within our imaginations—the loaf that could be bought for a mark coming to cost ten marks within months, rising to a hundred next week, to a thousand, a hundred thousand, eventually rushing on like a hurricane gaining speed to a million, a hundred millions, to milliards . . . What had bought a house the year before, a piano last month, a pound of butter last week, bought a newspaper in the morning but no longer on that afternoon. People who were in work were paid daily, if not hourly. People who went out to shop went in pairs to carry the laundry-basket heaped high with paper notes. Who had or held on to stocks and shares or foreign currencies, who had trustees and know-how and good advice, survived more or less. People with pensions or savings in cash were destitute, wiped out . . .

My father . . . Well, *he* had never bought shares, had never put coin in a piggy-bank; what came to him, he spent. Now it was real estate, bricks and mortar, a not inconsiderable amount of them. For him they were just there: immovable. *And* chock-full with antiques. His *collection*, *collected* piece by piece over his lifetime. Objects: rows upon rows. I did not learn to love them; knew that *he* did. As did a number of dealers—coveted would be the more appropriate term; the hoard was known, had been stalked, yet none of the sharks had as yet achieved access. At intervals there would come a morning—with another electricity bill possibly on its way—when my father, immaculately tailored, gloved, carrying a Gladstone bag, took a train to Freiburg or to Basle across the border. His countenance told one nothing. Questions were not asked. Answers throughout my childhood seemed to come through the air. Basle appeared most likely. Antique dealers at that period traded in foreign currencies only; to the Basle ones they would not be foreign: Swiss francs seemed natural, almost God-given. When my father came back in the evening—still secretive, secretively relieved?—the bag was not empty: out came treats, gingerbread and milk chocolate for Lina, salted almonds and good things in tins for me; for the dogs, dog-biscuits. He liked giving. He might look at the sideboard: 'Perhaps not that one tonight—'

184

and give me instructions for the precise vintage to bring up. I would strike match to candle.

\*       \*       \*

It had not been like that for me the whole time—the Robinson Crusoe challenge, the pleasure of contriving, the feel of a good crew, if unlikely matched, working hard each to their capacity to keep it all together. There had been a phase soon after the beginning of the new life when I was struck from one minute to the next by acute desolation, a deep unhappiness I was not able to explain or communicate. I did not know how to lift the darkness that lay heavy and autonomous inside me. (The hardest moments were sitting at table trying to disguise my misery while expected to tuck in.) I experienced the same sensation, the sudden obliteration of joy, in my later life, in my sixties, in London walking up Haymarket on a sunny June evening after a drinks party on the roof of New Zealand House with Richard, my well-loved editor and friend. There was no apparent reason. That time the eclipse lasted on and off for the best part of two years and I think of it as one of the worst experiences one might have. The childhood bout—also in full fine summer—resolved itself within weeks. One day I found a reason for that unhappiness: I wanted my sister, I wanted Jacko, I lacked feminine affection. They were good to me here, my father and Lina, they could hardly have been kinder . . . In their way. Lina was a shy, stiff peasant, to her I was both an under-servant and the employer's daughter; my father for all his affinity with animals wild and domestic seemed to reduce his contacts with humans to a show of material solicitude and good manners. What I needed came to me in a flash, complete with the knowledge of where to find it: I was going to run away.

At that moment the cloud inside me vanished (this experience leads to clichés), all became self-will, resolve, planning . . . Children, until circumstances, life and luck correct this at some points, are imbued with the sense that *they* and the instant fulfilment of their desires are at the centre of the universe, their only *reality*. I don't think that I was an ill-intentioned, let alone a ruthless child, yet when the time came, I behaved like one. No thought, no feeling, no questions about anybody else.

\*       \*       \*

Running away. *Getting* away, getting *somewhere*—uncaught—was an uncertain enterprise, odds of success low to vanishing point. I passed days working out ways and means with a mixture of cunning and uncertain

186

knowledge. Money and geography were among imponderables to be considered (with but little factual knowledge). What I knew was my goal—arrival feasibly before nightfall at Parkstrasse 10. *There* I could fling myself into Jacko's arms and all would be resolved and well. It was the address of the house in which my sister lived with her husband, the man of mature years, deputy mayor responsible for opera, the gardens and other amenities of Wiesbaden, the spa town in the Rhineland (somewhere north of us, or north-west?). I knew that the Rhineland was Occupied Territory, occupied by the French. Did one need a permit to cross from the Free to the Occupied Zone? Possibly. Maybe it did not apply to children. My brother-in-law, the deputy mayor, *Beigeordeneter* was the official title, was extremely Francophile and known as such, keeping open house to high-ranking French officers as well as to musicians and White Russian *émigrés.* (And was remembered as such when the really barbarous times arrived years on. He, Jacko's first husband who had been a Separatist, plotting or reported to have plotted for annexation of the Rhineland by France. Once in power the Nazis charged him with treason, charged him, convicted him, and had his head cut off. Literally. The death penalty under German law still being then by the axe. When I sought refuge at that man's door this was yet in more than a decade to

187

come.)

The first stage of planning was how to make an early and unnoticed getaway. It was June, daylight came early, I would have to be up and gone before Lina emerged from the poor room off the guest-wing passage where she slept. *I* was apt to sleep soundly and late for as long as they let me. An alarm clock toned down under my pillow might have been the answer had we had anything as up to date. The front-door locks and keys were heavy and ancient, and firmly ground shut at dark. The scullery door into the outer world was of a more contemporary design. I contrived to oil that lock. Then: the wall—the property was enclosed—high but not insuperably so: one might easily chip out a few footholds and I soon managed successful practice climbs. If observed I would talk about Everest. What next? When the day came, I would walk—quickly but nonchalantly—to the railway station on the road I had so often flown along by bicycle, hoping to encounter no one. Once there, I would have to buy a ticket . . . When I was commuting to the nuns, this had been done for me: well, I would have to do it on my own!

(In later life I heard Brian Howard—the naughtiest, he liked to think, of the Bright and Young—intone when persisting with some unlikely and nefarious enterprise,

Leggy over leggy, the doggy went to Dover
And when he came to the stile,
Hop! He went over

and it struck me that it had been in this spirit I
went forward on that childhood escapade,
leggy over leggy . . .)

I had decided on Frankfurt as a sensible
first destination, I knew it to be the nearest big
town to Wiesbaden. It might serve to cover up
my traces. But how far was it? In distance? In
hours? And what would a ticket cost . . . ? I'd
ask for half-fare which I believed was right for
children under eight. I was *not* under eight.
(Nearer eleven, if I am correct.) I was not tall
and if I stood close under the ticket window,
bending my knees a little, the man above
would not see all of me: I *would* have to have
the right money, be unsurprised by the amount
asked for. This caused much concern. I had
money, I had wads of it, unspent since the days
my mother's admirers generously tipped me.
But how much would it buy in terms of railway
ticket, what with inflation and all those
currencies? I panicked. One night I crept into
my father's dressing-room, found in the dark
his coat hung over a chair, found his wallet,
seized a handful . . . Crept back.

\*　　　\*　　　\*

I cannot forgive myself for this. Knowing the

isolation, the deprivations and anxieties of his new life, irreversible—he was well into his sixties . . . How could I, how could—and can—so many of us, children, adolescents, grown-up men and women, when our will flows strongly, do what too late we bitterly condemn?

That dawn I woke in time.

On the walk I was seen, and reported, by people working in the fields. I carried nothing apart from a book and a purse in the apron-pocket of my cotton dress which must have been on the short side, my wardrobe being infrequently renewed. At the station I was sold my ticket all right: half-fare, fourth class, as I had firmly said. There was still a fourth class on trains then: wooden seats and you could take your dog or a crated small animal. That official also reported me, to the police in fact: he had rubbed his eyes after a little while; but he was too late. I had been off in my fourth-class carriage. When it filled up, I held my corner, reading my book, keeping conversation at a stiff minimum. Where was I going? Visiting a relative. Back to the book. Certainly I had no luggage, I said irritably looking up, that was being sent on for me separately. I firmly refused any offers of food, declined sandwiches, bars of chocolate, sips from a thermos: fourth-class passengers are gregarious and hospitable. My refusal came from instinct and an entire cessation of hunger and thirst. After what must have been less than a couple of hours the train stopped for good. All got out. Fourth class was only on local trains. I had to change platforms, guess directions, board the next slow train. It was a confusing journey, hit and near miss, what should have taken a few hours or so went on well into the late afternoon. What I did not guess was that my travelling dog-compartment throughout confused the police: they searched the wrong (the actually right) trains. I made it. It was dusk. I walked again for the last stretch, openly now asking my way to Parkstrasse, on the other end of town in a quarter of gardens and trees.

My brother-in-law was at home, my sister was not. Oh, he said when he saw me, 'you?', more bewildered than cross: there had been a lot of telegrams . . . from my father, from the police, the crossing-point guards . . . Jacko was out of town at a tennis tournament, 'Perhaps we'd better get her back? I could send the car.' Yes, I said.

# CHAPTER ELEVEN

*A polyglot paradise—Jacko's future casts
its shadow—A year and more of bucolic
contentment at day and a fantasy evening
life: hard-worked stable-boy into lady
dinner companion—Sudden turning-point*

There ensued a great tumult which I did not
want to take in. My father arrived within a day
or so—yes yes and so had my sister, almost
instantly, that first evening duly loving as well
as vociferously upset. She and Borgman (that
was her husband's name: Hans Borgman) tried
to convey to me what my father had gone
through during the hours I was missing; from
cock-crow to late dusk when a telegram to *him*
had come at last. They insisted on his staying
to recuperate for a while. This had to include
me: I basked, shutting out my vision of a
future. My father did not reproach me, asked
no questions, entered into his grown-up
daughter's extremely privileged life. With
me—we were seldom alone—he showed little
beyond an aloof sadness. He never mentioned
his wallet, the missing notes. His one straight
reference to recent events was 'Billi—you left
the house unlocked, open to enemies and
thieves . . .'

The weeks following turned out to be the

most stimulating episode of my life so far. For the first time I found myself in a musically literate milieu. In no house we lived in had there been as much as a piano. My mother—curious lacuna—had no sense of nor desire for music; my father occasionally hummed a tune from *The Magic Flute*, a snatch of the tender catcher of birds, *'Der Vogelfänger bin ich ja, stets lustig heissa hopsasa'*; Jacko's tastes we know. And now she was married to a serious, erudite patron of music. It was he who is supposed to have achieved the engagement of a youngish Otto Klemperer by Wiesbaden Opera, and in the evenings he kept open house—every evening in fact—there was music, instrumental and vocal, by professional musicians and one would hear Stravinsky as well as Bach and Brahms. It had been ordained—Jacko was a (benevolent) disciplinarian—that I could stay up and attend those soirées; 9.45 p.m. was the limit fixed, after that I adroitly managed to retreat into semi-invisibility in which I succeeded to remain often until nearly midnight. Fair enough since that would be the hour when some of the musicians had only just arrived from their performances. Fellow guests were male and not young, except for Jacko and the occasional soprano. During my permitted presence I was treated with charming amiability by the French element (I admired their high *képis*, and *how* I was to love their country), I was unobtrusively snubbed by the Russian *émigrés* conscious that their titles, for most of them all they had to hang on to, were far grander than my father's. The musicians ignored me.

All were drinking brandy, in balloon glasses, genuine brandy, French, cognac, made available to the host by courtesy of the Occupying Powers. Those evenings went on into the small hours; if they became loud it was with music, not raised voices or drink.

The days—Jacko slept late, 'not to be disturbed', by then she and Borgman had their rooms in different wings of the villa, an ugly, reasonably comfortable house, from which I set out early to where it had been arranged for me to go: the tennis club—the days too were deliriously enjoyable. I was equally happy being coached to play (never well) or running after the balls of other people's matches. At lunch-time I went to pick up my brother-in-law at his mayoral office; he was one of those men who cannot bear to be by themselves for more than five minutes. Usually it was a woman, not particularly young, a post office employee, who walked him home. She was his mistress and had been that, unacknowledged if perhaps suspected by some friends and colleagues, well before Jacko aged not quite nineteen had thrown herself at his head. That liaison had been resumed a year or two after Borgman's wedding. During my stay, Jacko had still no idea of the postmistress's existence and position; by the time she knew, she had long not minded. His choice of myself as a stand-in midday escort may be explained by his not caring who was with him as long as he was not alone; he may even have been not displeased by my quizzing, 'Was Verdi or was he not greater than Puccini, and why?' 'What do people mean by programme music?' Thus Jacko had once seen him as the mature wise mentor who would elevate her future life, forswearing young admirers, dances, dreaming clothes. (She had been good at all of these and would be again.) They had met at some spa, she brought by the Berlin grandparents always careful about their health, he by his own strain of hypochondria. In my turn I was impressed by his knowledge, and grateful for his generous treatment of me. Unlike my sister, I did not fall in love with him. I do recall the little I knew at first hand of the man—host, musicologist, civil servant—with affection and conjecture. The awe at his ultimate fate, like something out of Grimm's fairy-tales, is too enormous to connect with anyone once seen in everyday human form. To Jacko he remained long ago a mistake (not her greatest yet) recalled with derision, wonderment at her younger self, and some bitterness.

*Then:* Hans Borgman and I walked amicably towards luncheon through a well-kept park.

The villa, much grander, next to his

belonged to the Henkels, the solid, decent family who owned the firm which produced, still does, the premium German champagne, Henkel Trocken. They were much distressed at the time by one of their daughters having insisted on marrying a young Rhinewein salesman, then thought worthless, called Ribbentrop. The one who in due course became German ambassador to Britain under Hitler, and was subsequently hanged at Nüremberg. I saw, over the fence as it were, the little Ribbentrop children playing in their garden. That was as far as I ever came into material contact with the future nightmare. (Unless one counts Issa.)

*    *    *

My Wiesbaden afternoons were spent at the races. Again with Borgman. My father was no racing man, indeed horses were the animals least loved by him, he saw them as a menace, the cause of many of the misadventures of his life. He had in fact endured a number of bad falls steeplechasing as a young man about to get engaged to an English heiress. The falls had caused concussion, so his logic ran: had he not hurt his head so often, he might have been better equipped to match up, among other things, to my mother's intellect. Here lay also the reason for his giving me a donkey rather than a pony; that she was a circus donkey of great guile who loathed little girls was just luck.

When there was no racing, Jacko and I with our father and the chauffeur went for country drives; in a Panhard, a large car, six-seater, open to the winds. Jacko drove too fast, hence her husband's insistence on the chauffeur. *He* was on her side: they swapped as soon as we were out of town, with my urging speed and our father caution. In those long-gone days when people's conduct was largely governed by their servants, there was no household of some size without its factions.

At Parkstrasse, the master's side was led by the butler-cum-valet, a melancholy Russian baron often disagreeable and in his turn somewhat at the whim of a handsome young guttersnipe he had recruited locally as footman. Together they refused to tolerate any housemaid. The head of Jacko's coterie was not the chauffeur but Nanny, a young nanny, sweet to her small charge and adoring Jacko. (Jacko was always nice to everyone who worked for her, seeing them as equals with whom one might also lose one's temper.) Oh yes! There was another child in the house, a resident child, unlike myself: the Borgmans' own baby. The little girl had been born at the end of the first year of their marriage. To Jacko it had come as the closing of the trap. She was already not only out of love with her husband; she had begun to he afraid of him.

*He* had a temper. He was proud of his wife as a possession—all his cronies fell for her vitality, her chic; and he *was* a jealous man—often not without cause, Jacko being a natural flirt, to put it at the most harmless—capable of rages. There were mutterings about his having torn his late mother's pearls off her neck on the dawn return from a dance (he never accompanied her on such occasions); he had been seen, the gossip ran, barring her entry on a winter night, snow and all, sword in hand at the front door. Did he *have* a sword? Whatever the truth of it, Jacko no longer liked the father of her child over-much: she had reverted to her nature which inclined towards the beach, the dance floor, men of her own age. Borgman, she maintained ever after, had cast a spell on her at that spa. To their little daughter she showed care and affection; that it had not the quality of the affection she had given to me spontaneously from birth was something the three of us were even then aware of. Inevitably Jacko was now supposed to be not a mere sister but a mother and as such she could see no door out to her kind of future. Escapades, possibly here and there, flings loyally alibied by Nanny or chauffeur. No serious attachment in view as yet. No serious attachment an acceptable solution. Borgman at that stage had not much of a rapport with his baby daughter; one could guess though that he would never let her go.

Would he let *Jacko* go?

*She* had nowhere to turn to. No money of her own. Her opulent grandparents existed no longer as such. Grandpapa had died; most of the fortune gone, through family decadence as well as the inflation; Grandmama's lavish establishment temporarily kept going by the bounty of a daughter-in-law, Jacko's middle-aged aunt, an heiress in her own right, financially astute. No rescue there. So what might be on offer for a young woman, possibly adulterous, abandoning or kicked out by her husband? Take up that Lieder talent she had spurned? Too late. A job? Jacko, though untrained, *had* skills in her locker. Too early. Gainful employment was still a very limited option in post-war Europe for a girl of her provenance. Give a hand at someone's dinner-party? Try a toe-hold in a dress-shop? Jacko had not acquired as yet the flexible fatalism of a Russian *émigrée*.

\*　　　\*　　　\*

So much for my sister's future. What about mine? A more immediate concern . . . *I* wanted to stay where I was, I prayed for the status quo. Days were passing . . . had already passed. How many? I dared not count. I tried not to hear what was being said, discussed—decided—around me. How was my father taking to his brief re-entry—even my ostrich nature perceived that it could not be other than *brief*—into what was in some ways the kind of world he had known and thrived in? Arrangements had to be made to allay his immediate concerns: Lina on her own, the animals, the safety of the house. Borgman took on the role of son-in-law to a man not very senior to himself. Borgman, a character not easily summed up, had already taken the necessary steps: efficiently, imaginatively, generously. He was spending money *en grand seigneur*. And discreetly. If one heard Jacko, this was not invariably the case. *Money*. Money poured into the running of the house, the ceaseless hospitality, the subsidies to novice violinists—figured in the ambiguities of the situation. It was English money and one did not know from one month to the next, from year to year, whether or not it was there. That English fortune, generated by a variety of English companies, had come to Borgman on his English mother's death, a large fortune at its moment—all fortunes large or small have one, as I learned early—the snag being that he, an only son, had inherited it shortly before the war and that it had been placed under embargo in August 1914 as enemy alien's property. And so it had remained in English banks and various institutions, producing or reducing dividends without distribution, for over a decade. During the latter half of which the complex and expensive processes of probate, unblocking, restitution began crawling forth. Oh, the law's, the accountants', the red tape's delays . . . Meanwhile Borgman, who had never attempted to live on a mayoral salary, had been steadily advanced substantial sums, on substantial interest, by German banks with firm faith in their English counterparts and the solidity of their client's expectations. Actual money, one understood, had begun to trickle in quite recently. The beneficiary himself, bored by the minutiae of the financial world and long accustomed to the irregularities of the position, insouciant one day, in near panic over one more bill the next, had left the unwinding of his fortune to the professionals and their hangers-on. A wife, who was an unrepentant spend-thrift, paid little notice to the uncertainties of the situation. Meanwhile down in Baden, our Lina was provided with enough strong young arms from the village to chop her firewood, guard her nights and feed the pig.

\*　　　\*　　　\*

I knew one thing I had to do. Urgently. Speak to Jacko. Explain, make clear to her. 'Please don't let them send me back.' 'Please make it all right for me not to go back.' For this I would have to see my sister by herself. Not easy. From the time of her levee, which was not far from the time we sat down to luncheon, she was rarely on her own. Almost with her breakfast tray—black coffee and the first cigarette: how stylish I thought that was—in streamed Nanny with my baby niece. I might have timed it better, found another moment— by her dressing-table before dinner? I never made it. Resolve every morning. Then failure of nerve. Another twenty-four hours lost. For the day that must come, I had another resolve: they would have to drag me down the drive, I would dig my feet in, they would have to lift me into the car, pull me into the station, on to the platform. When the train came in, I holding on to Jacko's arm, my father standing by tense, aloof I would howl. As I had howled at that eye-clinic when I was little: *that* had not been premeditated. This time people might hear—'Where is that man going to take that child?' They would help me . . .

Nothing like this happened. Indeed the day came. Did I walk a bit stiffly perhaps? I don't know whether I cried. At one point we were on a train, my father and I, sitting opposite each other on upholstered seats, not saying very much, I suppose. I don't remember the rest. It can't have been a long journey, shorter than the one I took—was there a picnic basket? 'How did we get back from the station? Fetched by one of our old carriages hitched on to a village horse? Lina's welcome I recall: tears, embraces, 'How could you have done this to *him*?' More embraces . . .

And after that? Complete reversal—how did it happen, how and how soon? I cannot recall what kind of a bridge there had been between that glittering visit and the long period of hard-working days filled with bucolic tasks carried out cheerfully and not badly, accepting contentment, a period that must have lasted for at least a couple of years. I had slid again into rural life as if I had never known nor aspired to anything else.

As rural life goes, it had its unorthodox moments. The evenings—the great doors locked, the animals asleep on the beds of straw or dried leaves I had made for them—belonged to my father's make-believe and past. Claret and roulette. Phantom roulette. The wheel with its little ball, the green cloth, the rake, the chips, were authentic, real, Monte Carlo, brought out from some cupboard recess which held his numberless paraphernalia. Monte Carlo also were the croupier's cries, in French of course. (Lina *learned.*) Less real were our stakes: my father held bank, we were the punters and the money we bought our chips with *was* money—not much by casino standards—Lina's wages, my pocket coins, but we were taught to shift the decimal point, as well as convert our paper marks into *louis d'or.* This heightened our emotion on winning or losing. Next morning—how quickly I learned the difference between an evening and a morning mood—regardless of how the luck had run, our original cash was unobtrusively returned. The night before, at dinner or *après les jeux*, my father had entertained us, his guests, with tales from his own life: his rural past—decorous and happy; his service in the cavalry—strenuous and unhealthy, it always rained on manoeuvres, and the etiquette! Above all beware of a turn as ADC; the Kaiser's barbarous way of scoffing his food in seconds with that fork/knife designed for his withered arm; when he had finished, all one's plates were whisked away. You never got enough to eat . . . Well, he escaped from all that—Paris: everything so beautiful; and Spain, the south of Spain: Seville, Granada, Ronda, perhaps he had loved Spain most of all . . . He talked about the monkeys he had kept, very attaching, some had difficult natures, jealousies one had to be on guard about like, well, French mistresses . . .

My father's speech was discreet, he used chaste words, though he took little account of his audience's limitations, my age, Lina's sense of sin. While he talked, it was as if he were looking at something that had been there. Once long ago I wrote of him, 'When he spoke, he saw what he had lived.' I think that this was true. A very simple way of presenting events as they were. Unlike my mother's verbal explorations which took in context, comment, judgement.

He talked of the Mesmerism he had once

been interested in. There was that man in Grasse . . . he *could* raise the dead; he spoke of ghosts, apparitions, coincidences . . . And then we were with chefs in their kitchens, he had once watched a Chinese cook. Come to think of it, he had never been out of Europe, well, Tangiers perhaps, and there was his life on Corsica, he did some painting there, perhaps more sketching, once there was a shipwreck quite near the shore . . . He'd made a sketch standing in the storm close to a sinking ship. Later he did make a painting of it in oil, had it framed. 'When your mother saw it, thirty years on it must be, she said her family knew of that ship—it had a name; her father had been on it when it sank off the coast of Corsica, he was on his way back from India, she hadn't been born then . . . No, no, he didn't drown, many of the passengers got rescued; the pearls he had promised to bring for his wife, they were lost, so your mother told me. Her mother, she said, was most upset.'

\*     \*     \*

Daylight life. I had one too: sorties into the village on my own. My father thought nothing of having me work as a farm-hand on our land; yet mucking-in at the potato harvest or the hay with a gang of other children, he found imprudent and unnecessary. Was I being exploited, was I being mocked? *I* enjoyed it greatly: the teamwork, the importance of tasks done, the cider, bread and thickly carved cold bacon afterwards at a peasant's house. I got on well with the boys, or thought I did; the girls I considered stupid, pious, meek. The boys could show some spirit: when the carts returned to the fields unloaded, we would snatch rides, two on each horse's back, trying to make them trot . . . Lina endeavoured to hint that the village frowned on my camaraderie with boys. Indeed there seemed to be some rule of segregation—at school and church as well as work and play. (We might have been living in Afghanistan.) As for my asking a few eleven- or twelve-year-olds into the park to see my Red Indian tent . . .

I was disturbed by Lina's insinuations—they were not about mere points of manners, there was something distasteful and obscure behind them; I felt offended, accused, unjustly—but of what? She had used a word: scandal. It was the word said to me gently by the nun who had taken me aside, 'We must avoid causing scandal, mustn't we?' It was to point out that the cotton dresses I wore at the convent school had become far too short. 'You *will* tell them at home . . .' That had given me the same feeling of something hidden and wrong of which I was ignorant though it was darkly there.

That shadow did not matter long. My father, badgered by inquisitive bureaucracy, thought it wise to let me do a spell at village school, seated of course in the girls' aisle. When I caught lice, a stop was put to it all.

*       *       *

From time to time—travel from zone to zone had become free again—my sister came, in Panhard with chauffeur and a few exquisite things to eat, to spend a week with her father. It turned out to be seldom more than one or two nights. These authorized parental visits served as pretexts for her escapades. I believe that my father knew and that although he would dearly have liked her to stay longer, he understood and did not disapprove. Jacko *was* his daughter. To me she simply said that she was going to meet someone. Nice? 'Very nice. You see, when you are grown-up there will be something quite delightful one can do—you can look forward to that.' Yes, I said, I will.

And that, come to think of it, must have been the only 'sex education' I ever had.

*       *       *

Certainly I should have liked my sister's visits to last longer. We both cried a little at each parting. It was no longer heartbreak. Even when confined to home ground, I enjoyed my agricultural existence. Then abruptly in a muddled confusing way it came to an end. It seems as if it all happened at the same time, as it could not. My mother claimed me. Divorced as the guilty party, she had nevertheless been given a right to custody for several months of every year. She had not claimed this for some time. Now she wanted as it were a lump sum. She was about to marry again, a man in the art world of some substance and reputation. There would be a home—in Italy. The courier was being engaged to escort me on the trains. More or less simultaneously my father fell ill. Appendicitis. The supposedly minor operation turned fatal by his bronchial asthma. He died within days. Borgman, with Jacko, came to take charge.

## CHAPTER TWELVE

*Cisalpine—A future waif: brief camaraderie—Confusion and delays— Holding one's own—A love trap— An instant of cognition—Naples v. Florence: a novel ecstasy—An affectionate pact—Financial and other realities— Houndings—Jacko's coup—What next?— Travelling lighter*

Having finished writing the previous chapter as I did today, today meaning in the twenty-first century, in my own old age, I am struck by the abrupt finality of the last page. This was indeed the point of no return: my father's lightning death, the severance from Germany (*that* was premature for persons of my situation or birth), my strange, defeated, formal father vanished (I am still trying to understand what he was like). So: disconnection of lines and life.

\*     \*     \*

That first Italian journey! Imagination anticipated Florence—the quattrocento, a house with a view, run on Borgman lines by a knowledgeable man, an art historian, not young: the prospective new husband whose presence as well as being a fount of instruction would dilute the perils of living once more with my mother. (There had been much amusement about my late rustic existence expressed in her communications with my father and myself.) More recently though had come a charming olive branch, a copy sent by hand of courier of Goethe's *Italienische Reise* graciously inscribed 'For my daughter, to remind her of her first Italian journey'. The journey, in fact, had not yet begun, indeed turned doubtful to materialize at all. True, when the train had crossed the Alps and engaged its slow descent into a sunlit fruitful valley, I had experienced a state of sheer joy, a fulfilment of a longing that lies dormant in many of us whose birth has been into the rain.

That was good. What was not was the message carried by the alarmingly slim young girl—today we would speak of anorexia—an hotel acquaintance whom my mother had persuaded to meet me at Vipiteno, the little cisalpine frontier post, in replacement of the courier who had been discharged the night before. I was told that we were to get off at Merano—after hardly more than another couple of hours' ride!—and wait there at an hotel. Wait for what? 'Your mother. She asked me to look after you, she's gone away for a few days.' *Gone away why and where?* Doris—that was the young girl's name did not know.

Merano. A place I had not heard of. A prosperous, *soigné* resort in a benign climate, surrounded by orchards and vines, with blue skies and a luxuriant vegetation in well-kept parks and gardens with well-dressed middle-aged people on the garden-benches. Paradise? *Where* was the quattrocento? Officially we were in Italy, in the province of Trentino-Alto Adige, physically we were in a former part of Austria, the Süd-Tyrol, annexed to Italy by the Treaty of Versailles in 1919: road signs, street names in Italian, native voices guttural. For me the great sights were puzzlingly delayed.

Meanwhile we, Doris and I, were lodged in a solid old-fashioned hotel, one that combined Austro—northern-Italian virtues of hospitable traditions—space, torrents of hot water, of *Mehlspeisen*, *Back-Hähnle* and *Schnitzel* modulating into *gnocchi* and *scaloppine* on the menus with *gelati à discrétion*. Waiters, young and old, were charming to children, especially so to a child who liked to eat. They were a new species to me (confidently approached ever after). And so was Doris, a new species, a member of the Weimar Republic's Jazz-Age generation, idealistic, liberated and liberating, mad for pleasure and, in contrast to their American originals, mouse-poor. Her provenance, Berlin, was one of distinguished men of letters and liberal-conservative civil servants; her mother, like Jacko's, had died early of TB. She talked night-clubs, Communism, films: avant-garde of course. Needless to say I had never been to a cinema, never mind avant-garde. It was interesting, if not up to the expectation of the Medici Chapel or the Ponte Vecchio. One thing we had in common: although Doris must have reached her twenties and I was still a child, we were each in some ways in advance of, as well as rather young for, our respective ages. One of the diversions in our Sister-Anne existence were late-night moonlit walks in the less kempt outskirts of Merano talking Utopia and munching stolen fruit. (In contrast to our being so nicely lodged and fed, we had barely any cash in our pockets.) The person Doris was on outlook for was a scriptwriter, member of a cinematographic unit, by whom she had been given hopes, plus railway fare, of

211

employment on location. Eventually it was my mother who turned up. In an abstracted mood, in two minds about something; one could not ask what. She did say that after all it might not have been quite the right moment to have sent for me. Later, one whole afternoon, she talked feelingly, unstoppably about my father, the past, the whole past. It sank in.

Letters, stamped express, kept arriving. After each batch, she proposed a move. Someone she had to see. Not here. So we moved. To Cortina. A short spurt sideways: eastwards, not south (I could read a map). Cortina d'Ampezzo, another resort, somewhat closer mountains, a not quite so 'good' hotel. Doris was persuaded to come with us. 'Never mind, these film people will find you'; meanwhile she could look after me. My mother herself would have to go away again. Before she left, I managed to ask, 'You *are* getting married? Soon?' The consulate at Florence had done the paperwork, she said, which did not mean that one had to be at their beck and call. She relented as far as, 'It may become rather a question.' Soon after her, Doris left as well. Those film people had found her. One hoped that some little good would come out of it. If it did it could not alter what was in store for so many of her kind, the future inhabitants of a mercilessly Occupied Europe. Doris (no Jewish blood) became unshakeably a resistant. With its consequences. There was still nothing of this in our minds during the brief weeks we spent, quite comfortable fugitives, at play together; nothing to indicate that this bright young waif would reappear at various intervals of our differing future existences. Hers mainly tragic and too short.

\*　　　\*　　　\*

My mother returned; not unduly disconcerted to find me by myself. (There had been no address to communicate that fact to her.) She saw me as fairly acclimatized, holding my own. I had managed to refuse hotel guests' kindly offers to join their table at meals and instead strolled nonchalantly—hair brushed, hands washed—to my own, a decent corner table for one, bringing a book. The food was still glorious (in my view), the waiters paternal; this, unlike lady-guests' caresses, I could accept. The wine—I would order a quarter-carafe—was not up to what we drank at what I thought of as the château, not as a lost home. My mother had left me a clutch of Tauchritzes, those pre-Penguin, English-language paperbacks for sale at every continental bookstall; she had also left some money. I bought an Italian grammar and a ball. I went for walks. Sometimes I felt a little queasy, uncertain, as though I was playing a part. 'And how are we this morning?' they would say to me in the garden. I had to push away a secret question: what if nobody came back? Even Jacko would not know where I was. How could she? The sole communications received were those express letters; they ceased when my mother was not there. She did come back. Then soon, she or we would be off again. There followed a period of weeks, indeed months, passed in journeys undertaken, it appeared, without foresight or plausible destination, of random sojourns in hotels of declining quality or in simple and clean *pensione* run by hardworking Italian women whose maternal affection I as naturally welcomed. Care for *a bambino* came lengths before curiosity about the *bambino's* mother's doings. This mother returned, from what must have been some encounter, glowing, elated, unseeing of all around, or serious, lucid, gloomily concerned. Contradictory patterns emerged, gathered from Delphic utterances, single sentences addressed to the air. 'How can they expect cut-and-dried decisions?' 'Yes, yes, I know what I *ought* to do.' 'A little patience might help.' 'Should one not accept what life offers?' 'Of course it *is all madness!*' On one of the euphoric returns she actually looked at me: 'I've been to Venice.' *Venice!* What I said was, 'Mummy, was it heaven?' 'It was.'

Gradually I made out that it must be more than one person she was meeting on these sorties she rushed off to. Put together later, it must have gone like this: on her way to the altar, as it were, of what was to be her second marriage, my mother had met a young man of great good looks who had insistently fallen in love with her at first sight. She had been dismissive, if amused. Apart from being the proverbial half her age, he was intellectually, she told him to his face, hardly above her own daughter. He was not her kind of man even if he looked as though he had stepped out of a Renaissance canvas—*not* off any contemporary Italian operatic stage—and disarmed by a graceful, easy, lightly teasing manner. She remained amused—of course they met again—became flattered by so much determined adoration, then attracted, allowed herself to fall a little in love, *was* in love. So—a fling. Why not? Her serious marriage could wait a little longer (they had already been openly attached some time); and once accomplished, good faith would require a closing of the doors. He wanted permanence; she was facing that perennial question: how far am I from forty? On such lines actions evolved. In phases. They met, face to face, she with requests, not lies. Be patient, please. He *was* patient; as well as tolerant, unreproachful, good-tempered. He must have been a man without much vanity, or very sure of himself, that phantom stepfather-to-be. (I never got a glimpse of him in person.) They met more

215

than once, at pleasant places; she still liked him, his company, the subjects they were able to talk about, yet she longed to be elsewhere. He did not prevent her departures, asked no questions, only refused almost serenely to take the fling as anything more than that. *'Tout passe: we* have yet a future to live.' She had told him the facts: Alessandro—his name was spoken—the son of a university professor on the verge of retirement, was an architecture student. This was somewhat problematical, as there were still brothers to educate and no help to be expected in the climate of the nascent regime to which the family, if not yet in open opposition was hostile. Such facts must have been grist to the elder suitor, a man of substance and some standing in the art world. My mother did not consent to discuss the material aspects of the situation. Her most urgent concerns were for Alessandro, who went wild with despair at their every parting.

Where? Was he still supposed to be a presence at home? How many lectures or tutorials did he cut short or miss? I did not know. My mother and I moved our base a good deal, if you could call it a base. She would need a rest, time for reflection, repacking of a suitcase. We got into *real* Italy by stages. I saw Lake Garda, I saw Vicenza, I got to know the conjugations of irregular Italian verbs. *'Avrebbe bisogna'*, trundled off smoothly when I required something. Then one day, we were at Verona, my mother told me to throw away or pack all we had accumulated during these last months—quite a few Tauchnitzes there were—we were to be off on a proper journey and it was going to be a surprise.

'Florence?' A sigh. 'You are a persistent child.' *Not* Florence.

It was a long train journey and near the beginning of it at a brief halt, I had not seen the station name, our compartment door opened and in stepped a young man more handsome than I could have imagined him to be. He kissed my mother's hand. That night the three of us booked into a small hotel in Naples. Two rooms; of which one I found—astonishment, relief—I was to have to myself.

We had dinner at one of a row of open-air restaurants on the bay: it was a new country. To him too, Alessandro said, a new, a foreign country. The food was being danced at us like so many circus acts, red wine streamed from double *fiaschi*, the noise was tremendous and so of course was the *view*. The quattrocento had been side tracked. *We were by the Mediterranean.*

\*　　\*　　\*

A predicament, familiar since early childhood, had been to decide what and how much my elders expected me to know or not to know. A

217

question of fine judgement and some tact.

Breakfast on our first Naples morning was being served on a terrace packed with tourists, English and Scandinavian as they mostly were, I'd learned, at such establishments. I was waiting at a table as my mother with Alessandro holding the door for her were coming in. I got up. 'Good morning, Daddy,' I said in a clear and cheerful voice. Heads turned.

I was left in little doubt about fine judgement and tact. My mother—good for her—took some time struggling not to laugh. When she recovered, she said, 'I think we ought to thank you for wanting to express support. Don't overdo it.'

Later when we were out of the public eye, she said gently, 'He will be Alessandro to you. As he is to me.' He and I looked solemnly at each other. Then he stood up and kissed me on both cheeks. The shades of the ceremony at Florence dissolved in my heart. It was all right.

My mother became more herself. 'We ought to buy you a new suit,' she said, 'to make you look too old to be my son. I always thought this must be your first communion suit. Is it, *caro*?' He looked at her tenderly and laughed. It *was* all right.

And this was how it went for a while. We moved to Sorrento, found another whitewashed *pensione.* Our fellow guests were a couple of Neapolitan lawyers with families of all ages on their summer holiday. We shared rowing boats; all meals were in an arbour. We ate the food of the Italian south, abundant, borne to table on vast platters: *melanzane*, thick-cut *pasta, calamari, frittura di pesce*, tough *bistecchi alla pizzaiola*, peaches, figs, *mozzarella di buffalo* dripping with freshness. My mother took Alessandro and me to the great sights, we spent a day on Capri, at Pompeii, went to Positano, to Ravello and, above all, to Paestum for the temple of Neptune.

One event reached us in that Elysian existence: the news of the kidnap and murder of Matteotti, the socialist leader of the opposition—there still *was* an opposition—his body had just been found. Our Neapolitan friends were eloquent with fury and hope: this could be the turning-point, the end of a dishonoured regime, Mussolini might fall. *Il fascismo* survived, as we know too well, with new strength.

We had an address by then. Alessandro, looking over the edges of his dream, was becoming aware of anomalies in the position, such as our apparent isolation—*he* had to appease, to circumvent *his* family—now he was seeking to detect some order in my mother's affairs. His first achievement had been to introduce her to the uses of the *posta restante*. In consequence we were now available to the outside world. Quite soon letters and

219

documents arrived, none of them welcome. While my mother accompanied, or not, by daughter had been racketing about Italy, presumably lost, the outside world in the guise of officials and trustees had not been asleep. Separately and jointly we presented them with a number of conundrums. The first to roost was money.

My mother's fortune, so-called, a family trust, had as we knew been much diminished by events, though thanks to astute management had also recovered to a modest degree. In view of her forthcoming marriage, the trustees had let her have a reasonable sum—supposedly not wishing her to enter respectable matrimony without some means of her own. (Subsequent arrangements if any to be got into later.) It was still the age before traveller's cheques, let alone credit cards, and the age of being able to get round the world with golden sovereigns was over, so what you went travelling with unless you were a student or a pilgrim was a Letter of Credit. This instrument consisted of a long sheet of thick paper—gentlemen carried it folded in their inside jacket pockets—issued by one reputable bank—your own—and valid at any branch abroad, stating the total sum allowed. So whenever you required a hundred or five hundred francs or pounds or lire, you presented your letter, were handed the sum requested which was then deducted from the stipulated total. So that was what we had been living on; at least my mother had not lost it; how much credit was left and whether more would or could be allowed under the tightly drawn rules of the trust was agitating my mother's minders' minds. They had *some* discretion; limited, as the terms of the trust would, ultimately, include the daughter. Consequently the question of maintenance for a semi-orphaned minor might arise. It had. Documents were arriving fast, 'apprising' us of my father's will. He had left everything in equal parts to his two daughters. Everything consisted of his collection and the château. (His ex-wife had never thought of going back on that: though the deed had been spontaneous, she had taken steps to make it stick. You could not rely on my mother's unreliability.) The collection had turned out to be, if not a great, a serious one. My father had known craftsmanship when he saw it. Valuation had been made and plans for sale by auction in a Freiburg or Basle house were under way. So far so smooth. However there was a clause in my father's will to the effect that the collection should remain where it was and be taken care of in perpetuity. As there was no provision whatsoever for maintenance, the clause would have to be fought on the grounds of unfeasibility. This was more or less certain to be successful, though would require legal expenses and time. What was far more serious was the fact, now revealed, that no taxes on the property and its produce had been paid during the last years of my father's lifetime. (The anxieties this must have cost him.) Some compromise would have to be arrived at, the cost might be considerable and it might take years to settle the estate. What my mother said to Alessandro was, 'My daughter is going to be an heiress, but will she be in time to pay for educating *all* your brothers? How many of them, did you say, want to go into medicine?'

Meanwhile, in present reality, worse was to come. Officialdom began inquiries as to *my* education. Waters had been somewhat muddied already in my father's time; the half they knew did not appease. A guardian should be appointed at once. No: my mother would not do. In the interim, authority over me lay with some local council in Baden. The guardian had to be a German, resident in Germany. The council had the courtesy to ask whether we had a suitable connection in mind. I saw rescue—Borgman. If he would. My mother was not over-pleased, *how* she had tried to prevent that marriage. But . . . Well . . . Yes. He, Borgman, agreed by telegraph, grasping the overall situation. His generous proposal was that I should live under his roof for the next years, visiting my mother whenever I wished to. He was able to arrange an excellent day-school capable of completing my unconventional education. Education loomed big with that council. So now did Borgman. A deputy mayor (a patriot for all they knew), who moreover made it clear that there could be no question of maintenance: his future ward was a near relative and would be a guest in his house. There must have been a great washing of hands and clearing of files.

I felt grateful, touched; saw reason. The time I had had in that house was a magical memory, once I'd have given anything to be allowed to stay on. Now it was a solution; I had become aware that one was needed. Life there would be interesting. Education I longed for. Why was I not jubilant? There lurked a feeling that this was a wrong road, leading to something I had already left. It was not what my life was going to be, already I had turned my back on the German past.

Chance or free will? Which is it that we the irreligious, the superstitious ones, mean when we say, 'in the lap of the gods'?

Then with another flurry of communications, my sister became a rogue factor. Jacko, we were informed, had left Borgman, left her husband and child without warning, had walked to the railway station in the middle of the night accompanied by faithful Nanny wheeling the pram loaded with Jacko's clothes—not her jewellery. That was left with the note—no address—on the dressing-table. (Nanny with empty pram had returned to her charge.)

Gradually we learnt what had triggered that sudden escape. Berlin Grandmama had died earlier that summer leaving a legacy. Enough, Jacko decided, to do as she longed to do for a reasonable number of years. (One may not live for ever. One cannot lay tram-lines to the future.) What she did not reckon with were her own extravagance and the ruthlessly expensive tastes of the young man she meant to share that future with. There were few delays and as soon as some money was in her hands, she was off in the manner we had heard to join him. Alessandro and I had to look for a lead from my mother. She saw; she laughed; she cried. Poor Jacko.

She tried to sum up for us. She knew about that young man, had met him once or twice. He was handsome—Alessandro got a sardonic look and my mother was laughing again—dazzlingly so, charming, very fair, imagine a *man-sized* Prince of Wales (she spoke of the one who became Duke of Windsor), good family, not much money but a title, German father, mother English, a playboy, a seducer, never done a stroke of work, lived off married women and I dare say the odd rich man. Jacko, she said, very sadly now, 'is making her second mistake, much, much worse than the first. In 1919 when there was that period of revolutionary turbulence in Berlin, he—a nominal student—is supposed to have taken

224

part in a piece of political thuggery, criminal tragical thuggery. And a cowardly part.' She was speaking in the tone she used about war. I respected her. Alessandro said, 'You are severe—we too have these kind of students here now.' 'He is morally worthless', my mother did not speak the nickname, a nice, a playful one, by which Jacko's Adonis was known. 'He will marry her if he thinks there's enough money, though her husband may well refuse a divorce.'

'Wasn't there a child?' Alessandro wanted to know. My mother enlightened us. 'Borgman could have sent the police after them if she'd taken it with her. Curious, I always thought Jacko was the maternal one—the way she carried on about you when you were born—and now look, it is I who have you with us on our elopement.'

I tried to take that in.

'By the way, what is she like that girl of Jacko's, you have met her, remember?'

'She was a baby then, quite a nice one.'

'Well, you will soon be able to tell us what she's like now.'

\*　　　\*　　　\*

I was not. If Borgman didn't divorce Jacko immediately—he did eventually, and quite harshly—he divorced me. Promptly, formally, by one letter . . . In the circumstances he was

225

not able to see his way to act as guardian to his ex-wife's sister . . . He wished me well.

My mother said, 'What are we going to do with *you*?'

That was not the only trouble hanging over us. There was Alessandro's position. By degrees, inevitably, his family had become aware that the woman he had run off with was not a cradle Catholic, was not an actual widow but a guilty divorcee, that he must be living off her, with whose money? There certainly was no settled home, was it true that she was old enough to he his mother . . . ?

*How* he dreaded his parents' letters. How he resisted their request of his coming north to see them and explain. Then his father, already in poor health, was struck by a heart attack. Alessandro had to go. My mother turned into something I had not known before. She turned mute. We sat opposite each other in the *pensione*—it was autumn, our lively Neapolitans were gone—she scarcely ate, she did not speak: she was shrunk in misery. One afternoon, on a walk, she stood still and faced me: He won't come back. They won't let him. He is weak.

He *will* come back, I told her, he said so to me.

More words came to her: and if he does, how *can* it last? The difference in age . . . She spoke about attachment, passion, how it is when there is only one being in all the world:

'*Chagrin d'amour.* There is no defence; it comes to us all; it will come to you. You will know.'

*Yes*, I said. She walked on, unsteadily, small ... For the first time in my life I was able to love her.

*       *       *

He did come back. It cannot have been easy, and our troubles—in battalions—were still with us; my mother herself again told us she was not going to try to remember which murderous French general—was it Foch?— when all around had failed gave the order to advance, but advance we shall. So we left mainland Italy and advanced to Sicily. Advanced? Retreated?

To me it was travel. I still respond to evocations of the names: Agrigento, Siracusa, the light, the skies, the nights already sharply cold. At the *alberghi*, boys brought in glowing charcoal braziers at bedtime and stood them on the marble floor. Such sweet and acrid fumes, so lethal if you kept the windows shut. And here too, the posts caught up with us.

Advance again? Fugitives must travel light. I had read enough about rafts and lifeboats and shipwrecks—I am no stoic; if I'd ever been unfearful, I had already forgotten such a state by then.

From one day to the next my mother

changed into concentrated decisiveness. 'I am not going to throw you among German wolves.' She solved the guardian problem in one swoop. What we needed was someone respectable and with clout who would above all trust *her*. She besought herself of a man, not young, she knew from the early stages of her marriage to my father, his wife happened to be a godchild of a member of her own family and he was presently in the German government—wrong politics: right-wing, never mind, he was an honourable man, a man of probity and he could stand up to those little functionaries down in Baden. She was pretty sure that he would respect her wishes. Which were?

She had worked it all out. If I wanted to become a writer—and God knew she had wanted to be one herself—it would be sensible for me to stop rattling about like a polyglot parrot. I ought to spend some time in an English, an English-speaking environment. I should go to England. To a first-rate boarding-school. Her German cabinet minister turned out to find this a sensible idea, and once he was roped in everyone else approved. The trustees became prepared to fund the fees and anything else required, in fact would provide for the daughter until that estate of hers was settled.

Now that all was in my mother's hands, we stumbled on to the next question. The school.

Which? Where? We expected her to exercise her magic with her English friends. Come to think of it, she had been singularly friendless during those vacillating months. 'Well, you see . . .' And it came out. She had been in hiding as it were, no one was supposed to know about that marriage ceremony in Florence, 'I'd given them all to think that we *were* already married for some years. *What* can I say to them now?'

She finally wrote to a couple she had met at an hotel, she didn't quite remember where, it must have been shortly before she had sent for me. 'They were amusing people, artists; he is a painter, not a very successful one—that is why they had to leave, ran out of money.' My mother was sure she had heard them speak of children back in England. They were nice people, kind, 'sure to be glad to look after you and help to choose a school. And that maintenance of yours may be not unwelcome.' She had forgotten where they said they lived, but they'd left her an address. (Which she found.)

And so it came to pass. We were at Palermo when Mrs Robbins's—indeed very nice—letter had come confirming that she would meet all the boat-trains at Victoria station on the date we'd given. Alessandro was to take me across to the mainland as far as Naples from where I would proceed alone. I would have a ticket as far as one could get which was the Italo-French border, after that I would have to deal with timetables and fares on my own. I would be given a bag to wear under my clothes with lire, French francs and a large crisp white paper which was a five-pound note. My mother was sure I would manage—you're good at improvising railway travel, *remember*? I said, 'That was when I was young.'

*Their* future was unresolved; they were still on the run as my mother called it now. Yet the running ought to be good. They planned to cross the sea to Tunisia: great things to see there. There were questions—naturally. Most were not spoken. Africa! Alessandro said; Africa, said I, a new continent! My mother looked at me benignly: it may well be that for you as well.


# CHAPTER THIRTEEN

*England, their England—A Midlands town
—Escapade to London—A grail: vision
opens—World beyond books—Tate
Gallery, Manet, a frisson: soldiers kill also
in Mexico—An afternoon's walk in
Querétaro twenty years on—Meanwhile
English perambulations continue—
Summons*

There has long been a considerable part of the inhabitants of the British Isles who were not born there. Into the lives of these, there had inevitably come a point of entry, whether on their own or with family or en masse, voluntarily or necessarily, by fighting, by flight. One need not think as far as Vikings, Romans, Normans—Huguenots, French aristocrats, pogrom victims, anti-Hitler refugees, Rhodes scholars, English tots shipped home by their India-governing parents, can more realistically be imagined. Each must have undergone some potent shock relevant to their own provenance: *it was all so different.*

As to myself, who could say that *mon amour des voyages* was not served? North Africa might have revealed some affinities with Sicily, England cannot; I was the explorer who had taken the wrong caravan, direction not towards the Sahara but the Poles.

Incidentally it *was* winter. How would the English domestic arrangements eighty years ago strike a native child born, say, in 1990? I at least had had the experience of those bowls of live charcoal on marble bedroom floors. However, my first point of entry turned out blurred, not sharp. Leggy over leggy that doggy, as in Brian Howard's nursery rhyme, got to Dover, but too sleepy to take in where it actually was. The journey had been confusing and long. Attention revived a little when the last train had stopped. Victoria Station. There ensued another uncertainty: Suzan, Mrs Robbins, my prospective hostess—she wore a name-badge—was unsure whether I was whom she was supposed to be picking up. I was not the expected age. (Indeed, as it turned out, her own children, two lots of two, consisted of a pair of toddlers and a couple of advanced adolescents.) Once accepted, I received a hug, was led straight into a street and taxi the shape of which made me sit up, the sight of flights of huge red buses did the rest. A hotel lobby, a room, a bed, white sheets, sleep.

The very next day I was plunged into what I can now identify, and need not describe, the life of a full-blown middle-middle-class household in the English Midlands in the early 1920s. The master, a manufacturer of agricultural machinery, and his wife, both fairly old and still active, grown-up sons with their wives and an assortment of children, numerous maiden aunts, a large complement of servants, all female, all in uniforms: starched caps and aprons, everyone attending in the mornings before breakfast a kind of religious service in the *dining-room* (the Catholic in me, though lapsed, was taken aback), four punctual sit-down meals a day, no wine in sight—water or barley water; no horses, no motor car, a (nice) pony and trap, stacks of bicycles all over the place.

My mother had talked of my going to live——at least until the gates of a boarding-school would close upon me—in an artist's milieu. Mrs Robbins, on the train bearing us away from London the first morning had tried somewhat ruefully to enlighten me as to our destination, or rather their own situation. You see? She said, Well you see . . . I tried.

Mrs Robbins, she did not remain that for long, Suzan then, turned out to be a light-hearted, self-deprecatory woman, ready to put up cheerfully, if not always effectively, with what circumstances threw at her. Which at present was the chanciness of making a living. Jack's last show . . . Not that it was much of a gallery . . . People don't seem to *buy* contemporary art. His posters ideas—very clever posters—for a new milk drink—for the Underground. Not the drink, the posters: on station walls, 'Well, that firm seems to have disappeared.'

I grunted small signs of sympathy.

'Oh, you mustn't think it's always like that, us being hard up, last winter we had a studio in London till we thought it would be cheaper and nicer to live abroad. It is of course—but one can't earn anything. So we went home and found a very nice cottage on the east coast. When we can't pay the rent Jack picks up a spot of teaching here and there . . . Once he was even offered an art master's post at a rather good school, but schools arc so stuffy, I don't think I would have done as a resident master's wife—I'm Irish—did you know?'

I did not. Nor did I see. Ireland, surely, was also England. The literature, I vaguely recalled, was regarded as something apart.

Then there came a good deal more of *you see* from Suzan. Trouble is Jack's father never approved of his not going into the Works like his brothers . . . 'My mother-in-law is very kind, she loves the children, she takes them in much of the time, they are happy there . . .' So: when they, she and Jack, were really up against it, 'Money-wise I mean, they take *us* in as well, till something turns up. The old man is never really cross at having us to stay, he's fond of Jack, he even lets him have the conservatory to paint in, it's a big house.'

And now I saw that this was where I was going to in that train.

*    *    *

They, the family, accepted me. No questions, little curiosity, natural goodwill, fitting me into their daily round like a not quite identifiable piece of jigsaw puzzle. 'The foreign child'. They made the elder children—girls whom I bored—take me along on their routines and treats. I learnt to play hockey, was admitted to tennis, shared their Boots' Lending Library subscription and a weekly matinee at the cinema. If my room was devoid of the means of heating, so was everyone else's as far as I could make out and I managed to read in bed at night, icy hands or not. Bacon and eggs, sausages, mushrooms to start the day pleased and impressed. Even at the sybaritic Berlin house of my infancy, no hot dishes appeared on that opulent table before 11 a.m., the hour of Second Breakfast, and was chiefly for the gentlemen. Now: the taste of crisp bacon with the sting of Colman's mustard and strong dark scalding tea (I spurned the milk) were an appreciated discovery. Even so I privately deplored the frizzled white of egg fried brutally in fat instead of gently settled in a little butter the way my father had once taught me to make an *oeuf sur le plat.* Ungrateful criticism of what so open-handedly was offered? Of course it was. I took it as legitimate observation. Well, it was that too. My penance is a Trappist's silence now about our other meals. Elizabeth David, pray for us. Whom she did pray for twenty years on were precisely such kitchens as the Robbinses'.

So much then about the resident family and their ways. The artist son and daughter-in-law, Jack and Suzan, who took shelter with them in times of need, were elective bohemians temporarily conforming with some degree of grace, having the talent to laugh at their own aspirations and failings. The English secret weapon. (So potent and so useful, in wars.) With them, I established an aloof intimacy, as one might among friendly aliens. Weeks, a month, passed, another had begun, decisions must be come by. Suzan's path through life was cheered by the recourse to Mr Micawber's favourite expression. What had turned up was in fact myself. Or rather that quarterly allowance paid by my trustees straight to Mr and Mrs Robbins to be handled in accordance with my mother's and my guardian's wishes. The sum—not an inadequate one—was intended to cover my eventual school fees, my maintenance at the Robbinses' residence during holidays, fares, clothes, books, pocket money. There seemed to be an assumption that the Robbinses were old friends, family friends more or less, of my mother's. We did not go into that aspect when the three of us sat together in the conservatory after tea. Jack liked company when he painted. Suzan did something with Plasticine, I fiddled with a book, it was warm, we talked. Suzan could be lively about the delights of abroad and the fun to be had in London, had I heard of Fitzrovia? There were artists in *her* family, composers, poets . . . Gradually we drifted towards solutions for our futures. Boarding-school? Suzan was uncertain from the start—their own girls had loathed and never lasted long in theirs (chosen mostly by the grandparents) and were determined at this juncture not to return to their present one, an establishment discovered, after so much else had failed, by their mother. An 'advanced' school, very free—perhaps *I* was more used to unconventional ways?—no one was made to work there, no fixed classes or beliefs, food was vegetarian . . . (I sat rigid.) The school was somewhere in Norfolk, a location meaning little to me; it jumped violently back into my mind years after when I first heard from a stage that line in *Private Lives*. Then: eventually, inspired by a sense of sitting in committee, we arrived at what must be the substance of my mother's and my guardian's intentions: to patch up my education and have me being looked after congenially by Jack and Suzan. Having established this premise, the execution of a plan could be put openly in hand. We would move to London, the three of us with the two elder girls, take a studio flat, engage private tutors able to continue with the girls from where they had left and work out a course for me. We would choose a first-rate man or woman whatever the cost, that was Jack's condition, or he would not fall in with what he saw as mainly of his wife's and my devising. Jack was honourable, and if not minutely practical, clear-sighted enough. Suzan was basically honourable too; in a more feminine fashion. What he called the child's money was only to be used within defined limits. The tutors' pay, my keep—not theirs while I lived under their roof. (Under his parents', I was, as they were, a guest.) After our 'liberation', it would have to be a paying guest, or lodger, no more nor less. Suzan put in that lodgers were strangers; paying guests were friends who chipped in, as well as helped one to a better flat and nicer food. I concurred. We could stretch our resources, I suggested, by not spending them on my clothes—the girls might let me have some of their cast-offs? They owned blazers and hockey skirts I rather liked the thought of. Jack did not take in such detail, but was firm about making sure of some adequate earned cash of their own, however temporarily. Living precariously was all right for artists, living off . . . well . . . a ward in chancery, was not. Things were stirring again . . . A gallery, a respectable one, had a proposal, not a one-man show, still . . . Interest in the posters was reviving in some unexpectedly solvent quarter, and now there was the friend, who had commissioned a portrait of his infant son, actually sending an advance of half the fee. Suzan said that the infant son could hardly be expected to sit for Jack in their present place . . .

\*       \*       \*

And so it all happened. London. A flat full of empty space in Belsize Park NW1. We arrived there one early spring day crammed into the front part of the van that carried some necessary bits of furniture collected from the attic by Jack's mother. New beds from Heals already awaited us as well as a gas stove, gallons of wall-paint, hand-woven mats

238

donated by friends. A bottle of South African sherry from nowhere. Suzan had made some curtains. At once we were all madly willing and busy. Jack set up the tools of his trade— canvases, brushes, easel: the smell of turpentine instantly persuasive . . . A kettle was at hand—it had travelled on one of our laps—and a Thermos or two. The first meal was Marmite sandwiches (for which I acquired a life-long taste), fish paste out of small glass containers, Jello for pudding and cocoa. For a week or two we worked cheerfully and hard at making things liveable according to our present standards. I gave a hand at whatever needed doing, mixing paints, washing windows, making a rice pudding with condensed milk in an enamel basin, it made me think of Feldkirch, the château, unbridgeably remote, and again not so. There the balancing acts, the making-do had brought sadness to my father; it was an ending, not a good one. Here, for them: a light-hearted venture, a rash and jolly beginning.

For me those snatches of English life were of a dual nature—gregarious, funny, undemanding, as far as the shared domesticity went at Belsize Park; exalted, solitary, pointers towards other worlds, at the times I spent apart. They trusted me; I trusted them; thus soon I was able to lead an existence of my own. With that I felt content.

Jack had quickly found me an excellent

tutor. A man who cast first light on many things and whose name I have forgotten. Being taught, *learning*, was all I had imagined it might be. Most mornings I walked to his Hampstead study for a couple of hours, some of the afternoons I worked. My room was the second largest of the flat, high ceilinged, good for pacing. Besides the brand-new bed there was an ink-stained desk, a wobbly bookcase, two chairs—one kitchen, one basket. Reading was pleasure given dignity by being called work. The tutor steered me away from much that had been already impregnated by my mother, such as the nineteenth-century French and Russian novelists and poets, I became inducted to the Victorians, to Fielding, to Dryden and Pope, to Gibbon. Gibbon loomed large for me. The pull of the Latin world. Notes, a précis, anything attempted in words of my own, was excruciating and left to the last minute. Hours of each day, well into the night, I spent walking. I had taken to London. To the parks, the scented flowering trees and bushes in back-streets and squares: it was early summer, the Season, I liked the smart shopping streets, Savile Row, Bond Street, the pavements crowded with good-looking people at the luncheon hour, I liked the handsome men, so well-dressed. The lively girls showed too much hat. I disliked the tawdriness of Piccadilly Circus and the gentility of a Lyons Corner House, instead I coveted the 'cut off the joint and two veg', but suffered rebuff at pubs because of my youth, then soon found a 2/6 lunch in Soho. Italian waiters. I had ten shillings a week pocket money, not bad at all. Some of it was spent on a bus ticket when it got too far or too late for me to get home on foot.

I was never molested or taken much notice of walking the streets after dark beyond an occasional leer from an occasional drunk or a 'Can you spare us a sixpence, Miss?' (It would take me a second to grasp that he meant me, I felt myself comfortable as a voyager or bambina: 'Miss' never sat well.) I only caught a late bus in case Suzan or Jack might notice or mind my being out after 11 p.m., at all other hours, I walked at ease along the Georgian terraces, elated by the glamour, historical and visual of Whitehall, enjoyed getting lost in the alley-ways and backyards of the City. I bowed to St Paul's.

And then came something else: one day I entered the National Gallery—and then at last, by what detours, I found the Quattrocento. *And so much else.* I was struck at that very first hour, by El Greco's *Storm over Toledo* hung in the small room on the right as one comes in: not a large canvas, projecting elemental violence and foreboding (occluding the luscious Titian nude), followed within minutes by the image of youthful courage, nobility and beauty of Piero della Francesca's

Archangel Michael having slain the dragon-snake. How tall he stands, how big the wings, how white, how proud the hands that hold the sword and the reptile's bleeding head, and how ambiguous that impish playful arrogance of the way the red bootees are stamping on their prey dismissing evil. Up till then anything that mattered had been apprehensible only by way of words, now the impact of two mute works had raised a curtain I had not known was there.

I saw, and I pursued. Headlong, unguided, carried off my feet by what this city of the north revealed to offer, I flew, I lingered, I flew again, in and out at Trafalgar Square, the Tate, the Wallace Collection—drawn to wide landscapes: Poussin, Claude Lorrain, to portraits of goddesses with glowing skins, to putti and clouds, cardinals, Infantas oppressively dressed, to mosques, temples, colonnades, and again and again I returned to Uccello's geometrical clash of arms.

There were moments when my euphoric encounters were perturbed by hints of menace, premonitions of man's implacability to man. At the Tate where huge exhibits in vast often near-empty rooms could be quite scary, I came across a large, awkwardly cut, fragment of Mallet's *Execution of the Emperor Maximilian of Mexico*—all that is there to see is a massed squad of soldiers with long rifles outstretched from shoulder towards an aim beyond the canvas' edge. I thought again of that scrap of the tragedy about to happen on the other side of the world: travelling across Mexico myself thirty or so years later, I had walked out of Querétaro, a provincial town on the Tierra Templada, in search of the hill where it happened—not all of it: just the end. I went alone. Maximilian of Habsburg, a weak man of good will, a liberal dreamer born into a sclerotic dynasty, having been pressed into acceptance of that improbable phantom, the Imperial Crown of Mexico, where after three years of overwhelming unreality he was sentenced to death by court martial at Querétaro on 15 June 1867 and shot four days later on a hill outside that town.

\*　　　\*　　　\*

What surprises me about that time of my first trotting from gallery to gallery in London, is that I seem never to have talked about what I was seeing and feeling to anyone. In a painter's house! Perhaps my position there was too ambiguous. Younger than their own daughters who had reached adolescent stage, I was not regarded as a child; or if so, as a child responsible for itself as well as consulted about household matters. Jack and Suzan were not disposed to look much further; I was part lodger, part alien. Part conspirator as well. Suzan and I consulted when there was a financial crisis. Jack's projects were not doing well. He was also scrupulous though unnoticing; it was Suzan and I who decided when it was to our mutual interest to use what was supposed to be my dress allowance (well above the ten bob a week) to round up the rent. I was fond of them, they were kind to me; when they felt flush enough to have dinner out at Bertorelli's in Charlotte Street—they had plenty of Fitzrovian chums, artists and poets—they would take me because they knew I enjoyed it. There I was, a young person at the end of the table, not expected, not suspected of any desire to speak. Had I attempted to do so, the company might have recalled Dr Johnson's dog standing on its hind legs spouting verse.

Might I not have written something of it all to my mother? Letters were not plain sailing during that first English phase, which lasted something like two years; I seldom knew where she—they—were. I can no longer recall at which point I learnt that she and Alessandro had married, were back on the Italian mainland (with his parents' consent?), were more or less settled at differing addresses from which at some point they would look forward to my visit: 'I suppose you have holidays?'

Jacko, too, communicated. At intervals. By brief letters on large sheets of crested writing-paper. She too was married, after a divorce, a vindictive one, worse than my mother's, being denied all access to *her* child. However she was by now in enjoyment of her grandmother's inheritance, had a *pied-à-terre* in Paris, most of the year she and her sun prince new husband spent at tennis, dancing and polo at resorts fashionable at the time, such as Schveningen and Biarritz and on the Adriatic, Brioni. To me she sent loving words and pieces of our late father's jewellery—the kind of watch and cigar gear men such as he had carried on their persons, goodness knows how she had got hold of them. Suzan and I would pawn them when the situation demanded.

Indeed we, the Robbins household, soon became as nomadic again as my own family, and with it my treasure hunting days did not last long. Avoiding—not always—a temporary refuge in the parental Midlands home, we drifted from country cottage to seaside lodgings. Tutors, of a kind, were usually found for me, as well as a London Library subscription. I liked country walks, and was not discontent to return to books again. When Jack sold a picture, as he did not too infrequently, we contrived another stay in London, good while it lasted. It was there that the actual summons came to join my mother and stepfather at an Italian lake. The trustees sent the fare. I had outgrown, once more, my clothes. Well, that must have been a minor dilemma.

# CHAPTER FOURTEEN

*Italy—In duo, in trio—Sweetness of life—*
*Settling into Anglo-Italian seesaw—A*
*chance encounter Private lives—*
*Pastures new*

The Italian years that followed my mother's invitation—few years and for me less than full length—were kaleidoscopic as well as domestically happy. *They,* my mother and Alessandro, were a married couple. Had there ever been any obstacles or questions? He adored her, visibly; watched over her, retrieved whatever she lost or mislaid, laughed at and with her. When she talked, he listened. And so did I. She liked to play us off one against the other with a simple conviction of our various inferiorities. We did not really mind. Neither father and daughter nor brother and sister, Alessandro and I trotted together well enough. She talked about the past: her friends', the world's, her own: 'No, not *he*, not really—it was *X* who was my greatest love,' she would tell us with reckless candour and Alessandro would take it as a natural course of events. His temperament was realistic in a very Latin way: both light-hearted and melancholy. (Never humble.) He was able to tease her with the reminder that under Italian law, ecclesiastical and civil, she was now indissolubly married. There is such a thing as an annulment, I put in. 'So there is, my pedantic child,' she said. 'We haven't got the influence or the money. What have I let myself in for!' Then she would smile sweetly at him: all was as it should be. *This* was her life. A far cry from the *Vénus tout entière* stage, the long months before the decision to jettison that other future, a far cry too from the bleak foreboding that overtook her when the young suitor was out of sight. Now, their difference in age did not seem to be a factor—not to her, not to him, and this was also the face they presented with complete naturalness to the world, and the world appeared to accept.

(As it turned out—as I came to see long after—when emotional catastrophe did overtake them, the difference in age was hardly a factor at all.)

\*      \*      \*

In those Italian years, they lived surrounded by numerous relations and friends who came to stay with or near them in the villa, the appartamento, the skiing lodge, rented or lent, they happened to be in.

Alessandro's father's death had occurred shortly after their return from North Africa; his mother, a cheerful, youthfully middle-aged woman, a monogamous Catholic, who had coped with bringing up six boys—or were they just five?—on an academic's salary, was coping on her own. She came to stay when there was room, which was quite often, well-meaning, trying resolutely to co-exist with a daughter-in-law of her own generation and worlds apart in almost everything else. She looked after the things my mother did not particularly regard as needing to be looked after, such as mending table linen or her younger sons' socks, as indeed they too, the younger sons, came to stay in their holidays from such studies they could still pursue in the teeth of Mussolini's growing hostility against anyone who did not ostensibly endorse the regime. That education was chiefly paid for, as I began to guess, by my mother's trustees. Their relinquishing some money to her new brothers-in-law was a feat of my mother's persuasiveness. And generosity. She and Alessandro at that point were living decently if on the modest side and without much show of anxiety. They had begun to do occasional decorators' jobs in lieu of rent in some of the houses they stayed in. They both had discovered and developed a talent: Alessandro, frustrated architect, was immensely handy with anything he touched; together they supplied taste and imagination. Some of the 'clients' were my mother's old friends arrived from everywhere to see her again. They were mostly women. (And indeed among them Issa, the young Issa half a lifetime

248

of history before her re-appearance on the island of Ischia as Martha Gellhorn's Kraut Baronessa, undid me. Before, in our remote Italian summers, she was already very hard, very seductive, chaperoned—absent-mindedly—by Mamoushka, her bright and amiable mother, and followed by a posse of tall young German suitors, Siegfrieds banished at nightfall to some nearby lodgings.) My mother's male friends kept, or were wisely kept, away. Alessandro anyhow did not much enjoy the company of men. The most spontaneous element of human intercourse for him was flirtation—*light* flirtation. He charmed, he teased . . . Pleasant enough as it were. One had to be a fool to expect anything to go further. My mother's women friends basked in her husband's company while respecting boundaries. They adored my mother too—she enlivened and amused them; there were no little asides, no jealousies, such was not the atmosphere. My mother was the core of this man's existence: that was understood.

Alessandro was a second son. The elder too had abundant good looks, sheer Italian dazzle without Alessandro's distinction and latent melancholy. That brother, only slightly senior, had already married. A rich woman—no precarious student he—a good deal older than himself *and* attractive. Sooner or later I understood that she had been Alessandro's first love when he was still practically a schoolboy. The elder brother ultimately won; the younger had scored a happy initiation. Late in our lives, when the women were no more and Alessandro began to see me as a daughter he had actually had, he told me that his serious attachments were always to someone much older than himself. I, as it turned out, had something of the same disposition: the snag is that as time runs on there is no one left to answer to such inclinations.

Whatever I may have been in those easy Italian years, it was not a family fixture, I couldn't feel myself as a daughter of the house. A child on holiday? Growing up in uneven stages . . . Holidays, often unpremeditated, from what? . . . The overall conception ran that I was being educated in England . . . Some of the time . . . The nature and locations of my studies, my position in the Robbins' household, were left ambiguous. At some point Jack and Suzan made one move too far and vanished from my existence. For ever. They went to Australia—it may have been New Zealand—to take up, backed by strong family approval, a respectably funded art mastership at a college. I think of them with some gratitude. Theirs was not the England I was seeking, one I did not return to. They had appeared fortuitously, and by casually allowing me much liberty became stepping stones towards a future. There had also been that connivance, unacknowledged though essential for permitting such a course, tri-partite between my mother, Suzan and myself (with Jack blankly keeping unaware), *a* connivance of half-truths fed to guardians, officialdom and Midlands kin. What each of us believed, or not, remained undiscussed.

And what were *my* aims in view? Divided certainly. To go on floating as often as I was allowed to in a delirious present. *Italy.* The great deeds of art set in great natural beauty, townships on hills, saints and warriors springing from the walls of quiet, dark churches, columns in the piazza, the cupola shining in the sky, the streets, the walking, the markets, the *people.* The cook in our kitchen, the purity of the food: *pastorale cantabile,* the wine on the table, the light . . .

There was as well a holding on to that stern and childish hope of writing, and for this among much else there had to be an anchorage of my own. Perhaps one firm language. By then I had begun to find a link with England, the England of the stupendous collections, the England also of cathedrals, of country houses, of landscapes—an England created by Englishmen, by English travellers, by artists and architects, by poets . . . There too I had left much love!

So it felt right, my being sent back quite often for varying stretches of time. It was

London again mostly where the Robbins half poised for flight hung on in lodgings, and from these as I grew older I managed brief tours on my own. (By motor-coach: cheap and anonymous.) Life became affected a good deal after a chance meeting. One afternoon I walked into a bookshop off Bond Street. What it in fact contained were rare books and modern first editions. A woman I took for a shop assistant, approached me, puzzled possibly about my customership. We got talking. What *was* I reading? Presently, I was asked my name. Oh, she'd heard it, she said, in Berlin; where she originally came from. *Berlin*—for me that was a long time ago, a long relinquished past. Hardly mine. (My father's provenance, if German, had not been that Protestant, Spartan-drilled, Prussian North but a softer belt of Catholic Southern provincial Kingdoms or Grand-Duchies such as Baden and Bavaria, a provenance mitigated, diluted, by centuries of marriage to women from the Austro-Hungarian Empire, Lombardy, the Veneto, Alsace.) Before I had a chance to growl, my inquisitor got on to say wasn't it the name of that girl who was seen at all the dances and used to live in that huge house with her maternal grandparents? *'Haute Juiverie,* you know, though unlike the Mendelssohns and the Reichenheims they have come down in the world quite a bit.' Intellectually, she meant. 'Any relation of yours?' The girl who bore my name? My sister, I said. Half-sister. Well *she*—the shop-woman, though I twigged by now that she was not one—had followed *her* sister to England quite soon after the war on her marriage. Her sister's, *not* her own. A marriage to a Scot. 'My erudite brother-in-law.' His name rang no bell for me; I gathered that he was a director of the shop we stood in. When at last I was able to get myself out of it, I was being asked to come to tea, invitation complete with day and address. Marylebone, NW1.

I went. Nearly missed it. The vagaries of London street-numbering. Misgivings, an impulse to bolt, then there it was: one of a row of lodging-houses.

I climbed linoleum-covered stairs to a large, well-lit first-floor front room handsomely furnished, unlike the Robbinses' b. & b.s. Much cheerfully painted wood, gracefully shaped chairs, shelves, chests—rustic continental eighteenth century it may have been. The tea I was presented with (kettle boiled behind a screen) consisted of a tray with unfussy good china, toasted cheese straws, strawberries, thick cream, Earl Grey in a white pot. I liked that tea. From a silver box I was offered a cigarette, gold-tipped, Turkish, and took it with a worldly, absent-minded air. It had happened before: avuncular men or forward boys in hotels. I acquitted myself neutrally. I never had the wish to smoke in

253

private; though sprang up to offer a light to any woman as soon as she put cigarette to mouth. (From a lighter I carried. One of my father's.) My hostess appeared to take me in her stride, which was more than I could do with her: I was struck by some incongruity—was it the set-up? It wasn't English nor did it seem exactly German either. It did not fit, socially or materially, into any context I had met so far. There was something askew in my 'new friends" position: somewhere, there might be a story. There was.

\*       \*       \*

It took time and chance getting to know it, if not all of it by any means. And one day—a long long time later on—I came to write it myself. As a story, inside another story, in one of my novels in fact: fitting it—the actual truth, the limited truth, as far as I had seen it—into fiction. One consequence of this was that another part of that story, a parallel past unsuspected, undreamt of by the two women whose existence it had been, came to light when a chance reader guessed the identity of the man, the centre in their separate lives, a man, long dead, a public figure much in the public eye, still remembered, still puzzled over in some quarters, whose private life—the relevant years were from 1910 to the death by his own hand in 1933—had been kept out of the maws and claws of the tabloid press in his own time and hereafter. Well, that chance reader—in the 1980s when my incomplete version was published—happened to be acquainted with a surviving member of the great man's family, a niece in fact who knew about one side of the secret life and nothing whatsoever about the other. He got her to read my book and also came to me for confirmation which in turn was imparted to other survivors of a precariously balanced double life kept under cover by then for some twenty years. Then these survivors appeared—literally—on my doorstep: an illegitimate son of retirement age—a nice man, with considerable achievements against odds put behind him; his wife; the niece; the chance reader. The new version of an already tangled tale was painful to take; inevitably it also had its farcical side. To the women protagonists, the discovery would have been tragic, an invalidation of relationships that had entailed, besides entire devotion, much social isolation and self-sacrifice. Both had died long since, and Rosie (the name I gave to the woman I met in a bookshop, who became a lifetime friend) has no known survivors. So it may be permissible to dwell now on the somewhat vaudeville character of the tale.

About the dominant personage, the man in the triangle, there is a certain amount in print: one or two biographies, fragments in colleagues' memoirs, reports of some of his own cases. Well, yes, he was a judge. He comes out as a man of considerable eloquence and intellect as well as immense charm. It was also known among a few of his friends that he was a gambler on a reckless and addicted scale. This too he had managed to get away with after a few major scares till ultimately it brought great grief to himself and those who loved him.

To the son, a little boy whom he had heaped with presents, seen to a good education, taught games, yet never recognized, he had appeared only as a welcome weekend playmate and his mother's visitor, whom he addressed as Mr H., a version of a name he believed he'd heard. 'Mr H' died when the boy was just fourteen—provided for; still ignorant. At the time he and I met, he, a man in frail health, sensitive, without a trace of his father's flamboyance, had already been working for some years on his autobiography. He let me read the work in progress. What he had just learned so late in life came as a bolt from an already not unclouded sky. Bravely, with good grace, he inserted Rosie in the account of his own and his mother's history. (For me, most likely the sole extant witness: a rum feeling.) He died before finishing the book. His wife, knowing its progress well and aware of what he wanted, decided to do what was still needed: some editing, a tying up of ends. She did it.

Sensitively and well. The judge's story was published in 2003. The title is *Mr Hardie*, and Rosie appears as Kate which was her real name. And so be it.

*       *       *

When I left Rosie-Kate's ambivalent Marylebone premises for the first time, I did not leave empty-handed. I was lent a book. Asked whether I had yet read this or that, I had said dismissively, 'I'm afraid I'm not much interested in contemporary literature.' Oh the pomposity! I still cringe. Kate had not reacted visibly. On the doorstep putting a book into my hands, a book without a jacket, she said, 'You might like to try this.' Outside I stopped at the first lamp post: on the spine I read '*Antic Hay* by Aldous Huxley'. Not a household name.

In due course Kate introduced me to her married sister Toni, and her husband. The sister was pretty in a fragile way—sharp-tongued, beset by grievances: a frustrated musical talent, a yearning for Berlin with a dry amusing way of talking about it all. I was made welcome. (In their Regents Park mews flat.) The sisters became set to monopolize me. Not the most propitious way to bring about an entry into the contemporary English literary world. And yet it was. Percy, the Scottish husband, Percy Muir was on his way to

257

eminence in the book collectors' world. He had friends; the friends lived in cottages, one or two had a country house. The last had cellars. Wine cellars. All had libraries. Some were eccentrics, most were learned, at home with the arts. They could talk. I was the young person at the low end of the table. But I was *there:* doors had opened. The Robbinses, still my official keepers, still trustful, kind, might as well have been already on their Australian boat.

# CHAPTER FIFTEEN

*Sands shifting once again*

Transitions worked out smoothly. Once again they were based on a few misconceptions. In good faith? Deliberate? Self-deception? All of these. There was an impression that the Robbinses had passed on *loco parentis* status to Kate and the Percy Muirs by a kind of Apostolic laying on of hands; in fact they had not met. Sister Toni took it into her head—I was encountering a strong streak of obstinacy there—that my mother was lacking in maternal responsibility, thus she and indeed the whole trio (childless) slipped into a role of what they saw as looking after me. This, anyway a bit late in the day, turned out to my

258

being left pretty well to my previous devices, such as the wanderings from gallery to gallery; to these Rosie-Kate and the Muirs respectively added some novel and instructive interests. Under Kate's wing I was one day dropped into the Law Courts in the Strand. My first case was a libel suit brought by a well-known bandleader, and at once I got captivated by the quality of intelligence and delivery of Counsel (then men of course) and the blend of gravity and theatre of it all. Transfusion of astringent reason with righteousness and a sublimated romanticism was most seductive. I was hooked for life. By the English legal system, by the supreme importance of a Rule of Law and the ways it was applied. I went again. On my own. Kate—favour of *her* judge's clerk—arranged for my admission to a back row in the well of the court. Soon I wished to become a barrister. Wrong sex, wrong voice, and where was the learning? Later however, a good deal later, those teenage court attendances led me to become a part-time law-reporter.

I had moved into a back-room of a lodging house in Marylebone a couple of doors from Kate-Rosie's more gracious establishment. I don't remember what was actually conveyed to my mother (one had not yet reached an age of frequent, cheap and thus unavoidable international telephonic communication). I had bought and sent her a copy of *Antic Hay*. She wrote back: an almost complete letter, pleased and impressed. This was brilliant, first-rate, *new*. 'We'll hear of this novelist again.' A kind of modern Swift. I should mark her word. Though—'*au fond* he is not a novelist'. I marked; I did not agree (then).

She must have been induced somehow to take a hand in the material arrangements necessary then. My allowance was now sent to the Percy Muirs (they, without touching it, handed it over straight to me); another change was that the money came no longer from my mother, but from my guardian, the German ex-cabinet minister (governments were short-lived in the Weimar Republic, then still struggling on). My father's estate had at last been settled: the château sold to some retiring diplomat; the collection, proved a good one of its kind, sold at auction by a reputable house; actual sums distributed. Some to Jacko, thus supporting that midnight exit from her marriage; some into my guardian's care. He, a scrupulous and punctilious man, arranged an allowance for my 'English education' during my minority. This turned out to be rather less than what I had been given during the Robbinses' period. Well, rather less was needed now, and I was good at handling money: cut down on but pay promptly for the fundamentals; then get the most pleasure out of the rest; make it last as long as it has to. Hence the back rather than the front-room at the bed-and-breakfast. Rosie I took to dinner in Soho: she was always free on week-ends.

I had another agreeable use for such monies as came my way. Whenever it was the turn for an Italian stay, my guardian's accountants sent funds for the fare. First class. I travelled third, emulating Sebastian Flyte and Charles Ryder on their way to Venice. (Come to think of it, the tale of those radiant boys was not written until much later.) What I did with the nice spare cash was changing into various slow trains after the Italian border to spend a few extra hours at places I had planned to see. When appropriate I ate in a restaurant or two.

*     *     *

That contented pendulate existence—England—Italy—England—came to a sudden end. Alessandro and my mother left Italy, almost from one week to the next, while the going for them was still overt and good. They defined themselves, casually, without fuss, as members of the Italian colony in France, were accepted as such and able to keep their Italian passports. This was possible at that point—1926—and there were a number of people, distinguished men among them, who had thought it prudent to assume this status. They had not belonged to any visible resistance to Il Fascismo, yet it was obvious that they were not *for*. Here and there, at increasing risk, they had done their bit—hiding a neighbour's manuscript from the night-searches, refusing to join what one was expected to join, posting compromising material to a foreign address, circulating copies of the London *Times*. (That could still be delivered to one, often censored—strips cut out by scissors.) How modest it all appears now, how minor, when one thinks of what actually went on: the beatings, the castor oil, the deportations to harsh islands; when one thinks of what was to come, of what had already come in the Soviet Union, what began in less than seven years in Nazi Germany . . . The universal consequences of it all: then and later and *now*. Poor tragic human breed.

By turning themselves into premature *émigrés*, my mother and Alessandro took a course many might have taken had they been able to or had had the foresight. My mother, among so many other things, was a brave woman. I am glad she did whatever it amounted to before she left.

Where were they planning to go? Planning is too definite a term. I have an impression that they were heading west towards the French Atlantic coast, somewhere near Biarritz, to friends who would put them up. There was some acute nervousness as they sat in their compartment at the beginning of the train journey. There often were menacing delays at Ventimiglia as one was waiting to move on. Once across the border, that tension changed into my mother's getting impatient. Were they sure to catch all those right connections? It was already evening and a damn long way to the other side of France. I never made out what exactly prompted their actions. (I have invented a few stories about that journey, pretending that I had been there. Still feel I had.) Of what went on in actual life, I can gather this: it was getting late and my mother, bored and tired, stated that the coast they were rolling along looked rather good, as far as one could discern as it had got quite dark. There were frequent short stops in unidentifiable stations. One might as well get off at one of them? They were travelling light. A conductor, a French one now, was taking an interest, giving a hand, shifting luggage into the corridor while my mother was looking out of the window. The stops were extremely brief. The train puffed on. More help appeared. 'If you don't make up your mind, we'll be at Marseilles soon.' *Not* Marseilles—my mother conceived it as a kind of Naples and she didn't want a Naples at this point. So at the next stop, they were cheerfully pushed off the train with their suitcases flung after them. They found themselves on the platform of a minute country station—Ollioulles-cum-Something, with no sea in sight. It was midnight. A bus was standing by. They were helped into the shaky little vehicle, a genuine adjunct of the SNCF (the French National Railways then as now) and after scarcely more than twenty minutes of a rattly ride, they were deposited on the quayside of a quiescent port.

There was an hotel. It still showed light. Hôtel de la Tour. 'Bien sûr nous avons des chambres.' They took one for the night. Next morning the sun came through the French window, the window gave on to a balcony, the balcony to a sea front: small boats bobbing at harbour. Pretty, my mother said. A breakfast was brought in, nicely laid. Seen to by the Patronne herself who lingered for a few minutes. We're out of season, she said, might they be interested in their special terms. Weekly terms. I'm afraid we're moving on today, Alessandro said. Very pretty, my mother repeated. What with one thing and another to be best done perhaps today: letters to get off, muddles to be avoided, decisions taken or the lack of them, they stayed for a great many years.

\*       \*       \*

The name of that pretty fishing port, their, and my, future home, was Sanary, Sanary-sur-mer. Subsequent events have given it something of an international reputation. That way was still a long way off. We were not quite halfway yet into the period of Entre-Deux-Guerres.

\*       \*       \*

264

In due course, I was summoned. The first couple of times I felt disorientated rather than eager. France was territory crossed so far only in trains, asleep much of the time. Its Mediterranean coast I found Italianate in vegetation and sounds; not in the least in architecture. My family no longer drifted obliviously in unsettled domestic ease. There appeared material worries—it was the beginning of a time when even if one still had a little money there were complications in getting hold of it. That first summer they were camping in a hot, ill-stuck-together bungalow on the edge of a narrow bay, all seaweed and rock, Port Issol, ten minutes' walk from Sanary proper. They seemed abandoned, though café acquaintances were beginning to sniff around them. When I had appeared, they addressed me as Mademoiselle with Alessandro's surname appended: we had aroused curiosities. Most openly such as the notary's and the house agent's wives and their brood. (I preferred to float the clear calm waves in eloquent solitude; I was beginning to learn Rimbaud by heart.) We had not yet got to know the painters, nor any of the Parisian or Anglo-Saxon summer residents, nor the ex-navy man who lived in a round white tower and said to smoke opium—not as yet the men and women who became friends, companions, lovers, rivals, detractors, mentors, guardian angels, for stretches of our lives.

## CHAPTER SIXTEEN

*South of France—The actual beginning of
a true compass point*

Now: as I shut my eyes, or when I keep them
open, I see it, compact and panoramic, as a
spectator might take in a theatre set—the
water front with boats and quays and coils of
rope, the crouching menders of nets, the
unceasing clank of some *parties de boules*, and
beyond it the backdrop, *'la place'*, lieu of
markets and encounters, the façade, a row of
mairie, church and bars tabacs, see it as my
mother saw it that first morning from the
balcony of the hôtel de la Tour. (Come to
think of it, I never actually stayed at the la
Tour, a place of mixed and varying
reputation—food on the sheltered terrace
always good, basic rooms, a clientèle of casual
tourists and naughty boys. Must have spent a
night or two there though, slipping out at dawn
as the fishing fleet got under way.)

Inland from *la place* rise a few narrow
streets of prospering shops, several
boulangeries, butchers, the quite outstanding
*épicerie,* the drapers, shoemakers, the *crèmerie,*
the *pâtissier,* and a cave hung from foot to top

266

with pots and pans. I hear the clang of their doorbells, feel the cobbles beneath my feet— past the post office all this peters out, the terrain gently climbing becomes semi-rural: a scattering of domestic houses, then villas, not many yet and quite ugly, some *pensions de famille*, the single serious hotel with tennis court and one large sad potted palm; the cemetery; and soon beyond, by one or another of the narrow rutted roads, one is in a back-country of archaic beauty rising towards the foothills of the Provençal Alps—empty country of harsh earth, sun-baked and fruitful, barely scarred by a scattering of low ageless stone-built human habitations, thyme-scented, terraced with olive, narcissi, wines. Sanary.

As it was.

It was there that I spent the end of my childhood, the years of adolescence, a near decade of early adult life, a time I stubbornly wanted to last and still long to live again, the happiest years, akin to the post-war Roman years in their exultation by environment though lacking the foundation of stable domestic contentment and the tough hard drive of work. The happiness in the south of France was one of place, not achievement, not events. Much of what happened there was good, even very good, some was traumatic. What I lived then, day by day, were the sea, the light, the sun, cicada sounds at night, first amorous pursuits, some exhilarating, some hopeless or mistakes, some attachments outlasting change—all punctuated by evasions of authority, evasion of evolving tragedy at home.

*     *     *

None of this was guessed at on this first stay I wrote about a couple of pages ago. By my second or third visit much had changed—my mother and Alessandro appeared if anything quite well pleased with the existence they had tumbled into . . . They were living in a largish draughty villa with a view, surrounded by eccentric new acquaintances and old friends; a kind of stability was shaping. Alessandro, by way of his wife's connections, had achieved a discreet footing in the contemporary art-market. For another of their friends he was converting the draughty villa into a civilized and comfortable house. They—we—were moving into a rather beautiful eighteenth-century provençal *mas* on the apex of a cypress alley. I took part in the home life—with my own fish to fry on the side, a good deal went on in those last years of the decade. As to what was happening to myself, I have already brought in fragments here, such as my relationship with the Mimerels, derisive and ambiguous with Oriane, loving, deep and loyal with Pierre; what I must not go into again is a more complete narrative of my early years in the south of France, for the awkward and obvious reason that I have written a version of them in a novel, written years after the actual and the invented tales. Yet the alembic of memory does not stand still. Perspectives shift. I treated that book as an autobiographical novel. Most of what happened *had* happened but was presented within the lax enough requirements of the novel: trimming, timing, concentration. What I am attempting now, a zigzag course from middle to beginning, back to middle, forward to a kind of judgement, seen by an individual with elective affinities not roots, are fractions of autobiography trimmed by a storyteller's mind. As for Sanary part one, I must try to be as summary as I can, compatible with coherence. I immediately see a difficulty with the Huxleys. Aldous and Maria: they had too large a part in my existence not to be brought into fragments of this text whatever the chronology, and this is the point at which I feel that I ought to write, briefly this time, a version of our first actual meeting.

One might ask how they got there, those nomads, from London to Florence to Forte dei Marmi to Paris, from rented flats, Italian villas, Swiss châlets, the French town house? They wanted to be near D. H. Lawrence who was attempting to keep alive in the South of France. That was at Bandol, the resort next to us. Lawrence did not get well at Bandol—any more than Katherine Mansfield did—as we know, he died on the other side of the coast, at Vence, in the spring of 1930. The Huxleys, who had followed Lawrence and Frieda throughout, went back to Bandol as a kindly disposed hotel keeper there had told them of a piece of land, with house in construction, the sea a few hundred yards away, for sale at La Gorguette—Sanary. At that juncture they wanted to get settled once again. *Point Counter Point*, the last of his iconoclastic novels, had just made them adequately well off. Italy— their first love—had become out of bounds (waxing Fascism), England was too cold, too dark for Aldous's frail health and sight. Maria with a local mason concocted an agreeable, slightly eccentric, house; Maria at solitary dawns planted a garden of gardenia bushes and strong-leafed artichokes among eucalyptus, vines and figs; warmth, sea and peace were all about them. At the Villa Uley in apparent stability.

The mason's mate to please and surprise— the Huxleys were liked, more often loved, wherever they went—had painted the gate-post with what he conceived to be their name in huge letters. Maria would only thank, not correct, him, and thus behind those wonderlandish gates, visitors from three continents would find them.

*    *    *

And so did we find them: my mother, my unliterary stepfather and my younger self, one burning summer afternoon, forced into this by Roy Campbell, the South African poet, mythomaniac, aspirant bullfighter and drunk, who happened to be staying with us. He had heard rumours that Huxley whom he had known at Oxford was building in the neighbourhood. Roy was insistent and so off we drove on what we surmised would turn out a wild-goose chase or if not, an unseemly intrusion. In fact, after some misdirections, we were at the house. An open door, behind it Aldous sitting on a red-tiled floor, grass-hopper legs neatly disposed, amidst piles of books he was trying to cram into a rotating cage. Campbell, sensitive enough, spoke at once—aware that Aldous's sight was not up to recognizing an unexpected face. Aldous smiled sweetly and said, 'Roy! *How nice* of you to come!', then turned to us, raising high both hands, 'There is no *horror* greater than the *First* Day in the *New Home.*'

Ever since that copy of *Antic Hay* had been put into my hands, I had read and reread every word published so far by its author, but had little notion of what he might look like—some shadowy presence in an ivory tower? Publishers at the time were less apt to exhibit their author's photograph on the dust-jacket. What struck me first was what I *heard*. I listened to that unhurried, silvery, expressive voice, the voice as spoken by the Jowett—Lewis Carroll Oxford generation, a voice already obsolete in Aldous's lifetime, and which remained unaffected by fashion, age and a twenty-five years' residence in the United States.

Maria appeared from nowhere—none of us had any idea that Huxley was a married man. And there she was. Floating white trousers, corals round the neck, large, intensely focused beautiful blue eyes, the face and figure of an El Greco angel. She coped with the invasion of strangers—Maria had the most unruffled manners. There ensued a tea party, my mother and Aldous hogging the entire conversation, and a call at our house the same evening by Maria bearing bread . . .

\*　　　\*　　　\*

Well the long of this is in another book, the biography I came to write, and *that* was in another age and they of course are dead. The future on that day when we sat around Maria's teapot, with Roy swigging *gros rouge* from a bottle in the shopping bag under his chair and myself sitting mute at the bottom of the table, was unforeseeable.

# CHAPTER SEVENTEEN

## *A malign concatenation*

My next account—not joyful—will have to be about a destructive blow of fate brought about through a blend of antecedents, chance, ill luck. I was returning to Sanary after another of my English stretches; there were still about two years to go till my majority and there was a notion based on some fragile fact, that I was sporadically engaged with obtaining a degree (something like an interpreter's certificate through an exam sat at some institution in the City). At Toulon station I was not met by Alessandro but by some minion from Pierre Mimerel's Garage Excelsior. There was nothing untoward in that, my stepfather these days was often a busy man. I had come bearing presents: tennis rackets and jazz records for Alessandro, Ivy Compton-Burnett for my mother, and this caused a certain amount of bustle. We sat down to lunch. Something was wrong. Heavily so. At first my mother hardly spoke at all; presently she became agitated. Increasingly: raising her arm as though looking for the watch that was seldom there. Alessandro sat tense and silent. We had not really finished when my mother got up and left the room. Alessandro followed her. In the

273

door she turned and said to me, 'I want to speak to you. He'll tell you when I'm ready.'

I found her lying on the bed, quite calm now. There was a glitter in her eyes though, unseeing? Triumphant?

'There is something I have to tell you.'

'?'

'Oh do sit down. Stop pacing . . .'

I pulled up a chair.

In a composed voice she said, 'He is having an affair with another woman.'

Oh my God I thought and blushed; there had been one or two—what?—episodes? kicking over the traces rather, the year before. I knew because in one way or another I had been involved in the cover-ups. It seemed all so natural or almost. He was a man, a young man. He was Italian. The fact that my mother was everything to him did not come into it. (The fact that she treated him, though lovingly, as her creation and possession, might have? Some slight diversions needed?) Women here and there—he went about a good deal on his building commissions—threw themselves at his head. He could be light-hearted as well as good-natured. There had been a tearful French girl to whom it would have been ungraceful to say an entire no. It was all so brief and unimportant, yet it did involve certain patches of thin ice, and that was when Alessandro's and my brotherhood came in, we just felt sure that it was better for

274

her not to know. His wife, my mother, to her ultimately enormous cost had the assurance of a long past of amatory supremacy behind her, an assurance become as serene as that of Queen Victoria's certainty of always finding placed behind her a chair to sink into.

Now all I managed to say was, 'Yes, Mummy?'

And then began a long, open, apparently rational narrative. The woman, 'well yes, the woman,' the friend of a friend sent to us, staying on the coast on her own—her husband too busy—she is married to a rich man—I saw her a couple of times, rather liked her, a pleasant woman, good-looking, chic—in an unobtrusive way—not stupid—though *no* intellectual, likes to laugh, my age, or pretty near it one would say. 'Well I hardly knew her. Then: it was exactly six weeks ago, Alessandro comes home very late one night—I found him on the sofa next morning, asleep, clothes all over the floor. I picked them up. Tidied his jacket . . . Something fell out: I glanced at it, suddenly saw what I had read. I shook him. He got half awake, looked confused. "What's this?" I said, "What's what?" he muttered. *"This letter!"'*

Here my mother turned to me, 'Don't look like that: I *did not* go through his pockets; the damn thing just fell out. It was not a letter, just a note.' A scrap of paper on the carpet . . .

She had not taken it in at that point;

275

surprise, yes; incredulity. She expected denial, explanations, the little note not meaning what it implied. Instead she got a blurred confession, 'Yes, he had spent the night . . . No, it was not the first time.' A promise not to see her again? Well, of course . . . Not at once though . . . How could anyone? A woman left on her own at an hotel in a foreign country. Can't we all be reasonable?

But that, as my mother went on telling me in the same rational, almost euphoric tone, she could not. She had made a frightful scene, she could hear it now. Outrage, misery, entreaty. As the day went on, Alessandro bathed and shaved, fully awake at last, became ready for affectionate words, reassurance. There was no one really beside herself, it doesn't mean much but it means something—let it run its course. In the week that followed she became calmer; she tried to think herself into his position, took an almost anecdotal interest in the affair, applauded her own tolerance. There came amicable luncheons *à trois* (my mother felt most at ease when 'the other woman' was actually there), yet on the days he went to see her on his own, she became agitated, miserable and, by the time he got home, furious. 'I was beastly to him.' She learnt to say what would wound him most, while recalling in the very thick of loud abuse what men had said about the main cause of the break-up of good marriages being tears, reproaches, unkind

276

words . . . while a brief period of quiet and forbearing rarely failed to bring back the status quo ante. My mother's mind agreed; her actions remained out of control. There were the grand scenes on his returns from an openly arranged encounter; there was the nagging when he had been out to buy some cigarettes; there were also her cool repentant comments on her own behaviour. Alessandro was too fine-strung for the emotional seesaw. She went to the chemist on the *place*, a clean establishment well-run by a kind humane man who had occasionally doled out sleeping cachets to her, and asked him for something 'calming to the nerves'. (The word tranquillizers had not entered common vocabulary yet.) She was given a bottle of some syrupy tonic, which had little effect beyond inducing, after too large a swig, more muzzy reproaches. Nor had other similar concoctions. My mother went to see the chemist in his backroom and told him that she was very unhappy. 'I am destroying my marriage by agitation and scenes.' She could not help herself—could *he* suggest some help? He must have realized her desperation. There was a doctor, he told her, one of the two local ones one was a jovial, steady fellow, well-liked—the other . . . *he* could be prepared to help her temporarily—he may find some ailment . . . She might go and see him. But to be careful . . . There could be danger (he actually used that word).

The doctor had a surgery—and presumably lived—in a little house among thin pines not far from the hotel with the sad palm. His appearance was both improbable and gruesome: emaciated, loose-hanging dusty suit, a transparent yellow skin, dark-circled sunken eyes—a figure out of some black comic strip.

So my mother had gone to the doctor in the woods. She didn't tell me much about the consultation. 'He hardly speaks . . .' When she left, which was quite soon, they both presumed that she had some trouble with her breathing, some kind of asthma . . . connected possibly with the heart—'so my heart needs easing!' She was told to pull up her sleeve and was given an injection, something from a needle. It was over in a second . . .' She was to come back next day and report. When she got home she went straight to bed and in no time at all felt an extraordinary sense of lightness, 'It was as if I did no longer exist, and nor did anything else, nothing mattered, only that floating, that all rightness, that peace.'

It lasted through that afternoon, well into the evening, the night; for the first time in weeks she *slept*, did not wake Alessandro. What was there to forgive? It was all so small, so remote. Next day Alessandro drove her back into the wood.

Here I had to ask, 'Did he come in with

you?'

'Of course not. He waited in the car. There is never anyone else in that surgery. I've never seen a nurse . . . only a half-grown sort of boy, a kind of servant . . .'

The doctor had appeared pleased. He wrote her a prescription. With that in hand they drove to the chemist who put together without comment a small parcel: a padded cardboard box holding two rows of some tiny phials—ampoules, a thin steel file, and a glass syringe. One, she was told, in the early afternoon, one before night.

But, I said, '*You?* How . . . ? Can one?'

'*I* couldn't—oh no.' The chemist told Alessandro how to give an injection. He is very adroit, as you know; does all the fiddly tricks. That glass thing has to be sterilized, *every* time. He boils it in a little saucepan over a spirit lamp, the kitchen stove is much too slow—it takes ages anyway. This is what is getting less good—the waiting for it (like today, because of your arrival). Perhaps he ought to teach you—good idea—more convenient when he has to be away to work . . .

\*　　　\*　　　\*

Among the questions I had not asked my mother then were 'How long has this been going on?' We were at the end of the 1920s, people like us were babes in the wood: one had heard about young women in night-clubs sniffing cocaine, one had read about opium dens. There was Sherlock Holmes, Jean Cocteau. Drugs were bad. Of course. Remotely; with a whiff of glamour: exotic docks, *fin de siècle* poetry . . . We were ignorant of all that is now common knowledge, ignorant of needles, of adulterated substances, of threats physical and legal. We did not know the meaning of addiction. Nor its signs. Nor that almost inevitably it comes sooner or later. Some 'subjects' are granted a long spell of grace . . . even years, others have a few months before the onset of the waiting, craving, the changes of behaviour, the screaming pain, set in. For my mother her time of grace turned out to be exceptionally brief, and this is what I meant by her having been undone, among other causes, through two pieces of ill-luck. One, purely accidental, was the doctor in the wood materializing at her time of need. (Rumours and conjectures there were many, yet nothing tangible was ever found out about his motives or his private habits; his fees throughout in no way exceeded those of a modest country practitioner's for a brief visit.)

The second piece of ill luck was constitutional. Unexpected, as her habitual animation was such that she—unlike my father or myself—had been scarcely aware of the pleasant effects of stimulants: it used to be the unfinished half-glass of claret on the dinner table or the champagne growing tepid in the hand it had been put into. *Now*, as I sat listening to her on that first day of knowledge, I should have been alerted by the words ' . . . it's getting less good—the waiting for it'. One question, though, I had asked, 'What is this thing you make Alessandro give you?'

Complacently, she had said, morphine.

\*  \*  \*

My mother lived on for another seven years; stretches of them tumultuous, pain-ridden, extreme; others subdued, conscious perhaps of impairment and loss or just hum-drumly unhappy. There were periods of cure and periods of recovery. Throughout she never quite lost the ability to amuse, to attract, to (briefly) seduce; often there came relief, absolution—by her own intelligent and compassionate interest in the public events then beginning to crash upon us.

\*  \*  \*

That initial stage of euphoria and tolerance—what's a little adultery?—punctuated by impatience, loud-voiced frustration, revived anger, had not lasted long into that summer. New visits to the wood, renewed prescriptions, increasing dosage, less intervals between their application. The other woman—who turned out to be much as my mother had first described her; nice-natured as well, tactful in behaviour, not too obviously in love—had left or rather withdrawn to the other side of the Côte, the smart side, the Riviera. Alessandro drove over at shortening intervals. This became practicable when I had mastered the fiddly little jobs—not breaking the minute ampoules, not omitting the surgical-spirit swab. As tensions increased, the other woman left the country. Total break? The question was felt, not asked. He had begun to need her, not so much as love affair than escape, an armistice of low pressure for the inside of a day, for thirty-six hours, from the increasing disorder in our house. When X was gone out of reach, he missed *her*. I am surprised to find myself unable to recall her name and don't wish to search or probe. I liked her, whenever there was actual contact, remote though she was from most of what interested me then (we both enjoyed swimming); I shy away from saddling her from an invented name: let it be bare X. To her too I owe some anonymity and peace. When she was gone—that first time—there was little relief. Absence. We all knew about that. What hung over us then were thoughts of the poste restante. Had he or had he not rented one of those slim steel boxes at the Sanary post office? There was a visible row of them on the wall, numbered in white paint, from one to twelve. (Years on, I once rented

282

one myself and every time I slipped in to search mine at some quiescent hour, I thought of Alessandro.) My mother was affectionate to him, it was he who had become restless and ruffled. Between them they were constructing a renunciatory drama, the tone rising and abating with the tides of my mother's euphoria, becalmment and plain fury. They were aiming at a dénouement: to her it had to be the end of the affair; what he needed was an *ending*. He saw it as a slow unmeasured slice of time on their own—he and *X*, weeks, perhaps a month or more, of fulfilment and unwinding. Travel . . . It might be Italy, it could be Spain . . . No fixed plan, no address: as they moved he would send telegrams addressed to me, for my eyes only, with a place name and its chief hotel; information resorted to in case of acute urgency. (My mother agreed to this airily.) Alessandro would be picked up, she would come with chauffeur, the chauffeur be sent back, and then they would be off. And so my mother would be off: on her own way of ending. She had promised to be en route to giving up what her prosaic family refused to speak of as her Artificial Paradise ('You are afraid even to think of it,' she had said to me, 'though you used to talk enough about having read *Les Fleurs du mal*'). Yes, and when the time was right, he would be back! All as before. Did they believe it? I think *he* did.

After they had left, I was supposed to be in charge. Between Alessandro and myself there had been no treaty, hardly words, just a kind of bond, some mutual reassurance. It was the feeling I had had the day he put me on the train at Naples on my first journey towards England. *In charge.* Up to what point? Then I had part of a ticket, a name card round my neck and a pocket with some money. Now I would be in charge of money I was unable (too young still for an account) to draw myself from a bank, which meant preventing my mother from writing more than a reasonable amount of cheques and taking care of the resulting cash. (As she used to do with Alessandro, as she had assured us she would do with me.) I had been left with our car—bought shining new out of Alessandro's earnings (a Ford cabriolet) the winter before. I had been barely allowed to touch it. Such driving experience I had came by way of the Pierre Mimerels' eccentric motoring stable, where most of the inmates looked, and quite likely had been, hand-made by Pierre. Just old enough— eighteen—I had passed my licence a few months ago, which meant that I was enthusiastic, not unpromising, lacking in experience. My mother, who never so much as touched a driving wheel, decided to make full expensive use of the car: she was going to lead a life of pleasure. We were at the height of August, very hot, the Côte from Cassis to Menton crammed with traffic, tourists, visiting friends. For us it meant ill-planned excursions—because we had to be back for what was now called her treatment, 'I didn't expect her to cut off *that* from one day to the next, did I?'

One might say there were problems. In that over-used word, problems indeed.

*     *     *

We had not reached the stage of her insistence of not leaving the house—her room, her bed— without taking her paraphernalia, 'Couldn't one stop by the roadside? All those cafés and places have a WC . . .' For a time, I objected. Strongly.

When it had come to the matter of sterilization, it was moved aside ('Just a drop of alcohol and a bit of cottonwool'). One part of the life of pleasure was treating me to dinner at a good restaurant. ('Look one up in the Michelin—never mind about kilometres, find a place with a view . . .') I protested. We were spending far too much already. Yet there we would be on the banquette of some suave place, ordering an extravagant train of courses, hardly noticed once they had got on to her plate, with me watching for the first signs of agitation, ready to ask for the bill, too aware

285

that there was still the order of an elaborate sweet omelette. And so a public cloakroom rather than the frantic night drive became a less frightening option.

Sanary then had one small branch of a bank open twice a week for a few hours. My mother often got there just after the door had closed. Relief: one cheque less cashed. Instead my clever mother began to run up bills. It was easy: at first we had credit everywhere. French mistrust of foreigners is quite near the surface—in the Midi it was often covered by a layer of joviality; anyway at one initial stage they chose to treat us as respectable visitors as well as sources of income. My mother began to enjoy the swagger of ordering or buying without producing actual cash. Ordering lavishly. She enjoyed the approving attitudes of the *traiteur*, the fish stall—the expensive one, the little bookshop, the *marchand de fleurs*, the boutique at Bandol a-flutter with silk scarves, how could I begrudge her, how could I *stop* her? There was such pleasure in standing treat, in arrival with presents. We still visited friends then—at the right hours, with her adequately covering up. (When we had first appeared at the Huxleys' gate, not that many weeks ago, the bad thing already going on full swing, both Aldous and Maria had been captivated within minutes; no suspicion of something out of joint.)

At the present point, my mother liked to

make her visits on her own ('What are taxis for?'). With her out, I was able to cope with another problem, the irregular arrivals of Alessandro's telegrams with their changes of address. These bald messages, which she had promised not to take note of—like those fire extinguishers marked EN CAS D'URGENCE—delivered from the post office by an old woman who bawled out her presence as she set foot on our doorstep, distressed my mother sadly. When she was in I had to be quick to open and take note of 'Hôtel Plaza . . .' or 'Villa Reale . . .' before tearing up the blue forms into small scraps. Then there came a howl: 'My health *is* a case of emergency: telegraph him to come back.' I tried to not leave the house before the post office had shut.

Soon I *had* to be—out and about, hours at a time, driving to Bandol, La Ciotat, to Toulon, once as far as Le Lavandou, to find yet again another pharmacy still willing or ignorant enough to cash the prescription I tried so nonchalantly to tender. Our Sanary man had told me compassionately but firmly that *he* no longer could: the doctor's reputation was not right. This had gone on far too long. Where was the medical reason? Was I aware of the frequency? The dosage? The *law?* All he could do was to persuade my mother to seek urgent alternate professional help. Which of course she indignantly refused. I did not understand

287

her suffering and her need, she told me, and was partly right: I had come to despise her making so much of a marital infidelity; I did feel pity, though not enough, either for her nor inside myself. I was exasperated, frightened, seldom kind. We could still laugh together, but not often. I longed for escape.

Meanwhile? What strikes me now as odd is that I did not even think of asking friends for help. I had quite a few by then, amorously and otherwise, most often elders and betters. Shying away from the whole situation? Some notion of standing guard for Alessandro? Unasked, our pharmacist told me 'Send for the husband'.

This I refused. He *would* come; sooner or later. When it was right for him. Meanwhile there was her need. She had reached the stage of finding my administrations clumsy and slow, preferring to do the necessary herself— sloppily and fast. There was no intention of cutting down now. I did what I had been advised: take these prescriptions as far afield as you can, and *never, ever* to the same place twice. I recall the stagefright on thresholds, the assumed nonchalance, the prepared sham answer to the questions which were not asked. I carried street maps so as not to park the Ford again in the same neighbourhood. One afternoon I came home and found the large looking-glass, a clock and the flower vases knocked down and smashed, the jagged pieces of glass all over the floor: my mother had taken a poker to them; it hadn't required, she said, much strength. 'This can be regarded as an emergency—*send for him at once.*' She pointed to the opened blue form on the table, I noted that it had come from Ronda, the graceful town in the south of Spain where she and my own father had lived for some months before I was born. (They left: childbirth insalubrious in those parts. Alas. Claiming Spanish birth would have given me much pleasure.)

\*　　　\*　　　\*

They arrived one mid-morning after days of forced drives in the still great September heat on crowded roads. *X* had stayed in the car outside. Alessandro looked distraught, underslept, covered in dust, streaked with sweat. My mother appeared in her nightgown, straight out of bed, dishevelled, haughty and cross. Each remained standing in their part of the room.

\*　　　\*　　　\*

What happened later? What happened *next?* That day gradually sorted itself out. Bath water was drawn, suitcases taken inside and dealt with. The femme de ménage came in unasked bearing a jug of citron pressé. My mother returned to bed. *X* presently was driven to an hotel (from which she was picked up by her husband's chauffeur before the week was out.)

The months which followed were chaotic, balanced between promises, hope, despair. My mother turned up for her third appointment with the local 'good GP' and walked out having called him Docteur Charles Bovary to his face. ('Oughtn't we look somewhat higher?' she said to Alessandro.) Our now quite disastrous money situation was coming to roost—tradesmen and restaurateurs do not like having *homard à l'américaine* dispensed unpaid. Oh, how bad had been my standing guard. That Alessandro did no better brought no solace.

At some long last my mother was persuaded to see a consultant at another end of the coast, 'to look higher' in fact. By then we had friends who *knew* (in fact we had no longer any other). Great and effective help came from Maria Huxley. She soothed, she persuaded, she showed authority. My mother became enabled to show trust and love. It was Maria who achieved the drive to the much postponed visit to the specialist; Maria who gave—and let us accept—the money. *Aldous*'s money, so hard earned, so much of it given away caused perpetual anguish to her. He—frail and indeed overdriven by the need to work—always said yes at once. A rash course for a man who seldom opened his bank or royalty statements, and a wife for whom they would have been Greek.

(Ah, but morally, Maria was numerate. She told her son, she told me, 'When a friend needs something, always give before they have to ask.')

That consultant, once we had reached his clutches, was brutal and direct. *'Pauvre femme,'* he said all the same, never had he had a case of such rapid addiction (he was headman of a reputable disintoxication clinic), she had reached a stage of dependance in months that would habitually take a subject a year or several years, a stage that affected not only behaviour, but brought a general deterioration of health. Retrievable? One would have to see. A question of constitution. Need for an institutional cure was urgent. Painful? This was when the hostile consultant had said, *pauvre femme.*

Urgency struck after it had been made clear to us that we were foreigners on French soil, about to become undesirable aliens (a term not yet familiar to people like us), and that it would soon no longer be possible to obtain a drug from legal sources (there was a snort in the way *legal* was dropped). Thus a stop to touring pharmacies with doubtful prescription, it meant instead bars on the water-front of Toulon (a girl slipping in and out appearing more innocent than Alessandro would have been). My mother complained about the uncertain quality of what was brought to her from these forays. We did not understand that for someone who has got into an untenable position, insolence however alienating is not arrogance but a last ditch of defence. She *was* lucid enough to take in the precariousness of her position. And so at long last came the day on which Maria succeeded in driving her to the awaiting clinic.

Neither her husband nor myself were allowed to visit her during the first weeks.

*     *     *

On her return she was helped out of the car by a young nurse, who must have been good to her. My mother did not want her to leave. Once inside the house, alone with us, she was near speechless, not interested in anything. She went straight to bed ('What else was there to do?' So there was a trace of astringency left.) That flatness—a desperate aura of failure gradually diminished.

She grew affectionate again with Uley, an offspring of the Huxleys' Siamese pair, given her as a kitten. Now, he lived on her bed, sat on the books—unread—we had brought, spat at the drops of sticky concoctions prescribed to her that she kept offering his delicate nostrils on her fingertips, and accepted her caresses with grace. Another indication of a partial return to living were the insults, still relatively mild, she fired at her medical attendant. The powers at the clinic—the lieu of her descent into hell of which she did not talk—had decreed professional supervision which in practice meant visits from our local good GP. A well-balanced chap, he turned out, *bien dans sa peau*, competent and confident: no Charles Bovary he. I don't think he paid much attention to my mother's barbed ironies, just went on supplying potions, some stimulating, some sedative, a return, we felt, to the initial valerium stage. What *she* asked for was some decent wine to be put on her tray. Give it to her, the good doctor told us. Though be careful. At some stage she will try to compensate with serious alcohol. Be careful about that too. We were. Others not. We did not quite know who. Gradually my mother regained her ability of getting her own way. Thus the bottles of gin, abhorred by Uley, found among the bedclothes.

For a time it did well for her. Within months she resumed a reasonably normal life, getting up on her own, getting dressed, going out, seeing friends. She was asked and went. (There was one rather Firbankian Christmas at the Huxleys' in Maria's new basement kitchen—an unusual eccentricity in those days—with little Matthew's toy railway clattering round the dinner table, my mother erratically made up, Uley on shoulder, Marie-

Laure de Noailles crowing with delight at the unconventionality of it all: *her* domestiques would never allow her to put foot in the kitchen.)

I looked across at my mother on that and many other evenings, and tried not to look at Alessandro. She had regained some of her confidence: one could not say that she was on the way to regaining the beauty she had worn so casually throughout her past existence. 'Losing one's looks' is a dicey thing for a woman beyond forty; what she was acquiring then was a kind of tragic grandeur, an imprint of suffering—expressed by an uncertain walk, emaciation, a ravaged nobility of face. How did she bear it? How much did she know? Was it more easily ignored out in the world of talk and take, or withdrawn in bed with gin and Uley? Her temper on the whole had become more even. Jokes exchanged with femme de ménage and postman; a placatory attitude towards me: no more pink chiffon, I was able to wear the kind of sailors' clothes I liked, was encouraged to write (in that realm my mother showed serious concern: *'Would* I be able to make it?'). She took little notice of my nocturnal escapes (climbing out of my bedroom window to go dancing at a late-night café on the port of Bandol; with perhaps worse to follow). Only to Alessandro was she consistently vindictive, nasty. 'He didn't work. He couldn't manage to find work. He was too cowardly to leave the house to work.' However, he had ruined her life, and who was he? When she did not attack, she ignored him. I didn't know how he bore it.

I knew that after those early first days in Italy, when he had so adamantly fallen in love with her, he soon began also to love her gently, dearly, protectively, beyond the dazzle and the attraction, with the wholehearted devotion of one human being to another. That was the foundation. One sexual side-step, natural to most men and many women, and (perhaps part retaliation to his youth?) he is cast into the role of a gigolo to whom one is still magnanimous enough to give house room.

*     *     *

He and I did not speak of the situation. If there was camaraderie, there was also reticence. Some things are too private for acknowledgement through speech.

*     *     *

One day there was a familiar smell in the house when I came in. It was the disinfectant my mother had come to use on her arm instead of going through the sterilization process of boiling the syringe. (Hers were glass, not plastic and disposable.) It had begun again.

How and where she got the stuff we did not know. Neither Alessandro nor I took a hand in it; at any rate she appeared to use it with some sense and moderation. It was her treat. For a time there was little change. Then one day we put up a friend of Alessandro's for the night. That year we avoided having anyone to stay, but he, a graduate student, was passing through, it was summer with everything affordable booked up. Dinner went rather well. The guest proved articulate and erudite; my mother and he got engaged in opinionated argument for and against Marx and Sigmund Freud which they seemed to enjoy. We all retreated to bed early. (I had renounced any attempt at a nocturnal outing.) Sometime in the night I was waked by a great noise. I crept in the hall and there was my mother in her nightgown standing in our guest's open door, shouting unstoppably. What I believe I heard went something like—'Do you realize where you are . . . ? You are under an adulterer's roof . . . !' I slunk away, shut my door. Bed, earplugs, blanket over head . . . When I woke it was bright dawn, Alessandro standing in my room, fully dressed, briefcase in hand, the motoring cap he liked to wear was on his head. What he was telling me was that he was leaving, he could not stay any more. I got up, we both stood for a time on the terrace above the cypress allée in the first light of another Mediterranean morning. The suitcases were already in the car, he said. The friend's car, they were going in that. Look after her, he said. I shall send some money when I can. We embraced. He was my brother.

*      *      *

For the rest of that year and beyond there came a good deal of help. From the friends around us; from Mamoushka, wicked Issa's generous mother, peacefully residing in the villa Alessandro had light-heartedly put together for her not so long ago; help from the Huxleys of course. The support given to *me* was above my deserts. I did what had to be done often without enough understanding and grace. Yet friends sheltered me well into adult years and thus allowed me to postpone efforts to stand on my own feet. (It allowed me space enough to learn to write.)

My mother's trustees inevitably had to put their oar in and so did—chivalrously, effectively—her old admirer, the German ex-minister who was still my guardian, by mobilizing medical as well as financial resources.

We moved out of our house into a furnished flat down the road. On the whole my mother managed not too badly. So when I came of age at last in the spring of 1932, it became possible for me to leave her briefly to go to Germany to settle my affairs; for good I hoped. Aldous

297

wanted to interview some scientists in Berlin, and so it came that I spent a week there with the Huxleys. It was a mixed-up and foreboding time, with daily clashes between Communists and Brownshirts in the streets. As for settling my financial future, I found bureaucracy off-handedly blocking the way, the present—financially very hard-pressed—government having already introduced money-export restrictions, so no question of transferring my modest inheritance to France. At least not without some lengthy wrestling with authority. I let the future take care of itself and left Germany with Maria smuggling a couple of my thousand-mark notes hidden in her shoes. These should do for a time. Don't tell Aldous.

\*　　　\*　　　\*

On our return, my mother was not in a good way back in the flat from a bridging cure in a private nursing home. For a time I was persuaded to move out. Later on moved back again. At one stage I needed someone in the house and appealed to my sister. Jacko, living in ambiguous circumstances herself, came. After their long drifting apart, they more or less accepted each other again. My sister, ferociously disgusted by drugs, had an aptitude for kindly and effective authority—it was largely she who had taught me behaviour when I was a young child. Now my mother gave in to her up to a point. For a while.

By the way, it was then that Jacko first met Pierre Mimerel.

Later still I moved from under my mother's roof for good, settling into an ancient farm house in the back country—simplicity, space, silence, with a painter friend in temporary permanency during which I wrote my two first novels (bad and derivative). My mother and I still saw a reasonable amount of each other; indeed shared some of Sanary's increasing social life. She had good periods—what is normality? (When I had a serious bout of bronchitis, it was she who arrived, in an old taxi for which she owed, bearing herbal teas and honey. The painter friend just wrung hands.) There were crises of course, from the inconvenient to the disastrous, cures and escapes from cures, and thus it went on. I shall not write about it any more, neither here nor elsewhere. Too many of us nowadays know, or are pushed into knowing, the nature of such devastations.

The last I saw of my mother was at Toulon station being lifted through the window of a wagon-lits carriage on a northbound express. Aldous and Maria stood with me on the platform.

She was taken towards a long cure in another country. Later, circumstances were not propitious for direct contact. I knew that she had a period of remission, living on her own, free of any artificial paradise. Her physical health however was ruined. She died in a hospital in her mid-fifties; I fear, though I hope not, alone. She and Alessandro had never met again.

## CHAPTER EIGHTEEN

*One turning of the screw—A compact—A civilized oasis—A literary royal family*

From the early 1920s on, here and there on that Mediterranean coast, one would find a handful of people who had chosen to live in places of benevolent climate and great natural beauty remote from the centres of commerce and government where one could play and work in the belief that History can have a stop. Was there not the League of Nations? Locarno? The searing still open grief of what had been endured and lost in the decade before?

By the early 1930s that illusion of safety had already become fractured. (Huxley, returned from a journey in Central America, wrote to an old friend that he was re-reading Wordsworth's account of his visit to France during the Revolution,

The land all swarming with passion like a

plain Devoured by locusts . . .

'Which is exactly Europe in '33—the awful sense of invisible vermin of hate, envy, anger crawling about . . .')

The 27th February 1933, the night of the German Reichstag fire, was one more in the long, long chain of dates in our progress, dates of an assassination, an invasion, a declaration of war, dates which would later be recognized as a point of no return before another giant wave of destruction and death. Through the millennia, the emotions—tribal, religious, ideological, acquisitive—which unleashed such suffering remained much the same; the means increased on unimagined scales. As did the number of the victims. First a stick, two stones, against another man, his women and a cave. How long did it take by way of the sword, the arrow and the cannon ball, the fortress and the armoured ship, the trench, the tank, the aeroplane to reach total war, mass subjugation, death camps, the bomb, the tyrant or the rabble killing a million or some millions here and there? What happened the next morning, the next days and weeks after that night of arson in Berlin: the seizure of power by Hitler and his crew, and all that flowed from it, was yet another (gigantic) stepping stone in human history. And now? Can we not see where we stand, overrunning the earth with our ever-evolving technologies and demands, now at the beginning of the twenty-first century AD?

*     *     *

At Sanary the odious events of that spring of 1933 became tangible by the arrival of several clans of distinguished, not to say, illustrious, writers in abrupt exile. Some, the prominently Jewish or left-wing or both, had managed to escape the Gestapo in time by crossing a land border in plausible guise. Some, not in immediate danger, possibly even liable to be counted as potential assets to German culture, had left house, habits, livelihoods and friends, moved by revulsion, foresight and their sense of honour. Many were internationally known, which meant translated; quite a few more, obscure or out of fashion, might face destitution; some were 'world famous': Thomas Mann, Bertolt Brecht, Lion Feuchtwanger, Arnold Zweig, Franz Werfel and his wife Alma who had been—and still carried his name—Mahler's widow. A galaxy indeed. And didn't they know it . . . Their entourage, a gathering of secretaries, housekeepers, agents, referred to them—straight-faced as *Dichterfürsten*, princes of poetry. (They split into cliques at once.) Some rented villas, Heinrich Mann with Blue-Angel mistress was able to put up at the Good Hotel, some made do with a couple of rooms in a

302

pension or managed to obtain lodgings with one of the none too willing locals. Dividing lines on the whole, though, were literary and political rather than financial or domestic. All had lost their library. *For how long?*

One may ask why Sanary? That modest fishing village now, more than half a century on, finds bestowed upon itself a kind of posthumous fame and is referred to in books and films as 'the one-time capital of German literature'. So a blue plaque can be seen on the wall of many a villa or boarding-house displaying an eminent or no longer quite so eminent name. (Tourist offices offer trilingual brochures with dates and maps.) By what quirk of circumstance had those troupes of what we the settled foreign residents—Parisians and Anglo-Saxons mostly—enjoyed calling the *haute culture* taken refuge in one obscure resort? It could hardly have been a planned move. Neither into a holiday nor a future. Too much, and too little, baggage for a straight dive into some capital city? The days were stretching towards Easter . . . the summer . . . The need was for somewhere quiet, not too expensive, a place to perch where one might carry on with work in progress, ruminate steps beyond . . .

Thomas Mann and his wife as it happened were away from their Munich home lecturing in Sweden in that crucial spring of the Nazis' first overt atrocities. His intention had been to

303

return and *remain*; he, an incarnation of German humanism, must be seen as such. He neither feared for, nor much doubted his own safety. His two elder children, Klaus and Erika, emphatically judged otherwise. Their father's Nobel Prize might offer some protection for his person, his very presence would help to legitimize the regime. They braved their father's not negligible authority and did their persuasive best—over uncertain international telephone lines—to convince him of his naïve and potentially disastrous error. They succeeded. Thus Thomas Mann flew out of Stockholm, over German territory, reached France. (The incidents on that air journey belong to history, not these pages.)

The 'Mann children'. When people spoke or wrote about them in those times as they did a good deal from their early and glamorous adolescence on, they meant the eldest pair. The other four, if proved in due course far from obscure, did not come to anything like the limelight, the notoriety, the actual talents and their influence on contemporaries and lovers. (When they toured America in their teens, they liked to bill themselves as twins, which they were not.) The Mann children then, adamantly anti-Fascist, anti-Nazi, foresighted, combative, had already been voluntary absentees from Germany for some years. Erika ran a political cabaret in Zürich, the Peppermill; brother Klaus, very much at ease in France, perambulated between Paris and the south, writing his novels in hotel rooms, smoking opium with Jean Cocteau at Toulon. Naturally he thought that this sea coast could offer some seemly refuge for his revered parents and the younger children. If not exactly *at* Toulon. Nor at that other naval port, Villefranche, recreation ground to the US Navy and home from home to Klaus. So he with Erika, the quick and organizing one, turned their small roadster westward in search of somewhere suitable: somewhere with fishermen and summer visitors, not sailors; nor opium.

Their first township was a row of shipbuilding yards, the next a centre of carnations grown *en primeur* hill by hill, the next announced itself as Sanary-sur-mer and looked more likely. They had thought of seeking advice from a contemporary of their father's, Meier-Graefe, the art historian, who had travelled to Spain early in the century to look at Velàsquez and returned enraptured by El Greco (somewhat mislaid for a few hundred years). He and his very young fourth wife—he had her elope with him straight from Swiss boarding-school, pursued by telephone and police—had a house not far further along, so they chanced finding someone on their way to guide them. The Manns, junior as well as senior, were used to coming across people they knew or who knew who they were. They rang the bell at the gate of a place on the main road where I happened to be (briefly) staying. It was toward the end of the siesta hours. What I saw were two young people in an open car, good-looking, a little travel-stained. I didn't know who they might be. They told me.

I said, 'You got away.'

'We *had* turned away,' Erika said with hard emphasis.

'For good,' her brother said.

'We shall never go back.'

'Never.'

'Never,' I said.

I stood, like the recruit, holding his ground, responding: PRESENT.

*      *      *

After that ineloquent Agincourt we returned to earth. I got into their car and we drove off to find the Meier-Graefes near Saint-Cyr. Not the Saint-Cyr l'Ecole of the great military school near Paris. Saint-Cyr-sur-Mer, a nearby modest native place. The house stood, old, low, of graceful proportions, on the apex of a cypress alley. Frau Meier-Graefe, on that unexpected arrival in the middle of the afternoon, looked still very young after what must have been half a decade of marriage; years younger than myself who was about to turn twenty-two. I kissed her hand. If somewhat unconventionally brought up, I still knew enough to follow, on this occasion, the custom of the German and Austrian upper classes which was that an unmarried woman kisses the hand of a married one whatever their respective ages. (Exception only if the unmarried woman happened to be both eminent and of advanced years.) Our present hostess had been née Epstein, father a well-known architect, the family Berlin Jewish upper bourgeoisie, *Grossbürgentum:* automatically we kissed hands, metaphorically that is: she slightly raised hers, I slightly bowed above it, blew lightly into the air. All the same, I was aware of the absurdity: the girl I stood in front of, dark-skinned, vivacious, sexy—not pretty—fitting the part of a runaway schoolgirl well cast in some French farce.

Later, much later, in her advanced middle age, when I had known her in another marriage, with other lovers—she specialized in famous writers and artists as well as Greek ship-owners—concurrent with discreet affairs with one of their young sons, when she had been chief confidante to that major Messalina, Alma Mahler: gradually through those years she and I had shared precarious times in many countries, England before the war, exile in America, post-war France; had become good friends. I have never met anyone quite like her. Inexhaustibly flirtatious, giggly, chatty, she was a graceful and imaginative maker of homes, who looked after—I should say served—her men (for richer and for poorer), a generous hostess, a helpful friend to those women who did not prefer to revile her. (Oh, the gossip . . . not to mention persecutions by poison-pen letters.) Above all she was a very brave woman, self-contained in grief, who bore tragic losses with reticence and dignity. Both her husbands died prematurely, the second suddenly on the day he was about to move into their new house; her own entire family perished in the Holocaust. (She herself managed a hair's-breadth escape from Vichy France in the middle of the war.)

It was in the late 1970s when she used to come to London—where I was living then—to see past admirers, an eminent Oxford philosopher, an equally so conductor—still bubbly she would say that I was her *aide-mémoire*: 'When and at whose house was the party with Jimmy and me and the screen?' It was by then that she enjoyed telling mutual friends (hers far grander than mine) of that past custom that had made me kiss her hand; she believed that this would make her seem younger.

\*　　　\*　　　\*

In that actual past, on that first visit, we were led into a large light room with long windows open on a balustrade and the receding line of tall dark cypress trees, a room almost sublimely uncluttered: a central table, some consoles, a plinth or two giving support to a few objects (so *far* from my father's serried ranks of medieval artisanery), none large, clay, terracotta, marble . . . Had I not seen their kind at the British Museum? Once again I felt myself at Paestum and Agrigento . . .

Later, on our way hack, I, still stunned, spoke about the beauty of that room. Poor devil, they said, those crocks and bowls are all he's got left, they took about everything, one after the other, those former wives, settlements, alimony . . . You should have seen Meier-Graefe's house in Berlin, the collections, his flats in Cairo, in Paris . . . Number three was the worst—opinions were turning against so many divorces—the family are north-German grandees, not *Junkers*, mines not land—the first wife behaved quite decently, not so vindictive and greedy.

I said, thank goodness at least no one was greedy about what he's got here.

Klaus said, in Berlin the walls were not bare, he had a Renoir, Goya etchings, no end of German Expressionists . . .

Earlier, he, the master of this house had come in.

I had read *Spanische Reise*, his El Greco book, so controversial at one time, and been much taken by it. There was a man who could see into paintings and then write what he had seen in a straight pared-down eloquently sober

German. (I read quite an amount of books in German in my youth, and after an earlier bout of Stefan Zweig—reneged on later—took to Meier-Graefe's handling of the language: terse at once and polished.) It was known that he had to work extremely hard at it. He rose and started to write literally at dawn morning after morning—the household geared to this—and worked until early afternoon, no papers, no post, no business, no talk; just concentration, at the end of the day, then there might be one paragraph, he has said that writing came hard to him: his first draft always read like schoolboy stuff.

So he came in, not strained, at ease, not particularly concerned with our call though agreeable enough. He was tall, strong-shouldered and slim, a vigorous man with hints of fragility (advancing into his late sixties) in a light tweed suit, well-worn though by no means shabby (an *English* tailor?), silk scarf, no tie. Polished shoes: an aristocratic bohemian. Straight hair, brushed back, fair into white. Fine hands. Fine face—handsome, worn, carved by restrained intelligence. A man belonging anywhere and nowhere, a man of his own, entirely. He spoke in educated German with an attenuated Prussian accent, turning mainly to Klaus, touching on contemporary politics, remotely, disdainfully. Tea had been brought in: China tea, very pale and clear in translucent cups; there was honey, some almonds, some exquisitely light biscuits. The schoolgirl Frau Meier-Graefe turned out a sophisticated *maîtresse de maison*. She, Erika and I were chiefly addressing ourselves to the matter in hand, finding an establishment suitable for Thomas Mann and his wife.

Saint-Cyr wasn't up to it, nor were the more numerous summer lettings at Sanary. An idea occurred and worked. The Villa Tranquille, the house Alessandro had civilized for Mamoushka, wicked Issa's docile mother, who—feeling herself in an ambiguous position as the mother-in-law of the German ambassador to Cairo, an old Foreign Office hand, who had seen his duty to remain *en poste* whatever the régime—had decided not to stay in her French residence for the time being. So La Tranquille it was. Wheels got into motion . . . That it might be equally ambiguous for Hitler's ambassador to have let his mother-in-law's house to Thomas Mann—instantly followed by the cream of anti-Nazi literati—did not occur to His Excellency at this point.

*        *        *

The impact of the German refugees, the droves who had rapidly followed the Thomas Manns and their train to Sanary, was, putting it gently, mixed. The working population, a compound of Italian and Provençal origins, customs, speech, were apt to be aloof as well

311

as quite pleasant to the various foreign hands that fed them; the more strictly French French seldom shed an inbred residual xenophobia. Swarmed upon by actual living Germans, distaste and instinctive fear rose readily to the surface. *'Un Boche, c'est toujours un Boche'*, could be heard when a cleaning woman had been reprimanded or paid late. Only the resident French artists, Kissling and *copains*, stood fiercely against what was happening in Germany and offered fraternity to its refugees.

As to the Huxleys: 'Rather a dismal crew,' Aldous wrote to his brother Julian, 'already showing the disastrous effects of exile. Let us hope we shall not have to scuttle when Tom Mosley gets into power.' His attitude at that stage of his own development was still a despairing detachment from most public events. Born with a sweet nature, tragedies in childhood and youth made him withdraw into an inaccessible inner shell, pouring meanwhile that brilliant acerbic scepticism into his work. He had been dismayed by Mussolini—with mockery more than heat—to the extent indeed of giving up living in Italy (where his health had thrived). Now, he did not let the Nazi atrocities invade his emotional consciousness. He deprecated what he saw as my excessive engagement with what went on in camps and streets, the victims and the thugs and maniacs who inflicted it. It *was* horrible, Aldous said, no more so than what was going on huge scale in the Soviet Union year after year since the 1917 Russian Revolution: Siberia, mass starvation, secret police, organized elimination of men and women.

Maria's feelings about our new neighbours were on an altogether different track. She herself, her family: mother and three sisters, had been Belgian refugees during the 1914 war. First in England (when she met Aldous and Aldous fell in love with her for good), then in Italy (when she had been torn from him by mother and authorities). Their position, hers and her family's, though often privileged and ultimately rewarding, had been precarious, penurious, often humiliating. One behaved with dignity, pliancy, showed gratitude, whereas the present refugees, the more visible ones, were throwing their weight about.

Some weight, one could say.

Maria remained distant, disapproving. (*Then*, not later: during the next war when the Huxleys themselves were expatriates in California and once more close neighbours, she and Frau Mann struck up a kind of solidarity, deploring some American habits on their walks.) In our Sanary days, I was ambivalent in my likes and dislikes. Together, Maria and I collected anecdotes, told Aldous, laughed.

Frau Mann's casual frequent statement, 'We owe it to our *Welt Ruhm*', was irresistible.

*Gloria mundi.* It was owed, among other things, a seemly domestic establishment. Caught on the port one Sunday morning, she pointed out to me, quite sharply, that the Villa Tranquille was not up to it. What had those friends of mine, she said, done without a *potato ricer*? The German Sunday luncheon for people of any standing was a roast of veal. How lacking such an instrument were they supposed to make the mashed potatoes? Muttering 'eat gigot and flageolets' under my breath, I had fled.

Thomas, the fulcrum of it all, accepted in a remote, stiffly pompous, not entirely unhumorous way, the friends promising, neurotic, vacillating between worship and rebellion his elder children kept bringing in. All called him *Zauberer*, Magician. Well, he *had* conjured *Buddenbrooks*, *The Magic Mountain*, *Tonio Kröger* . . . So what if the Goethe legacy sat a little too self-consciously upon him, complete to the black poodle nestling sycophantically at his side? I *know*: I drove the poodle, always a Nico, across the United States of America, coast to coast, east to west, Princeton to Pacific Palisades, in the Manns' car through a dense heatwave in July of 1940 while his owner was crossing the continent in an air-cooled train. Logistics: the Manns wanted the car without the ride; the train would not take the dog inside a human compartment. I had days and days of it—oh

314

the endless flat roads on and on through the corn plains of the Middlewest, the cabins we slept in through the brief nights—rejected once or twice: 'No dawgs'—the ice-cold Coca-Cola at the gas stations, laced from the quart of rum I carried; the sweating hot-furred animal clinging to me the last link with the human world he knew. He pressed against my driving leg, he tried to follow me into the showers, I comforted him in the air-thin altitudes of New Mexico; when we crossed the desert, I laid ice packs on his curly head. When at last I was able to deliver him, to the drawing-room filled with people in the Manns' new house, Nico went straight to his master, sat down by his side, head in air. When presently I came up to say goodbye to him, he ignored me. Slightly turned his head away. But I saw the terror in his eyes: am I to be taken away again? He was even afraid to snap. I guessed what the Manns thought about the nature of our journey. But I understood.

When we met, which we did once or twice again, we ignored each other.

I must not give an impression that I ever was or could have been a friend of Thomas Mann's. The distance was and is immense. I met him inevitably on that overcrowded Sanary stage and a cat does look at a king. I was told that he commented with pained disapproval of my intended abandonment of what he devoutly called the German

315

*Sprachboden*, the ultimate foundation of his work. I had indeed intended not to write in German. The structure, the run of the grammar would not bend to the ways in which I should one day want to shape what I would try to write. (By the time I was twenty, I had got on paper some laborious pieces in French.) To get into one language deeply, I found, one has to forsake all others.

When eventually I had been put in charge of Nico and the Lincoln on that transatlantic episode, it was because the Manns believed that I was reliable with motor cars and used to dogs. I had just then fled invaded France, made New York, and was seeking means of getting to California where there would be friends. On arrival in the early morning on the day of our separate departures at the Manns' Princeton house for breakfast, the Master was standing on the doorstep, hands raised high in greeting with impersonal Olympian benevolence: *'Willkommen.'*

\*　　　\*　　　\*

As to Klaus and Erika, the sudden bond on that first meeting by the roadside lasted in one mode or another throughout their too short lives. With Erika—quick-headed, breezy, robust—it did not go further than a sporadic camaraderie; for Klaus I came to feel much affection. I loved him as a brother in many

316

situations and years to come. At the beginning there had emerged some discrepancy, not just in age—I was five or six years younger—in experiences. They had lived a thing or two, so had I; though in some ways I was backward, and backward those Mann children certainly were not. They were travelled, pursued, notorious, they had married—one actually, one nearly—each other's lovers, they counted high in the *enfants terribles* circle of the time. Klaus, an Adonis during his short adolescence, had quickly become a published author, saluted at first as a precocious talent, so that the huge shadow of his father's fame had not at once cast its destructive wing on the son's work. ('So you also write, Mr Mann,' had been said to Klaus for the hundredth and the last time at a party in Cannes on the eve of his final and successful attempt on his own life.) *All, all of a piece throughout: / The chase had an end in view* . . . Already on the early first encounter in the south of France, so long yet before he wrote *Mephisto* and *The Turning Point*, before his brave war—a volunteer in the US Army—before another and another of his fractured attachments (and the rough encounters), before the money had run out for the next of his literary magazines, the refusal to be linked again with a recovering Germany, the biting disillusion with the post-war world, before all of these one was aware of Klaus's romantic—and contagious—bond with suicide.

317

'Half in love with easeful death . . .'

Love? Compulsion, a spell? One comes to see the power of another aspect of the paternal inheritance: what the son carried out in persona, the father had been able to integrate as one of the sources of his works. Think of Doctor Faustus, of the years upon years on that Mountain, of the gruesome remission of Lotte in Weimar, of death in Venice.

# CHAPTER NINETEEN

*Recall of a domestic life*

Turning back to the Sanary of the early thirties when many of us there still lived as if what Cyril Connolly has called 'the closing of the pleasure gardens of the West' might not take place. 'Here all is exquisitely lovely', Aldous wrote to Juliette, his sister-in-law, 'sun, roses, fruit, warmth. We bathe and bask . . .'

Such summers lasted well into October, and when the Huxleys were in residence at that Villa Uley I sometimes stayed with them. For a few periods I was given the grace of being part of such a life; not as an observer or researcher: I write of it as what I lived.

What troubles me is that I have already written about Aldous and Maria's domestic days before. Substantially. First, the year after his death, in a piece for the *Memorial Volume*, then, a decade on, a full biography, facts dispersed or fused according to its demands. I wrote *con amore*, and within the rules. Ought this not be enough? I have decided it is not. Not for what they were; not for me. I want to leave if I can a condensation of what it was: a *good* life by *good* people, in my old words, here in this book, compressed, conflated, with a flash here and there of a subsequent perception.

\*       \*       \*

The houses in California are no more, one burned down, the others not in recognizable form; the house in the south of France is still standing . . . shut up and in disrepair . . . For the stranger by the fence there is not much to see; a whitewashed house of no particular style, pleasant enough if of uncertain proportions . . . For the visitor from the past, the survivor, that residuum still bears the marks of a life that was once lived there.

There is the eucalyptus tree and the stumpy palms from which the hammocks used to swing. Here they came out into the timeless summer nights: Aldous; Maria; Matthew, then a small boy; the friend or two who usually stayed at the house.

Beethoven's first piano concerto played by Schnabel on the brief records of the hand-wound gramophone, and presently silence, leaves, the sky; then, as animation struck, Aldous talking in his clear voice, clear as a silver bell . . .

That Mauresque cube housed the fire-engine-red Bugatti Maria drove with such exquisite precision, and at that time *speed*. ('The only *new* sensation this wretched century has produced,' Aldous would say with relish.) He loved speed, which for him meant being driven fast. And above this garage is the studio built when Aldous began to paint regularly. In summer he painted every day in the blazing Mediterranean noon between lunch and tea. He had the flat roof whitewashed to deflect the sun and noted with satisfaction that the temperature inside did go down two degrees centigrade. Aldous used to have a model, so Maria, or Sophie their niece, a little girl of Matthew's age, or a friend, would sit for him. To make things pleasant for the sitter, one of us always read aloud. Aldous liked to paint and listen in one. Maria, whose English had a very individual cadence, had acquired a knack of reading extremely fast and without any expression whatsoever. Considering that what we read was never short—*Anna Karenina, Joseph Andrews*, half a shelf of Henry James—this was probably just as well. Victoria Ocampo, the Argentinian patroness of art who often came to stay, read excellently, but covered less ground. Moreover, as she was so very beautiful, she was required to sit rather than read. Once Aldous thought he would like to have a go again at *The Egoist*, but after one or two sessions Meredith was given up as unsuitable to high-speed reading.

The current of the house went with Aldous's working day. Breakfast about ten o'clock and everybody came down for it. There was China tea and it did not taste like tea in France because the Earl Grey was sent from Piccadilly and the water filtered. Aldous and Maria throughout their lives had an ambivalent attitude toward food (in theory and practice), Maria sometimes going through periods of positive revulsion, yet what was put before one in their house was never less than decent and good, and often quite delicious. (Roast duck and peas for Aldous's birthday.) It could also be eccentric. They were apt to fall for diets. At one time it had been the Hay diet (no mixing of proteins and starch at any one meal), and when that had been abandoned they still stuck for some reason to the Hay breakfast formula. So for many years there were two bare boiled eggs each one morning and no bread at all; toast, butter and jam next morning, but no egg. The jam, home-made, was mostly rose or quince. Maria would have been up for hours: looking after her artichoke bushes and scented tuberoses in the garden; Aldous still a bit groggy with sleep was comfortably silent. (Not in the mode of his formidable silences that extinguished talk.) There was no post. The delivery came at noon and even then no one seemed to wish to look at it at once. There were no papers. Aldous took no English newspapers at all. He subscribed to one Paris daily, and that too arrived later in the day. Yet Aldous always seemed to know pretty much what was going on—something Baldwin had said, the new unemployment figures, Musso's last speech, another French scandal, 'Poor old Tardieu . . .' 'Those Nazi lunatics . . .' His comments were summary and resigned. There were, inevitably, stacks of literary reviews sent to him from all over the world. The most part remained piled on a sofa not only unread but unopened. The only periodical coming to him on his own initiation was *Nature*.

Soon after ten, Aldous got up without a murmur and went to his room; the door shut behind him. It was a good-sized room, square, with well-shuttered windows on two sides and book cases up to the ceiling. The floor was red-tiled and bare. There was a roll-top desk with a swivel-chair, a very long chaise-longue and one deep armchair. Here, on a small typewriter, he wrote *Brave New World, Music at Night*—perhaps the most serene of his books—*Beyond the Mexique Bay*, and large parts of the far from serene *Eyeless in Gaza*. It was a good room, with its easy privacy and pacing space; it had all a writer needed, including the 1911 edition of the *Encyclopoedia Britannica*. Once during some winter months when the Huxleys were away, I was allowed to work in that room myself, and I have never known a better.

There was a gong for luncheon. First one went to bathe, walking the few minutes down to the pebbly beach on the bay, deserted at that hour. The children were already in the water. Aldous who carried the rubber boat was cheerfully anchored still, one felt, in his morning's work but ready for the break, willing to join the talk. From May into September, they swam every day and sometimes again at night, but there was never any oiling or mindless lying in the sun. One walked back, dressed—Aldous: khaki shorts, sandals, Egyptian cotton shirt—ate lunch. Off a rather disconcertingly modernistic table, designed for them, a long rectangle with a looking-glass surface; one saw oneself eating at an unusual angle. The midday leisure was neither hurried nor long—Aldous might tell some stories; he was well up on the local lore. Two of his favourites were Mademoiselle Casanova—a *jeune fille* with that actual surname, who Aldous swore was a boy in disguise, and Général Rose who at ninety built a folly for his mistress in a newly extended street officially called Boulevard du Plaisir Prolongé. There were often guests. The house ran with a civilized simplicity. In those years they still had the Italian servants who had followed them on their move from Italy. Rina, who had come to them at fourteen straight from herding goats, Rina plump and cheerful who was caught once with her hand in the pudding (whereupon she and Maria cried in each other's arms), Rina, who had learned to read and calculate, married to a neighbour's chauffeur, ran her husband's transport business through the war and after, inherited some of Aldous's paintings, one of Gerald Heard, as well as the two life-sized portraits of Aldous and Maria by his uncle Sir Laurence Collier; Rina who in middle-age travelled through the whole of France to comfort Maria, alone in an hotel in Paris a few months before her death. In the Villa Uley days there also was Rina's young sister, Camilla, savagely shy, and later Giulia, stately, mature, with a Roman profile and inflexible probity. Maria loved them. They loved Maria and the master, *il signore*, '*E tanto buono!*' they would say: he is *so good*.

They, too, were part of the tone: the courtesy, ease and dignity of all human commerce in that house.

After luncheon, the studio; or in the cooler seasons, the rarer hours of sunshine, the long walks. Aldous who officially, medically, could hardly see at all (consultants today still wax quite angry if you try to mention the Bates' Method) seemed to see much that we ignored: the caterpillar on the twig, the early leaf, the changing colour of the hills . . . And he enjoyed it so. Return. Five minutes granted. Standing or on a stool. China tea again and, invariably, some ginger-nuts. Then once more: work. Until about seven or half-past. On Thursdays Aldous had to write his bread-and-butter article for an American magazine. I think it was *Vanity Fair* and I think that he was paid the then very respectable sum of £10 a piece. He could write on whatever he liked. Maria used to explain that this arrangement came to £500 a year and ran the house and car for them. Although, after the penurious first years in London, the Huxleys always lived in decent comfort, they spent a good deal less on themselves than what they spent on others: his and her families, friends and supplicants, they must have regularly helped and kept a dozen individuals. Aldous did not like doing that weekly stint. He was supposed to be grumpy on Thursday morning; in fact he was too even-tempered and controlled to show anything except a more marked withdrawal. Yet those days must have been a strain—the effort of slicing into a new subject; the worry of getting it done and *there* in time—no e-mail, no faxes, to say nothing of the interruption of work in progress. By evening it was done, for Maria to drive it to the post-box at Bandol for the last collection.

Aldous used to complain about himself as a fairly slow writer in terms of Arnold Bennett's daily thousand. Actually he must have averaged five hundred words a day (less than Maugham, more than Greene, more or less than Proust?) and this with very great regularity. Every day he was at home, not ill, not on a journey, he worked. The notion of a workless weekend did not exist.

At dinner there was a sense of release, of being lightly *en fête*. One of their recreations in those years was dining with friends—in their own house on Maria's looking-glass table, at Edith Wharton's or Charles de Noailles's houses at Hyères, at their Sanary and Bandol neighbours, at the Kislings', the Willie Seabrooks', at my painter friend's, at the Meier-Graefes' at Saint-Cyr. And there were the picnics, those Huxleys picnics at sundown on beach or olive grove or cliff, when Matthew and Sophie and the fast and handsome Sanary young mixed with startled middle-aged French and ruffled eminent Germans. Never shall I forget the sight of Mrs Wharton, rotund, corseted, flushed and beautifully dressed, Paul Valéry and Madame Paul Valéry, frail sexagenarians, being led by Aldous towering and hesitatingly encouraging up a goat track on a rock face to the nonchalantly chosen picnic ground. There they would be given fried rabbit, zucchini flowers, and jugs of iced punch—white wine, lemon, rum—made by Aldous himself. There would be games under the Mediterranean darkness—often a kind of rather personal blind man's-bluff. Sometimes Aldous sang.

It seemed a good life for a writer. For a time it had a sense of solidity. I wished that it would go on for ever, that this was what life could be made to be. Aldous probably knew that it could not. The years passed and the bad news moved on . . . Even without the foreboding of what was approaching us, the Villa Uley existence would come to an end. Aldous was running towards something else, and it was not basking or scepticism. Yet those years must have been good ones for him; years of stable health and tranquil working, healing years between the wars, between the damaging losses of his youth and the struggles and losses later on. They *seemed* happy years. I was too young to know. For me then it was Aldous's intelligence that was the *ne plus ultra*; I was dazzled by his books (and what I took for their message); what I loved was the intellectual surface, the rest I took for granted: never a harsh word between Aldous and Maria; nor between them and others; the atmosphere of order, gaiety and grace; took for granted Aldous's unfailing goodwill, his patience, his readiness to help, the absence in him of any trace of pretentiousness or pomposity, his inability to lie or hate, to form a petty thought or a malevolent emotion, his fortitude. Only now can I see him then as the man who practised what he later preached. *Era tanto buono.*

# CHAPTER TWENTY

## *Hubris*

And what are we going to do about it? Klaus Mann, more active perhaps in 1933 than some European governments, moved every connection he had to bring out a new literary review. Purpose: giving a voice to the new diaspora. He succeeded. The language was to be German; the publisher Dutch: Querido, large and prestigious. Klaus, sole editor, moved to Amsterdam. He wanted impressive sponsors. He got those too. They were Heinrich Mann, very much endorsed as a major writer of the left, and perceived as less clannish as uncle than the father; André Gide, then near the height of his flirtation with Soviet ideology—his *Retour de l'URSS* just come out; and docile, if of small faith, Aldous Huxley. Their names looked well on the masthead. The title of the new review was *Die Sammlung*. (The nearest English word is 'the collection' but this lacks the German somewhat spiritual undertone of 'recollection'.) Klaus was a competent and dedicated editor and there was no lack of distinguished and internationally recognized contributors. The review almost at once attracted the notice, and some very black marks indeed, from the powers now ruling Germany. Coinciding with the first issue in 1934, Huxley's Central American travel book, *Beyond the Mexique Bay*, was published. I asked Klaus if he'd consider my writing about it: not just a review, an essay, a think-piece as we would say now. Klaus generously said yes. He knew I had published nothing at all before (my first novel had been turned down quite recently). I would be writing in English, and if it were accepted I would try to get it into German. One day there was a letter from Amsterdam saying that *Die Sammlung* had taken my contribution. Rapture. I had put into it about everything I ever thought I thought and the pages were bristling with quotations, beginning, I blush to remember, with Paul Valéry: *'La bêtise n'est pas mon fort'* . . . (fortunately put into Aldous's mouth, not mine). *Unfortunately* I had also dragged in words of my own, words hardly germane to a context of the paradoxes and absurdities of Mexico . . . There was one outspoken aggressive paragraph attacking current Nazi horrors. These indeed had been the themes of several other contributors, grandees of exile; I was aware of the futility of one by myself. I merely wanted—very strongly—to stand up and be counted (or more likely not).

Lion Feuchtwanger, the mainstay of the radical and prosperous clique of refugees, viveur and show off, well-known bestseller of two continents—whose writing I despised— put me on the carpet to tell me line by line how lousy my German was. I told him haughtily that I had originally written the piece in English which he assured me was not much better either: juvenile in concept, clumsy in execution. He was able to edit the translation of his novels whenever they were chosen for some hugely lucrative award, and was paid five dollars for every word he cut. An excellent bargain, he said smugly, German being so much longer. I knew *that.* He was smug, the little Lion, as his friends and detractors called him (he was *small* and short); smug about his

330

literary standing: he and Sinclair Lewis were the greatest novelists of the century, he told me; smug about his women—he had a good many, mistresses and casuals as well as a loyal and efficient wife; all were attractive, some beautiful. He did attract them, though many tried to deny having been to bed with him. He was smug about his wines. He did know about great wine. And liked being a good host.

During that dressing-down the little Lion gave me, I found out that he had a kind teacher's streak: he was holding a benevolent tutorial. My grammar and style pained him. Too bad that however inadequate I feared my own writing might be, I was not willing to accept the patiently suggested improvements from that source. (My kind of pride?) About that extraneous partisan passage he had said nothing at all.

When I wrote it, I did not think of consequences; if I had, I would have written it all the same. (The self-importance of idealists, so called.)

Consequences there came. Not at once. At the time the Hitler regime's prey were seen to be mainly Communists and full-fledged Jews; in fact the mills of oppression were already grinding slow and small. One early morning I received the brief information that any money I was holding had been confiscated.

That money: all I could ever expect, the capital from my father's estate, the release of which, legal if slow and subject to an export penalty, had been under negotiation by bankers and middlemen (conventional bureaucracy appeared to be still ticking on) was gone. Irrevocably it became clear. They— the régime—had taken connaissance of my partly Jewish descent. (I don't know to this day the actual percentage or exact provenance of my Jewish blood.) They would know now that I was associating with the prominent opposition, quite a few out and out Communists among them. They would not have looked if there hadn't been the insistent evidence in that review. There would be further consequences. Once one was on a black list . . . (How proud I was then, selfish young fool.) I still had no papers other than a German passport—musty brown paper with a kind of eagle on the cover—the French having done nothing at all about my application to become one of them. That passport had a year or so to run. Could I step then into a German consulate? Would I? I would not.

On that first morning of the news I was staying in the back country with my painter who was still asleep, and about to drive a crate of dawn-picked vegetables down to the Huxleys. Feeling more dazed than shocked, I arrived at their breakfast table. They knew as I knew that there was only a small, a very small, amount left of the cash Maria had smuggled out of Germany for me a couple of years before.

(Friends had helped to make it go so slowly: my painter more or less had kept me; Pierre Mimerel's garage put the petrol into my Ford.) Maria, very shocked, gave me some breakfast, to Aldous, very sleepy, she said, now we must all help Sybille. I? Gradually took it in.

*     *     *

During that period while adjustments and plans were more or less hanging fire, my sister Jacko also was causing anxiety. Vague, undiscussed. She had stayed at Sanary, moving into a modest little house by the beach at Port Issol. That something had gone wrong with her sun-god husband, one had felt for some time. Ask I could not. Infidelities there had been on both sides. Her affair with Pierre seemed to have petered out; she now saw a great deal of the Mimerels and their world of well-connected Parisian friends, a world fairly detached from the German refugees. When they talked politics at all, it was on the lines of 'Those ranters across the Rhine are bound to pipe down sooner or later . . . Meanwhile look at how they're solving their unemployment problem, look at their economy, their industry . . . Poor France . . .' When they mentioned Jacko's husband, it was as one of us. Such a good tennis partner. His absence? Some marital trouble quite likely.

Jacko living—for her—quite unextravagantly

did not exactly discuss my predicament, but tried to help by offering to knit something fluffy and elegant to fling over shoulders on cool evenings. (I got *my* will with a navy-blue pullover.) What it made flash through my mind though was: they've gone through her money. It had to come, oh well . . .

Meanwhile Aldous had read Meier-Graefe's *Spanish Journey* and longed to see El Grecos *sur place* himself. So did my painter. Thus it came about that late in the autumn the four of us were in Madrid. (Republican Spain pre-civil war.) It turned out an exhilarating and happy time. We took to what we saw. Long mornings in the Prado; hours in front of that miraculous painting, the *Burial of Count d'Orgaz*, at Toledo: excursions to Avila, to the Escurial; evenings of ease, theatre, late dinners, talk, affection, laughter . . . Come-uppance set in the morning we left Madrid for the flight back. We thought we had booked return by Air France, instead waiting for us sat a plane with a huge swastika painted on its tail, a Lufthansa plane. (The German line which alternated with the French.) So now, there I went again. I refused to travel in a Nazi plane. Aldous said it would be a fairly futile protest but gave way to my emotional indulgence. (My painter—of Jewish origin—shared my feelings.) There was no French flight on that day, so after some discussion and delays, a Spanish craft was rolled out. It was small. I did not see other passengers. It flew off all right. One settled down. After a while something happened: the plane made a sideways lurch and dropped, just dropped, to what looked like a few metres above ground and slowly clattered on. I had flown only once before, a neat efficient wafting from Zürich to Marseilles—a strange brief sensation that first *décollage*—one *is* in air . . . No images of Leonardo or Icarus had come to mind. So now: only an enquiring glance at my friends. For reassurance. None came. Instead, a sudden shattering engine noise. Persistent. (From *one* engine, it became clear: the other had shut off.) In that roar we slowly lopsided, hugging the rocky contours of the Costa Brava, just clearing bathing huts and cliffs, limped on. Minute after minute . . . After an hour or so, the pilot made Barcelona airport. Ambulance and a fire engine were waiting. We were helped down from the plane. Some Lufthansa personnel were also standing by—they saluted, faces closed, correct, irony just perceptible. Who could blame them?

We had planned to spend the rest of the day and the night at Barcelona. So we took a taxi to the hotel where we had reservations. It came as a bit of a surprise that it was still not yet very late in the morning. Dangers passed make for resilience: we had an enjoyable day—changed clothes, went sightseeing, sat in cafés—someone round a corner threw a bomb, sirens blared, 'Nihilists,' Aldous said with mild disapproval at such enthusiasm. That evening we were served a large *paella* in an animated restaurant. Next morning, we took the Air France flight back home.

*     *     *

And that turned out not so innocuous as one might expect. We were sitting in a still noiseless plane on some corner of the airfield, waiting for our start to take-off point. Aldous and I were sitting side by side behind a tall couple: one could see the back of their heads, showing well-groomed hair. The woman in a clear upper-class German voice was saying:

> *'Na, der D. ist also jetzt unser Kultur Attaché an der Pariser Botschaft.'*
> (Well, that D. is now Cultural Attaché at our Paris embassy.)

'D.' The woman had not, as I do, left it at the initial. D. was the surname of my sister's husband.

> *'Der kann doch nix,'* the man said. 'Fellow's never done a stroke of anything, our lot would have kicked him out if he'd showed his face at the Foreign Office.'
> 'Maybe they owe him now . . . There always was that rumour of his having been mixed up with some extreme right-

wing students' gang during our Revolution, so-called . . . Gave a hand when they put down the Communist putsch, some say he was in at the Rosa Luxemburg murder . . .'

'Too young,' he said. 'He may have been there—standing guard by the wall . . . ?'

'When the woman tried to get away through a window,' she said. 'You make me shiver. He's not the type. Not his scene. And a bit late to cash in . . . Mind, he's *very* decorative . . . international polish . . . adds up to a reassuring presence for the French. But aren't we forgetting that his wife is Jewish . . . ?'

'Half. Her mother was a Herz. Stinking rich—some time ago that was. Still rather prominent that lot: Herzes, Schwabachs, Bleichröders, bankers, financiers . . . Helped building the Kaiser's Reich . . . They couldn't possibly have a descendant now at a diplomatic post.'

She said, 'You know, I think I hear that the D.s are divorced. No one outside Germany is supposed to know.'

'Ah . . . that would square it. Racial purity at home, liberal attitudes abroad. A quick quiet divorce arranged by our authorities.'

'But would *she* take it—?'

At this point our engine sprang into noise, we began to roll off.

I looked at Aldous. I knew he had understood. (Aldous had picked up many languages here and there.) He put his hand inside his coat and pulled out that throwback to Edwardian habits, the leather-bound travelling flask; the man who did not drink spirits, who was near to allergic to whisky, carried a small neat flask of brandy. He unscrewed the cap and held it over to me. I drank.

*       *       *

Tears came later. At other hours, other days. Alone, in Maria's arms. Not Jacko's. I knew I should not, could not speak to Jacko about what I soon learned was essentially true. It fitted like some mathematical proposition: Jacko and D. had come to the end of her money; D. wanted to continue a life in the sun; D. obtained a minor diplomatic post by reason of the reassuring impression of a menacing regime he might give to some fairly grand French friends and connections of his part-Jewish wife (my sister—Frau Baronin, etc.— moved in circles quite different from mine); on the other hand a wife with evident Jewish blood *en poste* was not acceptable *inside* the new Germany; hence necessity of an immediate divorce on racial grounds, with

338

equal necessity of concealing this divorce from the ex-wife's French connections.

Query—how to obtain the connivance, the consent, the discretion of the discarded wife? They were far yet from the stage of sending some undercover Gestapo agent to the other end of France; and besides the whole thing was such a very minor matter, a tiny lick of gloss on a wide-strung construct of positive impressions. (Admittedly though, the chap was made for the job, an effective charmer, a ruthless social butterfly with a heart of steel, ignorant of ideals, other humans' pains.) As it happened there was no problem. Jacko vaguely hinted about some new woman—these things happen in the best of marriages: it will pass. She stayed on the Côte for the present, he in Paris, turning up quite frequently to see her. That they were no longer legally man and wife was not allowed to enter anyone's mind. My sister kept that divorce a secret. That too might be put into an equation: he wanted what was to him a glamorous life; he could not have it with her. She loved him—*that* I knew—loyalty was in order. She could show great strength, my sister.

As for myself, I just managed not to let on about what I overheard in that aeroplane. I admitted her fortitude, but could not love her as we had loved each other in my childhood and after. If she was *against* what was currently going on in Germany, she did not *detest* it

339

enough. This grieved me. Also I felt contaminated. During the next few years, we went on seeing each other. The friends we shared were the Mimerels and their visitors. There was an estrangement, one-sided perhaps, not open.

*      *      *

Jacko's silence held until the edge of the war. Her husband's actual position became general knowledge quite soon after our Spanish journey. The refugees had their network too. Some women were actually afraid to be noticed by D. on his visits. He was suspected to be an agent in diplomat's disguise come to abduct them. (Such things had happened, though not from the depth of Provençal France hundreds of miles from Rhine frontiers.) I avoided meeting him. Not always successfully. His job was about *culture*, Jacko told us, bringing him to dinner at my painter's house. Once—disarming charm disarms—he made his own way to a cup of tea at Maria Huxley's.

*      *      *

I, somewhat half-heartedly, had attempted to cope with my 'altered circumstances' by trying to earn a little money. This was achieved by going to London now and then where I had introductions to some—a growing number—of wise, middle-aged German Jews, professionals who had succeeded in leaving the Third Reich unscathed and still relatively rich. Their aim: the United States. They had immigration papers but no adequate English. The idea was that I might be able to give them a crash-course in easy, competent everyday speech. It worked. These tycoons and their families: wives, mistresses, sons ready to prepare for college, turned out to be clever, able, educated people, generous employers who became in my case friends. I discovered that I much enjoyed, and had an aptitude for, teaching. I craftily avoided having to write anything down by my own hand, and skated over spelling. They were trusting. (There were no blackboards in my clients' hotel suites.) I had one or two pupils per lesson and tailored methods to individual capacity and needs. Spoken words for some, others liked to read. With one man, an art-dealer of wide reputation, I improvised shop-talk to custodians and collectors; everyone, including the women, handsomely turned out and good-looking, was taught to be pleasant and competent when ordering in restaurant or bar. Our reading matter, beside newspapers, tabloids as well as *The Times*, were couplets of nonsense verse, easy to remember as well as a link of German Wilhelm Busch or Morgenstern to English Lewis Carroll and

Edward Lear. For prose we often read chunks of Hemingway or E. M. Forster. The fee for a private lesson then would be five shillings an hour or could be as low as 3/6 or even 2/6. I was paid 7/6 which felt and was quite a lot. They were open-handed my pupils, my friends.

I worked all hours. (Put up mostly in cheap lodgings, shades of Toni and Rosie.) When I got enough money together—this would have taken a couple of months, more or less, enough to see me through a good length of time, I would leave (with my pupils up to passing the US Immigration test), leave for home. Back to Sanary.

Once someone persuaded a London hostess that she needed me as a social secretary. A live-in job. I suspected that it must include my writing letters, answering invitations, cards and such. *I* wanted to write, was in fact starting a new novel. I said no, and instead—my painter friend having gone to New York, commissioned to do cartoons of politicians—went to spend the winter with the Mimerels.

## CHAPTER TWENTY-ONE

*A pleasant retreat—And a likely story!*

That turned out a peaceful and for me, so I believed, productive time. A well-ordered

342

existence in a spacious, impeccably kept white house, whitewashed inside and out, set among olive trees, well off the road, well beyond earshot of neighbours' sounds, comfort achieved by simple designs, wide sun-faced windows abolishing frontiers between room, trees and sky. That house was a product of an architect who knew to serve Oriane's modernistic affinities, and of her father's money. The result might have been hard. It was not. Living inside was living in nature without the roughness of the out-of-doors. Our routines were fastidious and calming.

Those were the last years of Pierre's and Oriane's marriage; neither of them knew this. For him, post-Jacko, Simone not met, it was going on doing the expected thing. For Oriane, still perilously acting out her extra-marital intrigues, Pierre was her pillar for life. Companion, protector. Of course she loved him. In *her* fashion; don't we all? The Jacko affair discreetly conducted—had met amused acceptance. The two women professed to be and were great friends. My position was different. There was still the gap of age between us—about ten years, but I was grown-up. My infatuation, so tiresome as well as fuel to her exhibitionism, was long extinct. I had become fond of her, and she of me. With all our various and quite different faults, we had a place in each other's lives: we too *were* friends. Not equals. With her unquenchable bovarism,

Oriane needed to find a new role for me: the page out of *Rosenkavalier* had become a fond joke between us (a flicker of a court, rejected yet once paid, sometimes remains); and so what now? She soon found it: I became for her '*mon jeune écrivain*', her young writer, whose career she nursed.

Well, in fact so she did—and Pierre—with their generous, their extravagant, hospitality through that winter. And there *was* a pinch of irony in her instruction to the *femme de ménage* to dust but lightly the sheaf of pages rising on my desk—'*Ne touchez pas ses oeuvres.*' They were rising those pages, the foothills of my second novel in front of which shone the ignis fatuus of an unexpected hope. Earlier, I had written a short story which Maria had pushed Aldous into showing to his American publisher, Cas Canfield, the head of Harpers, in Europe on a visit, for an opinion on the viability of a literary future for me. (Maria used to put that question—'Will Sybille make it?' on the visits to her various fortune-tellers.) Cas Canfield read the typescript on board ship home. In due course came a letter saying Harpers might be interested in publishing a full-length novel on the subject of that story. I squashed sloth and doubt, and sat down to write.

It got finished, and it had got long. But what was it like? And what was it about? A young man without slender means who loved art and

344

travel and felt badly about wasting daily hours of our short allotted span shut up in an office. (One of my seeds must have been the thought of T. S. Eliot's working in a bank.) My young man was a mere consumer, not a poet, no talent to waste, just down-hearted to be in the City of London when he longed to be at Chartres or in the Uffizi or in an Etruscan cave. Not exactly a universal need—as Aldous pointed out to me. (By letter.) My young man was spotted by a financier of great wealth and a somewhat convoluted wickedness who derived pleasure from hatching schemes, elaborate or petty, for humiliating and destabilizing people of whichever station, sex or age. He researched his specimens, their weaknesses and desires. He baited traps. Money was no object. The name I gave him was Procuransky, which was about as far as inventiveness went; a cardboard figure for the plot. I haven't lain eyes on the thing I wrote all of some seventy years ago and don't wish to. It turned up recently among some papers in the attic of a friend in France who had died, and the lawyer just shipped the lot to a Texas archive. Yet I still remember Mr P., who spends his leisure setting up recondite situations, getting on to our young man—I called him Francis—and finds him to be an insouciant atheist, say agnostic. 'One can never be quite sure in such matters, can one?' 'Quite,' says Mr P. and offers him a Faustian pact. A thousand a year—or was it twelve hundred? In return: a paper leaving his soul, or whatever retains consciousness, after his death, to the relevant authority or powers, if and where these exist, be they God, Demon, Devil, or omnipotent snake. 'A gamble,' says Mr P. 'Well hardly,' thinks our Francis. 'Perhaps,' says Mr P. who doesn't believe in anything much himself. 'All the same it will be interesting to see how you will come to feel about it. Well worth the money.' 'To *me*,' the young man thinks, 'and anyway it's all great nonsense.' And so a document is executed, complete with every legal quibble. The young man gives up his job, starts some travelling, rents an agreeable villa in Italy, invites his highbrow friends.

He begins an affair with a ravishing woman about twice his age . . . Soon he also sends to the London Library for an increasing number of theological books. Monotheistic, pantheistic, deistic . . . 'Rigmaroles', he thinks, 'no proof of anything really'. Yet men went on crusades, burned each other on the stakes . . . (*I* meanwhile had been looking it all up in Aldous's *Britannica* and found some scary stuff indeed. So I attempted to turn some of it into a novel of ideas.) The young man tries to chase it all away: there just could not be a possible connection with a scroll of tape-tied legalese . . . *Carpe diem* . . . The day went easier though with a drink in hand . . . 'Who's for a Bloody

346

Mary before we go to the beach?' Soon he tells a friend or two; they shrug it off yet seem to feel uncomfortable. He sees a doctor, for sleeping pills that is, though eventually he tells him; an abstruse anecdote. The doctor won't believe him; the next one, English, turns puritanical and gives him a dressing-down: he ought to see a psychiatrist. Eventually he does that too. Meanwhile he had told his mistress who turned scared and superstitious: he should see a priest. He does. More than one. A year or so elapses . . . Heavy drinking does not help by then. In due course, inevitably one might think, he starts on drugs. Morphine, what else? We have the acceleration and the cure, we have the recovery and the flatness after the recovery. We have the relapse and the railway station with the nurse in charge and the fast train coming in—will he end like Anna Karenina or did he only think of her when he hears the monster roar? I have forgotten which. Harpers turned the book down.

True accounts of my literary career are on the ironic side. In England at the time, Jonathan Cape considered publishing that novel. I was summoned by the great man to discuss it. He had his doubts, all the same he *might* venture . . . The decision was left to three editors. Two went against, one for.

As to Cas Canfield, he, almost two decades on, published the first of my books to reach that status. It went off, I believe, to some mutual satisfaction. Harpers then took the option on my next, *A Legacy:* Canfield read the typescript as was his wont on board ship . . . He is known to have said it was the most boring novel it had ever been his fate to have to read. Of course he turned it down. That was not the end of our seesaw. Another twenty years on or so he became co-publisher (with Alfred Knopf) of my Huxley biography on cordial terms. On the launch at the St Regis Hotel, homage was offered to three top American women writers of the time, Mary McCarthy, Janet Flanner and Hannah Arendt, each seated in a deep chair placed around the same big column, each with their queue of admirers lined up in front of them to pay homage. I, fond of all three in different ways, joined each queue in turn. Afterwards Cas Canfield bore me off to a private dinner party at his house: salmon trout and hock, agreeable intelligent men. *Sic transiunt miseriae mundi.*

# CHAPTER TWENTY-TWO

## *Nemesis*

While I was still wrestling with the poor young man's potential hells, the expiry date of my passport was getting nearer. The situation was serious. What does become of the ever-growing number of men and women without the right papers or no papers at all? There had come into being at that time a second version of the Nansen Passport for credible political refugees, a lifebuoy which assisted but by no means guaranteed the passage of frontiers or a Resident's Permit. That I would qualify for this document was more than doubtful. Lie doggo, as some friends advised, and hope that the French would shut their eyes on the expiry of my *carte d'identité* (issued only on the basis of the foreign nationals holding their own country's passport)? Dicey—at the mercy of a petty official or an anonymous letter to the Préfecture; the locals were prolific in poison-pen complaints. There were already far too many foreigners in Sanary. A go at reviving my old naturalization application? Pretty hopeless. It would need much powerful support over a very long time. Not the right moment, my French friends said. There was England: a British passport! What a superb idea. I did see myself by then—obstinately—as an English writer. One would have to go to England, live there, apply after five years, and then . . . Here I baulked. This was not where I was going to have my life . . . Five years away from the Mediterranean. At that impasse came news. Of Erika Mann. She had gone and married an Englishman. *He* had made the offer: a staunch anti-Fascist, anti-Nazi to the core; a young man, youngish, nearer thirty

349

than twenty, she thought, homosexual of course, had to be in the circumstances: a *mariage blanc*. She had been told that he greatly admired her father. His name was Ohden or something—she would keep her own name of course, his first name sounded odd.

That was Erika's account, as conveyed to her family. What was told by an eyewitness was the following: Erika, having received the offer of a helping hand to an instant passport, had arrived in England by boat train. Her first visit—the Mann children's Anglo-Saxon experiences had been American. Half a dozen young Englishmen were standing on the platform at Folkestone. Erika called out, 'Which of you is it?' The groom stepped forward. Whereupon she hooked her arm into his, pulled him aside and said heartily, 'Fine, let's go and get married.' The supporting cast rather gaped; Wystan Auden is reported to have taken it in his stride.

She got the passport, eventually grasped his identity; they became great friends.

*         *         *

Maria Huxley saw the solution for me and set to work. 'We must get one of our bugger friends to marry Sybille.' (That was the almost affectionate term Bloomsbury used for their friends; when it applied. Queer was genteel. It happened to be about the only Bloomsbury speak Maria had taken on and it rather amused Aldous.) The friends, however, were not at all keen. Oh, they thought it was a sensible thing to do and much applauded Auden's having rescued Thomas Mann's daughter. They also saw that such unions might lead to awkwardness in the future: even if one was not, one might feel that one ought to be, responsible. More so than to a mere friend. Ties tie. One candidate said he would 'if only she had two or three hundred a year of her own'. Maria related it all in letters to me, as the Huxleys were in London at that point. Not to worry was the general message: they were looking now for someone not quite so much 'in our world'.

She talked to their window-cleaner, a sweet young man, devoted to Maria, who would do anything she asked and had no wish to marry for his own sake as it were. He *was* a British subject. She didn't actually know from where, the West Indies probably, possibly from Africa . . . Aldous wasn't quite certain he would do. They decided to consult a great friend of mine to whom they referred—perhaps because he was like me too fond of food and wine—as 'Sybille's barrister'. They got on to him, he responded, and so I shall have to drag him into this ambivalent tale.

He was indeed a barrister at that juncture, though not for long. His articulate life had

351

begun with a scholarship to Winchester; at Oxford he *taught* Greek before reading for the Bar. A great future was predicted for him in the judiciary, in government, or where lay perhaps his deepest inclination, in academia. Eventually he became a highly successful grey eminence in the financial world. He died early, some twenty years ago, felled by the sudden death of his second wife. He was good-looking, with a mobile youthful head which reminded one of something between a cherub and a perky bird. His intelligence was as alert as it was incisive, never solemn. He had a fearful temper. This, one feared. He also had an easy, joyful laugh. I was extremely fond of him; often in awe; and for brief intervals attracted. In some of the pre-war years—between his marriages—he used to spend the summer holiday with us at my painter's place. Our friendship lasted to the end of his life. In more recent years, I used to run into his son at London wine tastings, speak to him on the telephone: he has his father's voice, an unexpectedly light voice—the same emphasis, the civilized case, the almost inaudible chuckle. The past is able to return to us by means of many triggers.

I will give no name to this friend I owe much to. If Aldous had been blamed for his involvement in the events I shall presently try to account for, he would not have noticed nor been harmed in any way that mattered to him.

I'm not sure that this would be so in the case of a man, alive or not, who had been a member of the Bar at the relevant time (and quite conscious of what he was letting himself so generously in for). He has, as I said, a son and other various progeny, and is known and regarded in circles which may nowadays well be hostile to his actions at the time. So I have chosen a synonymous first name orthographically allusive to him in round-about ways—Lysander.

Lysander put his foot down on the Huxleys' first proposition. One would have to look for someone of a more sophisticated milieu, someone less innocent, less altruistic in fact. This they did and quite soon found a designer friend who had a butler who had a friend— ex-friend in fact, a decent chap they would quite like to do a good turn to. He *was* hard up. And had grasped enough about the Nazi menace to behave sympathetically and fade back into his own existence. He also had the residence necessary for a fiancé-in-waiting. So Lysander saw to the necessary bureaucratic steps and I was summoned to England. Pierre Mimerel decided to come with me. I *was* nervous. We, so he said, might as well try to kill two birds with one stone: a schoolmate of his (Condorcet, Polytechnique, now an entrepreneur) was holding a concession for the recent cooking-cum-heating medium, bottled gas, and offering Pierre the opportunity to persuade rural England to warm itself by this novel device. Pierre would have the UK agency, I would act as his interpreter on a trial to set it up. Pierre's English was rudimentary . . . (His coastal busline meanwhile pursuing its expensive runs.) We set off by train and Channel crossing, and settled into a residential hotel in the Cromwell Road, Kensington; separate rooms, not adjoining, all on Lysander's advice. The Huxleys were at their London pied-à-terre, at Albany, Piccadilly. (Originally a set of chambers for bachelors, now bisexual flats for distinguished people. Still no dogs, no children, cats and birds selectively, busts of Byron and Macaulay in the vestibule.) E2 ground floor—never shall I forget that address. Next day on my own I went there. A man was standing in the drawing-room. Maria said, 'This is Terry.' I did not look at him in any focused way; later I took in someone on the handsome side, in his thirties probably, rather more masculine than Maria's b. friends. Then he and I were sent off to the registrar's office to fill in the form for a marriage licence. We trotted off. He guided me into a bus. My mother would have carried it off; so might Maria. (Lysander was in a rage when he learned of the arrangement: *the groom should have applied on his own.*) Eventually we got to standing at a counter with the clerk behind it requesting our particulars. He appeared neither affable nor interested.

NAME I wrote mine down.
FATHER'S NAME I wrote that too.
MOTHER'S NAME I wrote it.
FATHER'S OCCUPATION Well what? I wrote: 'Landowner'.
Now the groom's turn. When he came to FATHER'S NAME he wrote, 'Unknown'.
MOTHER'S NAME he put down the name I bear today.

We got to OCCUPATION. For me: 'None'. For him, 'Club Attendant'.

The clerk did not seem to take much notice. *We* had not looked at each other at all. Next came

ADDRESSES His, permanent, in SW1. Mine, since yesterday's date, in SW7.

Further question: a date for the wedding. Did we actually both say 'As soon as possible'? It was fixed for a few days ahead. 'That will be ten shillings,' said the clerk to Terry. Who for the first time turned to me. The look was such as seen on an embarrassed dog. 'Oh of course,' I mumbled, opened my bag, produced a note, tried a smile. (What I should have said is, how silly: we both came out without any money.) After this we turned our backs and marched out—me, thinking of Erika, heartily putting my arm into his.

We were to be married at eleven o'clock in the morning at Caxton Hall, Westminster, in the presence of Aldous, Maria and Pierre. Pierre was to be best man, Maria the second witness. In my room that morning, I had just about finished dressing, Pierre had come in, still in his silk dressing-gown, to wish me luck, *'Que le soleil d'Austerlitz . . .'*, when the telephone rang. I had been stretching out a leg to put on my left shoe: struck at once by a huge fear, I hobbled the few steps and lifted the receiver. A switchboard voice said, 'A gentleman to see you.' 'Who is he?' 'A gentleman from the Home Office, he's on his way up.' He was in the room within seconds, a tall man holding a briefcase and a bowler-hat. One contemptuous look at Pierre, and, 'Will you please leave us, I have business with this lady.' (Pierre vanished.) To me, 'I have to see your passport.' When he had it in his hand, he sat down and looked through it long and hard. 'So you have been living mostly in France over the last few years. And you intend to marry a British subject this morning?' There came more questions, tangential they seemed to me but then I was in shock. All the same I went to the telephone: I knew the number of Lysander's chambers, and his clerk came on the line: Lysander was in court. I managed to convey that I needed to speak to him. Urgently. The Home Office man sat, staring at nothing, listened. It took time for the

356

telephone to ring back. Lysander's voice: he had arranged a few minutes' adjournment. I said what I had rehearsed: 'Someone from the Home Office is with me here who says there's something wrong about Terry and I getting married.' Lysander—very quick—came back with, 'Go as soon as he's left. He won't take you with him—and go straight to the Huxleys, I shall meet you there.' The inquisitor indeed left quite soon. 'I'm afraid I shall have to take your passport with me.' Foolishly I asked, '. . . but I will get it back?' (The nasty brown thing.) He looked at my face for the first time, 'You will get it back all right, but you may not like what you will find inside it.'

*     *     *

An account of the days which now followed—days which were dramatic, farcical, morally ambivalent and for me, fragmented like a heavy dream, has been written by Maria Huxley to her son Matthew at great and vivid length. This letter, dashed off with galloping illiteracies, and very funny, must have passed through many hands: friends of friends', prospective biographers', academics'; now it is suspected to be buried in the archival depths of the Belgian National Library. How I wish I could see it again at this moment. Maria's coherent sequence of events. For me the factual, if not the emotional, memories, may

357

be blurred by past anxiety and panic.

The basic situation was straightforward enough. The British authorities—no Kafka here—were tipped off about the probability of an arranged marriage by the registrar's clerk, and that tip had been reinforced by further inquiries. I had not, they found, mentioned marriage as 'Reason of visit' at passport control on the boat. Then there was also an assumption on the presence of a likely ponce in my hotel bedroom (Pierre in his dressing gown invoking the Sun of Austerlitz) that I had been practising some fairly 'high-class' prostitution in France and might now be planning to transfer that activity to London.

Arranged marriages, marriages for the purpose of acquiring British nationality the quick way, if not illegal, were highly *undesirable* for a multitude of reasons: economic, political, instinctive—too many foreigners on this crowded isle . . . Indeed. That plight so urgent then, the need to escape from tyrannical regimes, hardships, deadly poverty is now overwhelming, desolating, hopeless. That human conception, the brotherhood of man—animals have no qualms fighting for their territory or so we believe—of everyone on earth free to go where he wishes: to enjoy, to work, to live, without arousing enmity or envy, is further from us than ever. Perhaps *for ever.*

Then as now there were ways of getting rid

of undesirable nationals. On that first day nothing further happened. I had moved into the Albany, sleeping on the drawing-room sofa, not quite long enough; Pierre remained in Kensington; Aldous did no work. The Huxleys and Lysander were trying to get on to probable sources of advice. (That November happened to be in the throes of an impending general election: people who might be able to help us were both more visible and more busy.) Next day we were requested to present ourselves at Caxton Hall. This we did. Terry with us of course. There we were informed by a nondescript official that the projected marriage was suspended. *Sine die?* For the present, there was nothing further. (Whiff of Kafka after all?) We walked back. Maria took Terry into her bedroom where he told her that he would see us through. Then, I believe, she embraced him. When they came out, she said, *'He is one of us.'* (Anteceding Mrs T.'s immortal words.)

We heard nothing over the next days and the weekend. Lysander roped in a solicitor friend (likeable); they talked about producing a statement by or about myself; they talked about a consular marriage in Holland? In Sweden? Such might become necessary and could be achieved if well timed. Then somehow we found ourselves in touch with the Quakers: they were known to help refugees. It would be splendid if I let them go public with my case, if I came out—would I? It might bring awareness of the fugitives from Nazism . . . It might lead to a prison sentence—a short one. Be brave, they said; I was taken to Friends' House in Trafalgar Square (earnest, kindly faces); I was taken to Lincoln's Inn; to tea and a drive with Lady Ottoline Morrell; to the flat of an MP (in the thick of fighting his seat) . . . Maria and I seemed to be spending hours in buses getting from place to place or shut up in the Albany with the telephone ringing, ringing again, *not* ringing back . . . A siege mentality is soon developed. It was believed likely that we were under surveillance. The Albany has two entrances, the main one giving on to the courtyard in Piccadilly guarded by porters in uniform and top hats (on excellent terms with the Huxleys); the back entrance, on the north end of the covered walk, is private, supposed to be used only by the tenants, who had the keys to a low gate giving on to back streets—Vigo and Savile Row. It was decided that I must on no account go out by myself, and always come and go by that locked entrance. Little good it did. One morning by messenger and main entrance my passport was returned to me. It was stamped with a Deportation Order. If I had not left the United Kingdom within forty-eight hours, I would be deported to the country of origin. (Germany.)

The first thing rapidly decided on that

morning was that Aldous—not Pierre, not Maria—*Aldous* would take me back to France that night. Newhaven—Dieppe night ferry. I saw them looking out his long winter coat for him. I felt overwhelmingly moved. Presently came instructions from Lysander, the essence of them being: there *is* time to fight back. So we ventured out to his friendly solicitor's office and sat round the desk (Terry as good as holding Maria's hand; never mine), the two lawyers much in charge. First let's give a reasonable slant to that accusation of her having lied on the boat, they said; get that out of the way. 'It hadn't occurred to me,' I said. It sounded feeble. 'What?' they said. 'Oh, do make sense,' said Maria. Then the solicitor tried: 'Could you do with a drink? Would you like some whisky?' Oh yes, I thought, I would. It came. A large whisky and soda. I drank it in one go. 'I had been coming to England every month or so for the last ten years,' I said, 'Don't you see?' I still felt weak. The solicitor gave me another look, 'Perhaps you need something to eat?' A clerk was sent out to the pub. A large plate of sandwiches appeared. I ate them. The solicitor cried out, 'You've been starving the poor girl!'

I realized that this must have been more or less the case: I couldn't remember anything about food during the last days. I got on my feet, strode about the room and talked.

'. . . That business on the boat? They had

361

always asked "Purpose?" and I always said "Visit" or "Seeing friends" . . . earlier it may have been "Continuing education". It didn't seem to matter much . . . A formality. It didn't cross my mind that marriage concerned them any more than seeing friends, a private matter.'

Plausible enough, the lawyers supposed: they may drop their point about the lie; the real crux is the purpose of marriage—if one could get into our statement that the marriage is not *solely* to obtain British Nationality.

There Maria came up to eloquence: *not solely* any more: we *can* say now that we all like each other. They certainly would try the 'not solely', Lysander said, in the statement they were preparing. More to the point was giving me a good character—a respectable future subject. (Even at that moment there was stirring faintly in my consciousness that obstinate conviction of becoming some day part of English literature.) The real crux, I heard them say, was my not turning into a financial liability. 'Can we say she's got five hundred a year?' Goodness no! Twice as much as my rejecting prospect had required! Aldous raised his hands, 'Can't we say *"private means"*, that's so deliciously vague?' Lysander said, 'She'll always have them. Somehow.'

They got on to who should go and speak to whom? Who had influence? Willing to use it? One of our neighbours in Albany was in the

Government (likely to survive?), Aldous, modestly reluctant, had already talked to him. (He had promised to try to help, and did so.) There were then in England large numbers of men of all parties ready to stand up for individual liberties. There happened to be on that night a large election do on the top of Selfridges. Aldous and Maria went, going from table to table, asking for support. Among some of their most intimate friends there was some strong dissent. Drop it, they were advised, let her drown; Aldous's work is far more important—too many such cases about . . .

Next morning was bleak. Not many hours left before the stay of deportation order expired. Maria now set out to what she had planned since the beginning—go to the Home Office and throw herself at the Secretary's feet, asking him to save her young friend. The Home Secretary then was a man not known for his liberal views; I met, in later life, at least two of the politicians whose career he had cut short after some minor unfortunate offence. Maria just went. Insisted on audience. Penetrated into an impressive office, went down on her knees in front of a non-committal figure, spoke, invoked mercy. Whether it was indeed the Secretary of State, or merely the minister, or someone below him, I cannot remember. Was she sure herself? It was all in that letter. Then she came back appeased: she had done what was natural to her: asked for grace.

Perhaps it had been so unEnglish that it worked. Some hours later came a message by hand—the Deportation Order was rescinded. Presently Lysander telephoned: our solicitor had been informed that there was no longer any obstacle to his client's marriage. Arrangements could be made with the registrar when we wished.

*     *     *

On the day when the five of us turned up again at Caxton Hall, all was smooth, closed faces. This time Aldous was best man, not Pierre (on lawyers' advice); afterwards I was handed the marriage certificate with a gesture of here's your saucer of milk.

For that evening Maria had arranged that Terry—who had been staunch and brave and honourable throughout—and I should have a big evening out. His choice of venues; she had slipped him a ten-pound note. He chose dinner at the Trocadero and a variety show afterwards. For me it was hard going. At the music-hall things got livelier: everybody knew him. The programme sellers teased—Why Terry, what have you been up to? Out with a girl! Is she your fiancée?

Maria insisted also on a real wedding party—to celebrate and thank all who had helped us. And a very mixed party it was.

When Terry saw the guest list, he said he would not come unless he could bring 'his own background'. Well of course. And so we had, among others, and I don't know why: Virginia Woolf, some minor politicians, our godfather designer, one or two Quakers, quite a few Bloomsburys and, led in by Terry, half a dozen showgirls, very pretty (delighting Aldous) and some tough males, bruisers rather than ephebes. Virginia Woolf came up to me, took mine into her exquisite hand (I had not met her before, nor after). 'This', she said, 'is a very queer party, I can't understand anything about it: one day you must come and tell me.'

That was not all. Maria still insisting—'He has become a friend'—arranged a *voyage de noces*, a weekend at the seaside, Brighton, or Eastbourne, or Blackpool . . . She was going to book the rooms: the official double for us: of course she would come to chaperone, the single for Terry. The hotel did not have to know. Eventually Terry turned out so unenthusiastic that we cancelled the whole thing.

\*       \*       \*

The bottled gas? Pierre and I kept some appointments in the City, met firm doubt—did rural England not have its coal kitchen-range and the evening fire in the sitting-room fireplace? We returned quite soon to France.

By day-boat, Dover–Calais.

*  *  *

For all the esteem, euphoria, warmth Maria had beamed at him for a few weeks, Terry, as predicted, melted back into his existence.

Every morning since, every day to this day, everywhere through all these years, when I stretch out my leg to put on the left shoe, there comes the pang of apprehension: for a few intense seconds I hold my breath—if the telephone does not ring, and no doorbell sounds, it will be all right: nothing bad is going to happen on this day.

## CHAPTER TWENTY-THREE

### *Guillotine—Wild oats*

There came again a beginning of summer. The Huxleys in residence; I living at my painter's in the hills, finishing that novel. The magic wand may have been somewhat crooked but it had done its work: I had become English from one minute to the next. At another office, another registrar's, they had put into my hand that stiff blue passport. It said what I now believed I was. (Maria had been annoyed with me over this conviction: for once we did not understand each other's views.) By now I know whose part was proved.

When I sent my current French identity card to the Préfecture du Var at Draguignan, applying for another with my new identity, they returned it with a *'devenue Anglaise'* scrawled by hand across a front page.

This had been earlier, soon after my return from that London phantasmagoria. Presently I had calmed down, felt settled, soothed by an inner purring which told me that it was *all right*, I would manage: it was here that I was going to live my life.

Then one day I was standing with Maria by the newspaper kiosk on the quay of the port about to open again at the end of the siesta hour, she was getting the *Petit Var* for Aldous who liked having the *faits divers* read to him, I about to fetch something from the still shuttered artist's supply shop. We were among the few people who did not keep siesta; during the heat of the day we used to typewrite behind closed shutters, she copying Aldous's pages, I trying to make my own. The sea two steps from us was quiet, the salt air light. *How good.* Maria, who often knew what was inside one's mind, said to me, 'No: we shall not stay here for ever. Our lives aren't going to be like this. You cannot choose your roots. This will not remain our home . . .' She added, 'Even if there isn't going to be a war.' (How often already one precisely used these words.)

'Anyway, Aldous is getting restless; he doesn't know it yet.'

That was in late June. By mid-July the Spanish Civil War broke out. We were having a picnic on the beach—it was a great summer for picnics on the playgrounds of the West—when the news was passed from mouth to mouth.

Before the end of the year, Aldous was in London working with the Peace Pledge Union. (He had met Dick Sheppard, had joined faith with him, with Gerald Heard and, on a parallel track, with P. M. Alexander, founder of the Alexander technique.) By the following February, Aldous and Maria had left the Villa Uley. For good, if unsaid. Next stage was London, the future was—for so many reasons, expressed and not expressed—America. With their son of course.

Aldous offered to give me an interview about his leaving. To my astonishment he sat down and wrote it himself: Questions as well as answers. The opening went,

Q. 'Going to America?'
A. 'Yes.'
Q. 'Lecture?'
A. 'No. Learn. Not teach.'

The seven-year lease on the Albany flat had still some time to run. I was in London on one of my turns of trying to earn my keep, or some of it. The Huxleys decided to have me stay in

368

the Albany by myself and try to find an eventual acceptable tenant for the remainder of their lease. So they moved into three service flats in the Mount Royal Hotel at Marble Arch—Aldous, Maria, Matthew, one small room, one bathroom, one kitchenette each: *no* house-keeping, how time-saving, how neat . . . In the evenings, after their mixed and many engagements, I went to the Mount Royal to say goodnight, to say goodbye, walking back to the Albany very late through a near silent Mayfair.

They sailed from Southampton on the SS *Normandie* on 7 April 1937. I went with them on the boat train and ferry on to the ship, staying on board until it was cleared to sail.

\*     \*     \*

Back in France eventually, having found a tenant up to the standards of the ex-army captain who ran the Albany, I found Sanary invaded—Sanary nightlife actually, as it rarely emerged, expectant, spruced up, for the first round of pre-dinner drinks—by a set I had so far more read and heard about than seen: the English Bright and Young of the last decade, no longer quite so young at that point, whose promise had begun to tarnish, whose comrades in outrage had moved on. They were semi-exiles now, still talented, still hopeful that tomorrow, or next year, that hard-set hurdle of sloth and *Angst* would be overcome. On offer *now* were the grand exotic looks of the mad-bad Englishman throughout the ages, on offer too, at the few hours between the sluggishness of the day and the excesses of the late night: verbal brilliance. Vertiginous brilliance shot out in what one could choose to hear as a seductive or affected voice. The prima donna of this set was Brian Howard—who else?—with two or three other men and their retinue of camp-followers and lovers, the latter either muscular central European oafs or sleek local pick-ups. Also appended were a few ravishing young women, English or American, between marriages or affairs, amusing even talented, bright themselves; they were neither fought with nor particularly well treated by the men. It was often these girls who dipped into their pockets when the saucers were counted as the cafés closed or the chits passed around at dawn at the night-clubs of the coast. When the men paid or asked to be paid for, money was often contentious.

The trouble with having had an inconclusive childhood is a likely drive into subsequent later ones. This is how I see my reckless turning during the last three pre-war summers *du côté de chez* Brian Howard. I was dazzled: the voice, the wit, the looks—there still exists that photograph of Brian as young Hamlet—although inwardly chewing at times a moralizing cud, both fascinated and appalled

370

by the goings on. I became witness and accomplice, joining them driving them night after night when Sanary had shut down, first perhaps to Suzy's bar at Bandol where one could dance, ambisexually, on a small floor-lit square, then on to a *boîte* or God forbid to others along the coast. My role: transport and *voyeur*. I had a vintage car then, open to the sky, with a running-board, the handbrake and the horn outside, and the carrosserie built in 1911 by Gallet. Pierre had got it for me, the ex-third car of a Faubourg Saint-Honoré friend of his, used only on rare estival country outings during the first quarter-century of its well-tuned existence. We paid for it with twenty-five pounds. Tyres to fit its wheels had been a problem. Large wheels held together by a spider's wheel of slender spikes. So it took some weeks of Saturday afternoons touring outskirts of small towns in search of half-defunct rubber factories to get it shod. It could seat eight, counting the jump-seats. How often it was kept waiting well into sharp daylight in some side street; I was waiting too; for the party or the fight to break up. Then I could drive them home (home being the Hôtel de la Tour, or some villa), never entirely sober myself though still careful and in control. One night when Brian insisted on Saint Tropez once too often, *he* drove off with the car. He came back without it the next day, and the car came back eventually in a sorry state, towed by a rescue vehicle sent from the Garage Excelsior. How Pierre disapproved. *Cette bande d'Anglais . . .*

We did cause scandal. The worst one was the Abdication party given belatedly the summer after that event when Brian had got hold of a gramophone record with Edward VIII's farewell speech. The party was held at a villa shared by Brian and oaf, Eddy Gathorne Hardy and Klaus Mann happy for once with a quiet American academic. They had asked, perhaps not wisely, a number of French people, a serious playwright, Paris art dealers, a local lawyer, a naval officer and a woman said to be part Russian part Swiss, said also to be apt to bite when drunk.

The party didn't go very well. The extraneous element stood about, not drinking over much, Brian in near-ecclesiastical get-up, officiated at an improvised altar on which stood the rented gramophone. Eventually silence was asked for, Brian knelt, we were hearing a snatch of the National Anthem followed by the voice of him who was by now the Duke of Windsor: 'Now at long last . . .', the well-known words rang on, the record or the setting made them sound like a parody, solemn and squeaky. The guests hovered between bewilderment, distaste and nervous giggles. ('For Heaven's sake what was that all about?') They left early, stiffly, politely. The rest of us drank a great deal more. It was very late and very hungry that we arrived at the backstreet Italian bistro, still open to us. A friendly place, family run, cheap, and there we were, the sole customers in a narrow whitewashed room sitting on two sides of a long wooden table, all men except for Marcelle, a glowing young beauty, the second, already, ex-wife of Peter Quennell, and the Russian-Swiss biter who with her escort, a maidenly Parisian sophisticate called Sacha had hung on, and myself. Unfortunately, very unfortunately, this Sacha addressed some down-putting jibe at Brian's oaf, oaf squealed, Brian intoned a regal reprimand, the man called Sacha seized a jug of water and poured it over oaf's head, Brian leaped up, took a knife, an Italian dinner-knife, a knife all the same, and went for Sacha's chest, a scrum of men tried to restrain Brian from the back pinning down his arms . . . Within seconds a general fight had broken out. The table overturned, carafes of red wine flowing forth, plates of spaghetti pomodori sliding on to our clothes and the floor, the biter-woman wriggled over the slippery tiles trying to get at Brian's ankle, the room had become too narrow to choose opponents, all the men seemed to be fighting each other: with fists and kicks, not glass. Marcelle and I, each on our own accord, threw ourselves between them, arms and open hands motionless down our sides (we might have been trained by the

Mahatma himself) trying to keep them apart.

'Stop it,' we cried, 'Peace please, oh please,' and I could hear how small our voices sounded below the din. Suddenly it was all over: one more wild shout then all rushed out past the petrified *padroni* into the street on to the port, burst into the Café de la Marine, near midnight, still half filled with middle-aged locals. And there we were, panting, bloodstained—most of it wine and tomato paste—subsiding on to separate tables. There was an upsurge or two of hostilities, a raised voice, a menacing pointing of soda-water siphons, an actual squirt aggressively aimed. That was all: we were spent.

\*　　　\*　　　\*

We *had* caused scandal. Of long-term consequences. In that summer just a formal summons to the Mairie; the powers that were had been reached by a variety of rumours, yet judged that British *lèse-majesté* was not within their competence. We, Brian, Eddy, myself, were arraigned for the fracas at the bistro and our revolting irruption into Sanary's most respectable café, and of course were sent to pay, not very much—for the broken cutlery and dishes.

Brian's divertimenti were not always so silly and so ugly. To brush aside that memory I should recall one night, irresistible in a

374

sophisticatedly outrageous way which would have gone down well in the still far-off Sixties, was much enjoyed by nearly all, and visually captivating. Brian had written—actually sat down and written—a play to be performed by ourselves, called *The Secret of Mayerling*, a key to the true causes of Crown Prince Rudolph of *infelix Austria* and the Countess Vetsera, his mistress's double suicide at that hunting lodge. The play was performed out of doors at my painter's house. The stage was the long terrace with steps into a clearing framed by a grove of trees in which the spectators, a near hundred, sat on rows of hired chairs. The lighting out of tree-tops and bushes was designed, constructed and worked by skilful Pierre. The Crown Prince was played by Brian in black satin court-breeches (another of my father's random relics) and a Byronic shirt, the doomed Countess, Marcelle Quennell in a turquoise dressing-gown, Eddy Gathorne Hardy, over six feet tall, played the Empress Elizabeth (of the fabulous tresses), in a transvestite gown, a rented wig and a Woolworth crown. Oaf was a coachman who had to announce the arrival of His Royal Highness's or Her Imperial Majesty's coaches and took much care not to mix these up. The Secret, a rent-boy picked up at the Viennese Municipal Baths, was played by me, another transvestite in a tight drainpipe trouser suit, shaking with stage-fright. (The little Lion,

Feuchtwanger, had kindly sent me an imperial pint of Krug to drink while I was being made up. It helped.)

The audience was reasonably multilingual. The Mimerels, the Kislings, estival artists, most of the still present German Haute Culture (we were late in the summer before the Munich Crisis), the theatre critic of *Le Petit Var*, the Adjoint au Maire, a Communist bon-vivant. The play (length a short hour) was in English of course. When it was over the audience clapped and laughed so much that we gave a—totally ad lib—second performance in German which the principal actors did rather well; when there was more clamour afterwards, we chaotically gave a third in French (it showed up where the Bright and Young had mainly sowed wild oats: Berlin).

For all the grotesqueries there was one great theatrical moment—when the audience had been bidden silence and the spotlights came on out of the dark trees, there was the Prince and his love sitting side by side, ineluctably, magically beautiful, she with a lazy hand on a book.

Silence.

Then, the Prince: 'My dear! Reading again. What is it?'

Vetsera yawning, slowly turning over a slim volume: 'Anton Chekhov.'

\*       \*       \*

So much is known, has been written, is performed around Brian Howard. There is of course Marie Jacqueline Lancaster's excellent—and sad—biography, *Portrait of a Failure*. What he failed to write, others have. There are the hundreds of his letters to his mother—I was asked to read them when the estate was being settled after his suicide in 1957—cartons of them, all evasions, reassurances, demands. (He loved her, feared her, inevitably.) There is *Brideshead*: there is his world naughty and ineffective, also intellectually, artistically, passionate and sincere, in *Vile Bodies*, there is Cyril Connolly in what is surely the best of his incomparable parodies, *Where Engels Feared to Tread: from Oscar to Stalin*.

And here I am, late in the day, adding more words. They are fractions from the beginnings of an affection which lasted—*malgré tout*, on my side at least, for twenty years. Enough now.

I must add one more fact: Brian's early and courageous stand against Hitler. Industrious stand: he wrote wake-ups for the *New Statesman*, spoke inside Germany. Once he escaped within hours of being seized by the Gestapo at Munich. Unity Mitford—the ironies of mixed loyalty!—arranged smuggling him over the border in female fancy dress. Brian Howard was what officialdom came to call later on: a premature anti-Fascist.

# CHAPTER TWENTY-FOUR

## *What can we ever do?*

Within weeks of that amiable folly, not the
worst but the forerunner was upon us.
Ultimata, démarches, speeches rampant,
speeches about preparedness, huddles around
every audible radio—*the Munich Crisis*. In
France, all in their ways prayed for No War,
No War *Now*. Peace was too much to think
aloud of. That came later when Chamberlain
had flown off once again, when Mussolini had
put his oar in, and Hitler his signature: *Peace*,
in our time. Relief, immense instant relief?
Yes. Fears resurged soon after, prompted by
reason, by events, and thus divided with each
other and within our inner selves we limped
on, lived on, weighed practical steps, through
the last year of No-War (Did it feel like such in
Spain? In Prague?)

\*     \*     \*

Some of that time I spent in Paris for a need of
other friends, city lights. I found a garçonnière
with four square metres of garden and a live
fountain in the yard of an English clergyman's
widow's house in the unfamiliar territory of
the 16ième *arrondissement*; had new America-

bound pupils nervously in transit, did volunteer work for a group of hard-up, left-wing refugees. (It was then on New Year's Day after *Munich* that I had first met at the *sortie* out of a literary salon Allanah Harper.) The rest of the time it was Sanary with the English set gone, my painter friend packed up and returned to America, choosing California where the Thomas Manns had already arrived. I lived in the Villa Uley empty although not put up for sale, sharing it for that last summer with Maria's sculptress sister, Suzanne Nicolas, and her artist family. Brian had stayed on to take care of his beloved boy, so blatantly Germanic, so blatantly of military age, who could not be taken to England having already been deported for unseemly behaviour when staying at Brian's mother's house in Surrey.

Local attitude to foreigners had been tangibly hostile: France was held to be pushed into war by the City of London and the Jews. During the thick of *Munich*, Brian and my painter friend had been spat upon walking on the port.

Eleven months. And there was closing time. In August that unexpected bolt, the non-aggression pact between Germany and the Soviet Union; a week later Germany invades Poland; Anglo-British Ultimatum; September 3rd Chamberlain's speech. We are at war.

Now there is unspeakable evil to be defeated. By mass suffering, mass destruction does it balance? *Can* it balance? Another war to end war? I did not think so then.

Nor during that first winter, the Phoney War, *la Drôle de guerre*, when nothing seemed to happen except men disappeared by call-up, men on stand-by, restrictions, blackout (what about Finland? about the convoys at sea?). On the Côte, all male German refugees under the age of sixty were shut up in a camp, a disused tile factory in open country near Aix-en-Provence. Lion Feuchtwanger . . . Brian's poor boy of course. The elderly and the women were treated with coldness, contemptuously served in shops, all bills called in. Hard to tell what now rankled more: accounts unpaid or past money lavishly spent. Recent English misbehaviour was also laid on our doors. More grievously, we refugees when not treated as warmongers were suspected of being spies. Many were under surveillance. I was being interrogated by the bank clerk who used to negotiate my mother's cheques; now revealed as a member of the secret police. My changed nationality might well be a cover. Thought to be on the side of what one most abhors is very bitter.

\*     \*     \*

Plans aimed towards return. England. For the duration. To move out of one French *département* into another required a permit; as did doing it in one's car, as did petrol coupons: each from a different authority and of limited duration. When the real thing broke out, when Germany invaded Denmark, Norway, Holland, Belgium, and in mid-May France, we—that was Brian, Allanah Harper and myself—were still dithering in the South. German armies marching, advancing . . . Did I then still feel in terms of the horrors of war? I could not get them out of my mind where they clashed with the urging desire that *this* war must be won. Which meant fought. The recurrent dilemma of the pacifist.

Now we had to think of flight. Our own. Brian managed to reach Marseilles and the chock-full cargo boat which took him, with Somerset Maugham among the escapees, safely to England. Allanah and I got to Genoa where we spent some fraught days slinking about before Italy's Declaration of War, expected any moment. (In which event, we would be arrested and interned, the American consul had warned us—the British one had already left.) We crept about waiting, few lire in our pockets, saw Chamberlain in effigy burnt one night in a Piazza, until allowed at almost the last hour (the Declaration came on June 10th) to board an American passenger ship, already loaded to the gills with Polish refugees and the womenfolk of US officials, on which the Huxleys and my painter friend had cabled passages for us from half a world away.

A neutral ship, technically out of bounds for U-boats, held for search at Gibraltar (the vessel carried half the gold of the bank of Italy; we passengers did not know this), the voyage took some twenty days. On each, the telegraph brought dire news—Pétain's speech asking for an Armistice . . . France signing an Armistice . . . Britain alone holding out. Were we at the beginning of the end of life as we had known it? When we reached New York, emerging after hours of grey docks and dismal proceedings, into summer midtown Manhattan at noon, the streets sunlit, glittering with bright awnings where tall doormen lifted hats to smiling men and well-dressed women. A new exotic opulent world evoking the more attenuated image of the Mayfair London lunch-hour in a frivolous decade.

## CHAPTER TWENTY-FIVE

### *Cut off—The omitted future*

Had I but world enough and time . . . I have not. And shall not write now about the life that followed. Nothing more about the War, nothing about the next seven years in America, six of them in the United States, one in Mexico. About what happened on my post-war return to Europe, I have already written a good deal, as much as I wished to, covering stretches of time, places, events—connected though not chronological—until another point of change in Rome. What derived from that, what happened in the fifty or so years between then and now, I shall merely catalogue, and I want to begin this summary of a long future from the view of a day at the beginning of this book: from the middle.

The single day, the neutral floating, not bound by aims or hours, when I was immersed only in what there was to see, yet unknowingly sustained by where I had arrived at, one published book, a novel with perceived dimensions in the course of writing; the prospect tomorrow of holidays by a Swiss lake; return to Rome and the loving friend who had sought me on that ramshackle shed on a rooftop on Piazza di Spagna, and with whom I was now living in the same quarter in a real appartamento. So much for that present. The future, a long one, is only summarily evoked now.

The Roman years harmonious, happy, hard-working, deepening my sense of belonging. I have loved many places, their architecture, their countrysides, the cities, the lives lived in them—the abiding hours of my rootless existence though are three: Rome, Paris and the French Midi. How I love them, how I long for them.

Evelyn and I spent part of our summers on

the Alpes Maritimes side of the Coast, with Allanah Harper in a house she had bought. The Mimerels, Pierre and Simone, returned from making wine and giving it away, were back at Sanary, living in a centuries-old ruin in the back country they had grandly restored. When I came to stay with them, which was often, Oriane usually insisted on inclusion. I also spent winter weeks in Paris at my old friend and Mexican companion E.'s, E. who had settled in an apartment in the *septième*— run for her, extravagantly but superbly, by my sister, who needed a home and a job—E. still trying to progress with a biography of first Madame de Pompadour where Nancy Mitford overtook her (they became good friends, lugging sackfuls of books between the rue de Lille and the rue Monsieur). E. then switched to Madame de Maintenon.

When we gave up Rome, Evelyn returning to ailing parents in New York, where she achieved a most reputable position in publishing, I went to England. There I returned to my early fascination with the Law. It started with my achieving a commission for an article on that archetypal Criminal Court, The Old Bailey. *For Vogue.* (The contempt of my fellow reporters.) After this, long rounds of Magistrates Courts, County Courts, Assizes. Then a book about the trial of the reputed Bluebeard of the time, Dr Bodkin Adams. Intention: a comprehensive, unsensational account of the facts and atmosphere of a major murder trial. The prosecution, the police, the press, public, fellow GPs were convinced of the foolish, greedy doctor's guilt. The judge (Lord Devlin), the chief crime reporter of the *Express*, the doctor's patients, myself—and of course the jury were certain quite early in the case that he was innocent. I still think so.

Obsessed—postponing novels—I went off on travels to write a book about the practice of the Law in various countries from the human as well as the spectator's view. England, Germany and France, with some brief comedy thrown in about proceedings in Austria and Switzerland. This led on eventually to my covering in earnest some of the most ostentatious cases, criminal and political, of the Sixties and the Seventies. Such as *Lady Chatterley's*, poor Stephen Ward's of the Profumo scandal, Jeremy Thorpe's, Jack Ruby's trial after the Kennedy assassination at Dallas Texas. The most devastating experience was the prosecution of twenty-three men— survivors, plucked out after nearly two decades of anonymity or hiding, who had served as staff (innocent term) at Auschwitz concentration camp, by a *German* court at Frankfurt which was then still West Germany: a hundred and eighty-three court days from the end of 1963 to the summer of 1965. The closing speeches alone took thirty days. The quiet determination, the strict adherence to legal process, the icy impersonal politeness, the sheer *endurance* in dealing with the unspeakable, the daily routines of the suffering inconceivable to a normal human mind, proved step by patient step by judge and prosecutors (four young men) achieved an almost consoling display of human decency and stamina.

In between I wrote two—connected—novels. Living then, from the mid-Fifties into the mid-Seventies, when she died, with Eda Lord whom I had first met when we were very young at a wild Berlin party; it was when I had been there with Aldous and Maria in the year before Hitler, pre-Brian for me and I mostly sat prim and shocked—reading a review. Eda, like so many Americans I got to know, was a casualty of Prohibition, who had blazed through it at her college age. Eventually with unrelenting effort—and the crutches of cigarettes and caffeine—she achieved to become a late-writing novelist with her three books published in what had become a wrong decade. Hers are subtle, delicate, moving in an understating way. Her first novel, *Childsplay*, was called a minor masterpiece by that tough-spoken colleague Martha Gellhorn. I agree with her; and so do those who get to read one of my two remaining copies now.

During the time with Eda, we were living in years' or half-years' snatches in rented houses or flats in Dorset, in London, in Portugal, in Essex, then London again, then Italy: the Browning Villa at Asolo, an intolerable mistake with a sudden recourse to where we should have started: the South of France. And there we found the only both loved and permanent home I ever had: a conversioned annex built on Allanah Harper's property: a rural patch in that triangle of Mougins, Cannes and Grasse. We had adjoining studios, a pergola, a terrace, jasmine and honeysuckle, night-flowering climbers, tree frogs, set in an olive grove. A near decade of it, into which fell alas a very great deal of travelling—uniquely interesting though, during the six years it took to research and write my biography of Huxley.

Inevitably, gradually, half-heartedly, the move away—the sunlight was getting more and more painful for my eyes, I could hardly go out of doors in full day time, no more swimming in a glittering sea, my gardening (and essential watering by hand) began when Riviera society were at cocktail. London at least two or three times a year had become necessary for work, for stimulation. More and more I wanted to be part, a small part, of the English political process. Thus eventually, the move. Many regrets at first . . . We had to give up for good the abode in the olive grove. I longed to get back. Too late. Then I began to enjoy myself. Eda was heart-broken. The sea was her most grateful element. Her life—without alcohol, with lapses into alcohol, with constant long-term changes of attachments dramatically severed—had not been happy or smooth. In the best of our times, and we had them, she and I led a simple, walking hand-in-hand existence. When I set off on a journey, there was always a note tucked away in bag or pocket to be found *en route*. Our last year or two was not good. Her defeatism, the resentful unhappiness had become a burden to me. I wanted out. And she felt it. When she became ill, all this changed. After months of treatments, a time of hope which she was able to spend in Provence with two of her greatest friends, Richard Olney and M. F. K. Fisher. Return. Relapse. She said, 'Better if we had not called the doctor'. At the hospital they spoke of discharge and six months to live. Instead deterioration set in within days. Then the end. The last words audible between us were a line from the Jabberwock of Lewis Carroll's *Through the Looking-Glass.*

\*     \*     \*

Friends were good. Evelyn came over from New York; Christmas I fled from to Allanah's. English life, London life, gradually took over. The PEN Club, the R.S.Lit., committees, a (very brief) First Day's Joining of the Social Democratic Party, literary journalism, another trial or two, much happy involvement with cookery and wine; work for *Time–Life* as assistant consultant on their volume of world wines, dinner parties: as guest, as kitchenmaid, as chief cook. Friends *retrouvés* or new. I chaired lectures, dined out inspecting for restaurant guides, throwing myself into it all. It was an interesting new life for a couple of decades. (As long as one could hop about.) There was often grief: loved ones die. I worked, slowly often, or too little. It took long to get into, to write, to finish what will have to be my last novel, *Jigsaw*. I took even longer to evolve this book. I would like to have been able to say something more about that half of my life from today's perspectives, to tell some more stories. The plight, the brutal injustice to the Sanary Germans at the Armistice, onset of the Vichy Regime, the background absurdities of the Ruby trial at Dallas, an account of interviews with Aldous's Swami, his devotees, his and Maria's families, are cases in point. Wish I could tell the half of it . . . But, I repeat, there seems to be no time.

*Epilogues*

Fast Loose Ends

*Jacko*

She, openly divorced by then, had taken refuge in Paris throughout the war and subsequent Occupation. French friends of all shades of alliance sustained, sheltered and, when the worst Edict came, took turns in hiding her— half Jews, of which she was one, were now officially recategorized as Full Jews. Jacko was on the list of those to be deported. To what end we know. Her ex-husband had long left his risible diplomatic post and joined the Kommandantur, the occupying German government of Paris. Of what and how much he did there, what were his powers, I am still in ignorance; I know that he is considered a war criminal of a minor sort, who was enabled to escape into well-kept lifelong exile on Majorca thanks to a high-placed English patron of his —herself not uninfluential—French mistress. What is also known is that at the height of Jacko's peril, he stepped in and saved her. She was struck off the fatal list—untouched for the rest of the war. For this she paid with a long shadow of disgrace with the French: near two years in a camp, suspected of collaboration, freed eventually and able to live on in France (with her papers never quite sorted out). All of this I minded irrevocably, not just for her, for myself. She was no collaborator, *pauvre femme moyenne*, she loved France as much as I did,

393

was alienated by most things German, but had little conscience about what she called 'just politics'. Some of her connections, men and milieux she was capable of associating herself with, were to me a source of deep distress, and this unspoken discord underlaid our relationship. On her side, she remained the loving, generous sister often seeking my advice, more often mocking my preoccupations, '*Oh,* la grande intellectuelle!*' On my side there was a good deal of cowardice, sad to admit. Her uncertain standing with the French authorities never ceased to resurrect my own fears.

### My sister's child

And now what about the little girl Jacko left behind when she ran away from her first husband. After his gruesome end, sentenced to a traitor's death by the Nazi regime, she, Alix, joined eventually a resistance movement, spent the war on the run, had two children, each conceived from rape by unidentifiable soldiers—boys whom she brought up devotedly and well. The American Occupation Forces in Germany took on her and them, giving her a good job, leading to a career for life. Did she ever see her mother again? Yes, once or twice. I was with them. Alix looked up to her mother as an unobtainable glamorous figure, discussed childhood jealousy of me without rancour, enjoyed her French holidays.

Jacko was very nice to her daughter. Yet we three were worlds apart and knew it. 'She's become a middle-class Americo-German,' Jacko said to me. There was talk about meeting the boys some day. As it turned out, my sister never saw her two grandsons.


*Brian's boy*
Brian, an anti-Nazi on record having to flee himself, could do nothing more. However there had been a little money and some previous strings pulled, so the boy escaped from his tile-factory camp by enterprise or help and reappeared in the temporary safety of north Africa. From London Brian as good as blackmailed every influential person he managed to approach. The boy got on to Mrs Roosevelt's list of US visas granted to the most prominent and endangered German refugees held in Vichy France. So by 1941, bullied by desperate cables—Brian had improbably joined the British air force (ground crew)—threatening to hijack a bomber, it came about that he whom we no longer liked to call the oaf, was seen through Ellis Island Immigration by Wystan Auden, Cyril Connolly's first wife Jean and myself.

*The Roman marble bath*
The hut on the roof-top passed on to me by the Constantine FitzGibbons had a splendid

marble bath. I used to sit in its cool water, book in hand, during the noon hours. Unfortunately a chunk of it had been broken by Constantine and Theodora in one of their ferocious fights. It didn't seem to matter over-much, it kept stuck in like a very large tooth. When I took over, the arrangement included my paying for the FitzGibbons's damages' repairs. When I left in turn, the chunk of marble turned out ruinous to replace. The landlady was implacable. The cost—for my finances—was almost a last straw. The repayment, gradually achieved, took ages.

### The vintage car

During the last searing days before severance from Europe, I gave it to Madame Guerinier, our rough and kind-hearted *femme de ménage.* She had a son of motoring-passion age; transport might be of use to them in what lay ahead. It was. Not least by eventually selling it to an ambulating pork butcher. The custom-built exterior became converted into a shopping van. The car survived. I saw it on a square, surrounded by a queue of customers, some years after the war. I recognized the fine webbed wheels.

### Multilingualism: je ne m'accuse pas

To remain monolingual reduces the mind to the confines of a tramline. The civilized mind needs alternatives for its expression. The civilized mind by individual limitations and the aping of the media has seen better days. Any language acquired opens song-lines. How I repent not to have learned a little Greek and Russian, not to have attempted at least one Oriental path to thought.

*Apprenticeship*
Fragments classical and contemporary of masterpieces—style or lines—if we have the chance to come upon them at the right times, will enter into our own perceptions as part of the foundations of our future works.

\*     \*     \*

Evolving in darkness and time like the essences of the spirit-still, the myriad contents of the quiescent memory mature, expand, until triggered by some auspicious jolt some fragments are released into the outer air of words and feelings.

\*     \*     \*

'Have another glass of wine?' they say. I don't think so. 'Why not? You might as well.' Perhaps I will.

\*     \*     \*

A friend has brought me a pair of lemons off a

tree at Sorrento. As a young child I played on the sands at Sorrento: that was in another century. Or is it today?